PLATO'S PROGRESS

PLATO'S PROGRESS

GILBERT RYLE

*Waynflete Professor of Metaphysical Philosophy
in the University of Oxford*

CAMBRIDGE
AT THE UNIVERSITY PRESS
1966

PUBLISHED BY
THE SYNDICS OF THE CAMBRIDGE UNIVERSITY PRESS

Bentley House, 200 Euston Road, London, N.W. 1
American Branch: 32 East 57th Street, New York, N.Y. 10022
West African Office: P.M.B. 5181, Ibadan, Nigeria

©

CAMBRIDGE UNIVERSITY PRESS

1966

Printed in Great Britain at the University Printing House, Cambridge
(Brooke Crutchley, University Printer)

LIBRARY OF CONGRESS CATALOGUE
CARD NUMBER: 66–15278

CONTENTS

v

CONTENTS

CONTENTS

v

CONTENTS

CONTENTS

CONTENTS

CHAPTER I

THE DISORDERS

I. ARISTOTLE AND PLATO

When Plato died in 347 Aristotle was thirty-seven years old
and had spent the last twenty years first as a student and
then as a teacher in Plato's Academy. How is Aristotle's
philosophical thinking related to Plato's philosophical
thinking?

(i) *Disciple or rebel?*

One is tempted to suppose *a priori* that Aristotle is the
heir to, and continuator of Plato's philosophy. How could
the pupil of a philosophical genius fail to be his disciple?
Yet it is notorious that in his very early productive years
Aristotle is already making vigorous and radical attacks
upon Plato's Theory of Forms. Even where this Theory is
not in question Aristotle is nearly equally vigorous in his
criticisms of, *inter alia*, Plato's account of the notion of
Pleasure and of the geometrical chemistry of Plato's
Timaeus.

One is then tempted to suppose that Aristotle developed
by early reaction out of the receptive disciple that he must
have once been. Aristotle's philosophy is, perhaps, a
philosophy of secession. Yet scholars have looked in vain
in Aristotle's most juvenile writings for any convincing
traces of the desiderated early pieties. Nowhere does
Aristotle talk like an acolyte. Nor even does he seem any-

where to talk like an angry or a guilty rebel against his old master. He discusses Platonic doctrines like an exacting critic, but not like an apostate; and while often arguing against Platonic conclusions, he often wields Platonic arguments against the errors of others. The polar notions of the limit and the limitable are cardinal in Plato's *Philebus* and *Parmenides*; and they are cardinal in, among other things, Aristotle's *Physics*. The very unpartisanship both of Aristotle's rejections and of his sharings of Platonic thoughts should make one suspicious from the start of the hypothesis that Aristotle was a loyal disciple, but also of the hypothesis that he was a renegade disciple of Plato.

(ii) *Aristotle's description of Plato*

In his survey of the history of philosophy in his *Metaphysics* I Aristotle gives an account of Plato's philosophy which baffles us in two ways. He describes a Pythagorean stage in Plato's thought to which in our Platonic dialogues almost nothing corresponds, save for some hints in the *Philebus*. Secondly, he says nothing here and very little elsewhere about that important stage in Plato's thought which is very fully represented in his *Cratylus*, *Theaetetus*, *Sophist* and *Parmenides*. It is true that Aristotle's survey of previous philosophy was confined to the ways in which his predecessors had anticipated or failed to anticipate his own doctrine of the Four Causes, and these four dialogues were not upon this particular track. None the less Aristotle's omission of any mention of this development in Plato's thought is surprising, and all the more surprising because Plato's thought here seems to us to be at its least other-

worldly and at its most Aristotelian in tenor and even sometimes in diction. In the *Parmenides*, Part I, Plato assembles
some powerful arguments against what had been his own
Theory of Forms, and at least one of these arguments is
closely akin to one which Aristotle himself employs. Yet
Aristotle nowhere mentions this fact. Actually he
nowhere mentions this dialogue by name, though he
almost certainly alludes to some points in it in his *Physics*.
Nor does Aristotle mention the argument in Plato's
Sophist, that the Friends of the Forms would have to concede the unqualified reality of at least some non-timeless,
mutable entities, namely thinking beings. Not only the
other-worldly is fully real. Aristotle fairly often alludes to,
draws on or mentions, though not by name, Plato's
Theaetetus, yet he does not discuss the philosophically
most original things in this dialogue, despite the fact that
in his *Categories* and his *De Interpretatione* his own interests
and even some of his own semi-technical vocabulary are
closely akin to those of Plato when he composed both
this dialogue and the *Cratylus* and *Sophist*. We get the
impression that Aristotle, so far from having been brought
up and moulded on these dialogues from his late teens,
was at best superficially acquainted with them when he
wrote his *Categories* and the beginning of his *De
Interpretatione*.

(iii) *Non-Platonic influences on Aristotle*

Conversely, there are cardinal ideas with which, from his
early productive years, Aristotle operates confidently and
systematically, which have their provenance in nothing

written or taught by Plato. For one thing, Aristotle seems almost to begin his philosophical life fully equipped with an elaborate apparatus of categories. He employs this apparatus for, *inter alia*, his criticisms of the Theory of Forms. It is difficult to see how this apparatus could just have occurred to the young Aristotle, and equally difficult to see how he or anyone else could have developed it out of any Platonic doctrines or even out of any revolt against such doctrines. For another thing, Aristotle was, from pretty early in his career as a philosopher, quite at home with the notion of Potentiality *versus* Actuality, and with the kindred notions of Possibility, Contingency, Necessity and Impossibility. That the stimulus to Aristotle's thoughts on these modal notions came from recent or contemporary Megarians is a tempting guess. At least no such stimulus could have come from anything written by Plato with the dubious exception of his *Hippias Minor*. There seem to have existed some powerful non-Platonic formative influences upon the young Aristotle; and Plato's formative influence seems to have been both slighter and patchier than we had assumed.

(iv) *The remote Plato*

Next, while we must admire the studied impersonality of Aristotle's lecture-manners, we should still feel some surprise at finding in the course of Aristotle's voluminous works not one certain echo from Plato's tutorial voice, hardly one anecdote about Plato as a man, and hardly one mention of any trait of Plato's character. We cannot tell from anything said by Aristotle whether Plato possessed or lacked the endearing approachability of his own Socrates. Aristotle took notes of Plato's unpublished *Lecture on the Good*, and we know something of what Aristotle had there recorded, and of his comments upon the contents of this *Lecture*. Apart from this we hear almost nothing from Aristotle of Plato's spoken instructions; of his contributions to discussions; of his replies to questions and objections; or of his jokes or repartees, if any. It is as if Aristotle knew as a reader many, though not all, of Plato's dialogues; knew as a listener Plato's *Lecture on the Good*; but did not know Plato the man. Incidentally, it is something of a puzzle that Aristotle shows very little knowledge of or interest in Plato's *Republic*. Outside his *Politics*, which contains moderately full discussions of the political gist of *Republic*, Books II–V and Book VIII, Aristotle very seldom mentions or draws on the *Republic*. Our students, in their study of the Line, the Cave, the Sun, the Idea of the Good, the relation between dialectic and the sciences, can get little reflected light from Aristotle. He is silent about what is for them the heart of Platonism. The *Republic*'s definition of Justice as Minding one's own Business is not even mentioned by Aristotle in his *Rhetoric*, *Topics*, *Eudemian Ethics* or *Nicomachean Ethics* V, which is in its entirety a discussion of the nature of Justice. By contrast, Aristotle incessantly mentions, echoes and controverts things in Plato's *Timaeus*.

In his *Politics* II Aristotle two or three times complains that in Plato's *Republic* certain cardinal questions were left unanswered, and certain cardinal doctrines were left indeterminate. Neither he nor his colleagues seem to have asked Plato personally for the needed amplifications. Was Plato unapproachable? Or was his *Republic* unknown to them while Plato was alive?

(v) *Plato and the Topics*

Finally, at the end of his *De Sophisticis Elenchis*, where he makes his solitary excursion into autobiography, Aristotle says that unlike the composers of other Training Manuals, for example of rhetoric, he himself in composing his *Art of Dialectic*, that is, our *Topics*, had had to start from absolute scratch. He does indeed draw specimens of dialectical points, good and bad, from Plato's dialogues. But for the theory or methodology of dialectical argumentation he owes no debts to anyone. It follows that Plato had not taught Aristotle dialectic and therefore that he had not taught Aristotle philosophy in Plato's prevailing, though not his terminal sense of the word. Aristotle may have sat at Plato's feet for instruction in the scientific content of the *Timaeus*, though even this can be contested. But not for instruction in the strategy or tactics of the Socratic Method deployed in the *Charmides*, the *Euthydemus*, the *Gorgias* or Book I of the *Republic*.

It seems then that many things are wrong with our habitual picture of Aristotle studying philosophy under Plato's personal tutelage from the age of eighteen, and absorbing from about the same date even the latest of Plato's dialogues.

2. PLATO

Apart from perplexities and dubieties about the connexions between Plato's and Aristotle's philosophical
thinking there are independent reasons for doubting the
standard accounts of Plato's own philosophical life.

(i) *Plato's Floruit*

It is often assumed that Plato was a self-moving philosopher when quite a young man, and in particular that
he was composing Socratic dialogues soon after, if not
before the death of Socrates in 399, when Plato was about
thirty. As there exists no evidence whatsoever to confirm
it, it looks as if the assumption rests partly on the *a priori*
idea that a philosopher, or at least a great philosopher, has
in the nature of things to have launched himself on his
vocation when full of the vigour of youth. But this *a
priori* view is easily demolished. Aristotle, Berkeley and
Hume were indeed early flowerers; but if Locke and Kant
had died in their middle fifties, histories of philosophy
would hardly mention their names. The question Was
Plato a Hume or a Kant? is an open question.

There may be, not another reason, but an unwitting
motive behind the standard assumption. No one can read
Plato's early Socratic dialogues without loving Plato's
Socrates. The hope that the real Socrates was like Plato's
Socrates can tempt us to bolster up Plato's biographical
credibility by dating the composition of his Socratic dia-
logues very close to the lifetime of Socrates. Hoping that
Plato was a Boswell and not a Landor we welcome the

7

idea that when he wrote his early Socratic dialogues the voice of the real Socrates was still ringing in his ears. There is nothing unworthy in this hope. But it is not evidence and in fact there is no evidence at all to support the hope. It will be seen that there is conclusive evidence in the other direction.

The same doubts can be raised about the date of the foundation of Plato's Academy. We can be sure that this foundation came after Plato's first journey to Sicily at the beginning of the 380's. But we have no evidence at all to show that it came soon after his return. We know that the Academy was founded before 367 when the young Aristotle joined it; and before 369 when Theaetetus perished, having already become a teacher in it. But the prevalent supposition that Plato founded the Academy when he was in his early forties and not in his early or even late fifties is quite unsupported by evidence. It will be seen that there is very strong evidence in the other direction.

(ii) *Plato's Platonism*

Platonic scholars and commentators sometimes present their philosopher in a shape into which no one would dream of trying to squeeze any other philosopher. It is made to appear that fairly early in Plato's philosophical life, if not at its start, a special doctrine occurred to him. This doctrine, often dubbed 'Platonism', from then on remained his creed and no other important philosophical problems or ideas ever occurred to him. The bulk of his philosophical life was occupied in keeping this banner nailed to his mast.

8

Scholars and commentators have tried hard and with some success to trace the course of the philosophical development of Aristotle and to describe his exploitations of new equipments that he had provided for himself and his relinquishments of prepossessions of which he had become critical. Aristotle grew. Yet save in some minor matters no such growth has been generally permitted to Plato. Though praising Plato as the Master Thinker history has commonly allowed him no important new thinking and certainly no radical re-thinking. He had nothing more to learn from anyone else or even from himself. He never had to correct any serious mistakes of his own or to clear up any confusions in which he had formerly been. He started his explorations with the discovery of his Treasure Island; he had no need or desire to explore any more. In giving his latest philosophical writings to mankind he had nothing of importance to do save to repeat his habitual message.

That Plato's dialogues cannot be construed to fit this picture of the static philosopher needs to be argued in detail. For the moment it is necessary to state the *a priori* truth that being a philosopher cannot be like this. In theology a man may be captured for life by a doctrine. There is some tenet in which he is just a lifelong believer. But, *pace* the majority of historians of philosophy, philosophy is not adherence to a tenet or membership of a church or party. It is exploration. Only a *Terra Incognita* is interesting. It is a matter of course that a philosopher, like any other inquirer, is all the time learning at least from himself, at best both from himself and from others. If Plato was anything of a philosopher, then he cannot have been merely a lifelong Platonist. His problem of today cannot have been just his already solved single problem of two or twenty years ago. If Plato's late dialogues contain nothing of philosophical importance that was not already present in his middle or his early dialogues, we should say bluntly that Plato's philosophical arteries hardened regrettably soon, and that he was not a philosopher after his composition of those middle or early dialogues.

To say this is not to prejudge the question whether Plato's Theory of Forms is or contains the right solution to his then problem, whatever this problem was. It is only to say that if Plato had solved his then problem or thought that he had done so, then either he was intellectually sclerotic in never being teased by any ulterior problem; or else he was not sclerotic and so did not remain a mere partisan of Platonism. Either Plato was, after his adoption of Platonism, not much of a thinker, or his champions have misrepresented his thought. Either new problems did not force themselves on him—or they did. But if they did, then the story of Plato's philosophical development still awaits the telling. In justice to Plato we should ask not 'Did Plato grow?' but rather 'What was the course of his philosophic growth?'.

(iii) *The crisis*

In Plato's early and dramatically lively dialogues the argumentative action takes the shape of Socrates driving his interlocutors by sequences of questions into admitting the falsity of the theses that they had been defending. The dramatic climaxes of these dialogues are elenchi. Both for forcefulness of confutation and for dramatic power Plato reaches the peak of his genius in his *Gorgias* and in what would have been his *Thrasymachus*, namely what is now the body of Book I of our *Republic*.

Then quite suddenly, perhaps when halfway through composing his *Thrasymachus*, Plato abandons the elenctic dialogue. From now on the interlocutors of Socrates or of the Eleatic Stranger are only occasionally and perfunctorily defenders of theses; the dialectical checkmating of them virtually disappears. No longer employing strategies or stratagems Socrates himself flattens out in some dialogues into a professor or a preacher. The torpedo-fish has submerged and for a long time jollity disappears from the dialogues. It is natural to connect with this sudden abandonment of the dialectical dialogue the startling veto laid by Socrates in Book VII of the *Republic* on the participation in dialectical disputation by the young men, with his violent assertion '. . . they themselves and the whole business of philosophy are discredited with other men'. This Book, which announces to the world the education to be provided by the Academy, declares that dialectic is not to be any part of its curriculum for students. The young Aristotles are to have no philosophical training, but training only in mathematics and theoretical astronomy, for all that in some of Plato's quite recent elenctic dialogues and in his *Apology* the young men had been represented as benefiting supremely from training in the Socratic Method.

What is this public discredit or scandal which has come upon philosophy and upon the young men who have hitherto been participating in elenctic disputation? What bearings has Socrates' new veto on dialectic for the young men upon the relations between the philosopher Aristotle and the philosopher Plato? Have we to suppose that the young Aristotle, so far from being a philosophical disciple of Plato, was never even his philosophical pupil? Above all, did the scandal, if historically there was one, besides somehow forcing Plato abruptly to give up composing dialectical dialogues, affect the course of Plato's own philosophical thinking?

There are signs here of a crisis in Plato's life. What was this crisis; what differences did it make to him? History yields no answer. It does not even recognize the problem.

(iv) *Natural science*

In his *Timaeus* Plato expounds in considerable detail physical, physiological and pathological doctrines, many of which derive directly from the Italian scientists Archytas, Archedemus and Philistion. The description of Timaeus of Locri, at 20A and 27A, is the description of Archytas of Tarentum. After Socrates' renunciation of physical speculations in the *Phaedo* and after his contemptuous treatment of observational astronomy in the *Republic* VII and of medical science in the *Republic* III 405–410 it is matter for surprise that Plato now produces a full-scale treatise *On Nature and the Composition of Man*. That the contents of this treatise quickly became a basic study for students in the Academy is shown by the fact that from his early days Aristotle draws on the *Timaeus* far more frequently than on any other Platonic dialogue. Early in the *Timaeus* Plato does indeed aver that inside the field of Nature nothing better can be expected than probable conjectures; and he describes the search for knowledge of Nature merely as a recreation and a permissible pastime (59 C–D). But he soon forgets these apologetic sentiments, and in his later dialogue, the *Philebus*, which often exploits doctrines given in the *Timaeus*, he treats natural science as science and not as merely probable conjecture. The *Timaeus* is the first work that Plato wrote just for the Academy, and he wrote it not to entertain but to instruct.

Transcendent realities no longer monopolize science. The universe of things that move, alter, begin and end is no longer a kaleidoscope of semblances. Archytas, Philistion, Eudoxus, Speusippus and Aristotle can after all both pose their questions about Nature and hope to find the answers to them. To the writer of the *Timaeus* this world is no longer a place of exile for the philosopher. It now competes with the Transcendent World in both interestingness and investigability.

Opinions are divided whether the *Timaeus* is one of Plato's latest compositions or whether it belongs to the middle of his philosophical career. The latter view will be argued in Chapter VII. But if the latter view is right, then the Plato who wrote the late dialogues differs fundamentally in outlook from the Plato who wrote the *Phaedo*. The pious idea of reading the nostalgic otherworldliness of the *Phaedo* between the unaccommodating lines of the *Philebus*, *Cratylus*, *Theaetetus*, *Sophist*, *Politicus*, *Laws* and *Parmenides* founders on the reef of the *Timaeus*. Scientific understanding of Nature had formerly been despaired of.

Now the young Aristotles are brought up on the physics and the physiology that Plato has recently imported in his *Timaeus* from Sicily to the Academy. Doubtless the young Aristotles are duly awed by the Creation story with which the *Timaeus* opens. But what they study, discuss and correct is its astronomy, its chemistry, its human anatomy and its pathology. The Plato who compiled what is in large part a textbook for medical students has undergone a major conversion from the Plato who wrote the *Phaedo* and the *Republic*.

The orthodox picture of Plato as the stay-at-home Platonist leaves no room for this conversion. Even Aristotle, steeped though he is in the natural science of the *Timaeus*, makes no mention of it in his sketch of Plato's doctrines in his *Metaphysics* I. Presumably he correctly credited this natural science itself to Plato's Italian teachers, but it is still surprising that he says nothing here about the *bouleversement* given by this teaching to Plato's ontology and epistemology. Between Plato's contempt for observational astronomy in the *Republic* 529–30 and his lament over his earlier ignorance of it in the *Laws* VII 821–2 an intellectual revolution has occurred which has hardly ruffled the surface of the history of Plato's thought.

(v) *The Theory of Forms*

The Theory of Forms is given an honorific, though brief treatment in the *Timaeus*, from 51 C, though Plato does not put the Theory to any positive work. Plato seems to be defending the Theory of Forms against some actual critics of it. His one argument for the Theory is that the differ-

ences between Knowledge and Opinion require that there
exist eternal and immutable objects for the one and merely
temporary and mutable objects for the other.

But in his *Theaetetus* 196, without drawing any explicit
morals for the Theory of Forms, Plato proves two things.
First, that even about eternal and immutable objects, like
the number 7, we can be in a state of mere opinion. For
it can erroneously seem to us that, say, $7 + 5 = 11$.
Secondly, that about mundane happenings like crimes or
accidents an eyewitness can have knowledge, where the
jurors can achieve nothing better than opinion. What I
have knowledge and you have only opinion about may be
an eternal and immutable thing or it may be a mutable
thing or a momentary happening. Knowledge and
opinion, even true opinion, do indeed differ, but not in
having different provinces. The sole prop provided for the
Theory of Forms by Plato's *Timaeus* is tranquilly removed
by Plato's *Theaetetus*.

In the *Philebus* 15 the Theory of Forms is again mentioned with deference. Not only is the Theory obviously
now under heavy fire but in fact the argument of the rest
of the dialogue is based not at all on this Theory of Forms
but on the quite different principle, almost certainly
learned from Archytas, of the limit and the limitable.
Aristotle, always an antagonist of the Theory of Forms,
unquestioningly adopts, systematizes and develops this
theory of the limit and the limitable. Latter-day
Friends of the Forms sometimes try to affiliate the theory
of the limit and the limitable to the Theory of Forms, but
Aristotle knew that the rejection of the latter Theory is en-

tirely compatible with acceptance of the former theory.

In the *Sophist* 248-9 Plato speaks with surprising detachment of the Friends or the Partisans of the Forms. He demonstrates that they ought to acknowledge the full reality of at least some impermanent and mutable entities, namely the human minds that acquire, at some moment of time, their knowledge of the Forms. It is interesting to speculate who in the 350's these Friends of the Forms are. For neither Speusippus nor Xenocrates nor Eudoxus nor, of course, Aristotle champions the Theory of Forms. Does even Plato?

Finally, in Part I of the *Parmenides* Plato puts into Parmenides' mouth a series of objections to the juvenile Socrates' Theory of Forms, and specifically to his accounts of the relations between Forms and particulars and between Forms and human intellects. Parmenides' argumentation is so careful, drastic and philosophically professional that its very style reminds us of Aristotle at work. More than this. At least one of Parmenides' destructive arguments is the brother or first cousin of the famous Third Man argument that Aristotle also employs against the Theory of Forms. These arguments of Parmenides are sometimes, very oddly, written off as devoid of cogency. Sometimes, even more oddly, they are allowed to be cogent and yet denied to affect the position against which they are cogent. Plato himself represents Socrates' Theory of Forms as a juvenile theory which betrays Socrates' lack of the required dialectical discipline.

Thus we find Plato in the late dialogues, the *Philebus*, *Theaetetus* and *Sophist*, at least detached from his old

Theory of Forms, and in the *Parmenides* apparently de-
molitionary of it. Yet Aristotle nowhere mentions an in-
fanticidal Plato. Even the possibility of such a stage in
Plato's thought is ignored by the orthodox view of Plato as
the lifelong Friend of the Forms. The first part of the *Parmenides* by itself is conclusive proof either of the falsity or
else of the prematurity of Aristotle's account of Plato's
thought in his *Metaphysics* I. It is by itself conclusive proof
also of the falsity of the orthodox view of Plato as the
philosophical stay-at-home.

Whether with disappointment or with relief we have
to recognize that Plato's thought moved. We have to try
to chart an intellectual odyssey which took Plato from the
elenctic dialogues, through and past the *Phaedo* and the
Republic, *via* the *Timaeus* and the *Philebus*, to the *Parmenides*, Part I, the *Cratylus*, the *Theaetetus*, the *Sophist* and
the *Parmenides*, Part II.

(vi) *Dialectic*

In Plato's early dialogues up to, say, the *Gorgias* or the
would-have-been *Thrasymachus* the argumentation is so
constructed as to terminate in the confutations of theses.
Whether the answerer's thesis is a definition, like 'Justice
is the Interest of the Stronger', or just a general proposition,
like 'Virtue is Teachable', the application of the Socratic
Method to his thesis culminates, if successful, in its demolition. If an elenctic argument is compelling, it compels the
answerer to abandon a position. The Socratic Method
cannot terminate in the establishing of a definition, in the
demonstration of a thesis or in the resolution of an *aporia*.

Its achievements are the exposures of inconsistencies. They are not yet what Aristotle or the terminal Plato rank as 'philosophy'. Now the elenctic debating which these dialogues exemplify is identical with the dialectic of which Aristotle's *Topics* is the *Art* or Methodology. Here Aristotle develops the methodology of the rule-governed battles of wits of which Plato's elenctic dialogues give us dramatized specimens. Aristotle is the Clausewitz to Plato's Napoleon.

We can be sure that for a time Plato had not only composed dialectical dramas; he had also taught elenctic argumentation to young men. He had tutorially conducted eristic Moots. Indeed his dialectical dialogues should be read as case-books of recent Moots, dramatized partly to help students to remember and digest the argument-sequences that finally crystallized out of these Moots. Yet before Aristotle joined the Academy, indeed before the Academy was started, Plato had been compelled, somehow, to stop composing eristic mimes, because he had been compelled, somehow, to stop conducting eristic Moots for the young men.

In Book VII of the *Republic* we are told that there is to be no training in dialectic for the young men in the Academy. It is not until the early 350's that Aristotle himself introduces into the Academy's curriculum the dialectical training for the young men from which he himself in his own student days had been screened.

Though withdrawn from the practice of the Socratic Method Plato never lost his passion for it. In his *Apology*, *Republic*, *Philebus*, *Phaedrus* and *Sophist* he continues to pay high tributes to the exercise. In the second part of his *Parmenides* he presents as a curricular paradigm an elaborate, virtually undramatized argumentation-chain terminating in the multilateral confutation of a single thesis and of its negation. What the *Parmenides*, Part II, exhibits is just what Aristotle's *Topics* requires of philosophically rewarding dialectic. Here Plato and his young colleague, Aristotle, are entirely *en rapport*. Parmenides' young interlocutor has the name 'Aristotle'. Plato does differ from Aristotle and also from himself in his accounts of the theoretical profits of this elenctic debating. But as in the 370's, so in the 350's Plato still sees dialectic as the coping-stone of education.

Aristotle's polemics against the Theory of Forms obviously issue out of formal disputations *pro* and *contra* Plato's old thesis. We may surmise that like Socrates in the *Gorgias* 458 A Plato relished the compellingness of the dialectic more than he lamented its demolition of his own old thesis. In Part I of his *Parmenides* he makes his own contribution to that nexus of destructive arguments. He cares more for a conclusive rebuttal than he cares for even his own, once darling doctrine. This Plato is not the Plato of the Neo-Platonists or the Plato of later commentators. It is not even the Plato of Aristotle's *Metaphysics* I. But it is the real Plato, a Plato who has been overlooked by his antagonists no worse than by his devotees.

3. CONCLUSION

If we are to determine the effects of Plato's writings on the thought of Aristotle, we have from the start to be suspicious of their accepted chronology and to be prepared to find that Aristotle, so far from having been brought up on all of the writings, was himself producing logical, scientific and philosophical ideas before he had access to most of Plato's later dialogues. We have also to be suspicious of the congenial picture of the youthful Aristotle sitting at the feet of the Head of the Academy.

If we are to make philosophical sense of Plato's writings in themselves, we have to renounce the supposition that Plato was the lifelong warder or prisoner of a tenet. Plato travelled. The reconstruction of his intellectual journey requires for its own sake drastic revision of the accepted chronology of his writings. It also requires a drastic revision of the accepted account of his visits to Sicily, together with the rejection of the authenticity of some of the so-called Platonic Epistles on which this account is based. Sicily did indeed make all the difference to the course of Plato's thinking, but the description of this difference has to be founded in an examination of the new qualities of that thinking.

Most important but also most hazardous of all is the duty to discover, against the resistance of a totally reticent history, the nature and the effects of that crisis in Plato's life, which abruptly terminated his production of elenctic dialogues, made him forbid the teaching of dialectic to young men in the Academy, and even, perhaps, caused him to found the Academy itself with a curriculum which gave no teaching role to its Head. What was the disaster that broke Plato's intimate association with young students and forced out of him his lament in the *Phaedo* at Heaven's ban on suicide?

CHAPTER II

THE PUBLICATION OF DIALOGUES

I. BOOK-READING

How did Plato, Glaucon, Aeschines, Xenophon, Aristotle and the many other writers of dialogues publish their compositions? Certainly the 'book of the dialogue', like that of the play, was often procurable by readers. But the fact that we ourselves can often purchase from bookshops the texts of songs, plays, sermons, Reith Lectures and Third Programme discussions does not make us think that such productions are composed for readers. They are composed for listeners. Their reading public is epiphytic upon their listening public. If there existed no congregations, there would exist no volumes of printed sermons. So perhaps Plato and the others composed dialogues for audiences, and later made them available also for readers. This was certainly true of the composers of successful tragedies, comedies and mimes, of panegyric, funeral and forensic orations, and of some sophists' lectures.

Our familiarity with print inclines us to forget that in Plato's day every copy of the text of a tragedy, an epic or a panegyric address had to be separately handwritten by a copyist, much as until a couple of generations ago boots and shoes were separately hand-made for individual wearers by individual shoemakers. We have no contemporary testimony that during Plato's lifetime there yet existed bookstores exhibiting stocks of ready-made books; and though we get a few allusions, we get oddly few allusions from fourth-century writers to the purchase, ownership or use of books. We know that booksellers existed, but we have to guess whether as yet a bookseller was more than a copyist who would write out his personal copy for a customer who had bespoken one. It is in the *Life of Zeno the Stoic* by Diogenes Laertius that our earliest bookstore is mentioned, though we cannot argue from silence that such stores had not existed in Plato's day.

In his *Phaedrus* 274 B–277 A Plato surprises us by deploring the use of books, save as mere *aides-mémoires*. At 257 D he treats book-writing as a thing done by sophists. In his *Memorabilia* IV, 11 Xenophon's rich and ambitious young Euthydemus is regarded as exceptional in being the owner of a library of books. He even owns the whole of Homer. The other books mentioned all seem to be vocational training manuals, that is, *Arts* of the sort that sophists wrote (cf. Plato's *Sophist* 232 D–E and *Hippias Minor* 368 C–E). Euripides was famous for the possession of a lot of books, which shows that in his time book-ownership was a rare thing. He seems to have kept a personal copyist of his own.

We know that literacy was almost universal in Athens, else the jokes against Spartan illiteracy would not have amused. We do not know that there existed a book-buying public large enough for authors to write merely for its pleasure and improvement. No books are bequeathed in Plato's own will. The young Aristotle seems to have been nicknamed 'The Reader', as if inside the Academy itself during the 360's book-reading was still an uncommon hobby.

Besides suspecting of anachronism the idea that Plato or anyone else composed just for the eyes of exceptional people like Euthydemus, Euripides and Aristotle, we need positive evidence for the opposite idea that Plato, like the dramatists, orators and composers of mimes, wrote for audiences. We have no contemporary testimony for this idea, any more than we have it for the idea that he wrote for book-readers. We have to make do with straws.

2. THE RECITATION OF DIALOGUES

(a) Plato's dialogues are dramatic, his earlier dialogues much more dramatic than his later ones. Some of these have been recently performed by schoolboys and students and, as we should expect, they act extremely well. It is natural to suppose that their author designed them to have the theatrical excellences which they do in fact possess. Conversely it is unnatural to suppose that Plato was requiring readers to imagine themselves hearing dialectical mimes, who had never had even the chance of hearing any. Divines do sometimes publish volumes of sermons that have never been preached; but only because their readers already know what it is like to listen to sermons from the pulpit. Berkeley, Hume and Landor write dialogues for readers only; but perhaps they are trading on a previously existent art of writing dialogues for audiences. The literary simulacrum has to be posterior to the real thing and to lack the life of the real thing. It smells proleptically of the reader's lamp. There is no such smell in Plato's earlier dialogues.

(*b*) Aristotle frequently contrasts 'exoteric' discourses with other discourses designed for academic recipients. Assuming that Aristotle is referring to things in writing scholars have been puzzled to give sense to the contrast. How could writings be channelled towards and away from different classes of readers? But if Aristotle is talking about spoken discourses, the problem vanishes. Dialogues are exoteric since they are recited to the general public. Lectures are not exoteric since they are delivered to students in the school. If 'exoteric' means 'extra-mural', this can be an epithet only of things spoken. Some scholars have equated exoteric discourses with compositions endowed with literary elegances. This is right enough but only *per accidens*. Exoteric compositions have to entertain audiences of non-students, and audiences already habituated to dramatic and rhetorical performances.

(*c*) Diogenes Laertius tells a few stories of philosophers, including Plato, delivering dialogues or other discourses to audiences, in his *Aeschines* 62; his *Plato* 35, 37; his *Antisthenes* 2; and his *Democritus* 39. Two of the stories, both about Plato, must be falsehoods. But the fact that Diogenes takes the occurrence of such recitals as a matter of course has a little evidential value. We know from Aristoxenus that Plato delivered his lecture on *The Good* to a mainly non-academic audience. It was not a success; perhaps for that reason it was never issued in book-form. We do not know whether it was in the shape of a dialogue or of a monologue, like the *Timaeus*. In his *Politics* II 1263 b 16

24

Aristotle speaks of the recipient of Plato's *Republic* as a 'listener'.

(*d*) In the *Seventh Letter* 341D Plato is made to say that the lecture, συνουσία, which he gave to Dionysius II was not to be given to the general public either in writing *or in speech* (italics added), though it might be given to the few who had learned to research. The laity would either despise it or else get inflated with empty expectations.

Galen, who knew the history of medicine better than anyone, says that Plato gave his *Timaeus* only to the few with scientific training. The general public would have despised it. Galen makes it clear that the contemptuous public would have been a listening public (p. 757 of vol. IV of Kühn's *Galeni Opera Omnia*).

The facts that the lecture mentioned in the *Seventh Letter* was about Nature, φύσις (341E, 344D), and that the *Timaeus* is the only Platonic composition on this subject, indicate that Galen and the *Seventh Letter* are saying the same thing about the same Platonic work. Plato's *Timaeus* was exceptional in not being intended for issue to the general public at all, either in writing *or in speech*.

(*e*) In Plato's *Parmenides* 136D–E Zeno says that it would have been wrong to impose on Parmenides the heavy task of demonstrating the dialectical method in front of Hoi Polloi, since he is too old and Hoi Polloi do not realize that only by such lengthy argumentations can we reach the truth. Since, dramatically, there is no question of Hoi Polloi being present in Pythodorus' private house, it may be inferred that Plato is explaining why the *Parmenides* is not to be heard by the general public, but only by the members of the Academy; that is, why he is making an exception to what has been, apart from the *Timaeus*, his regular practice.

(*f*) In the *Laws* 811 the Athenian Stranger, discussing what poetry and prose should be learned by boys and young men, says:

I think I am not wholly in want of a pattern, for when I consider the words which we have spoken from early dawn until now...they appear to me quite like a poem...of all the discourses which I have ever learnt or heard, this seemed to me the justest and most suitable for young men to hear...the director of education...cannot do better than advise the teachers to teach the young men these words and any which are of a like nature; if he should happen to find them, either in poetry or prose, or if he came across unwritten discourses akin to ours, he should certainly preserve them and commit them to writing.

Plato, in referring to the *Laws* as 'unwritten discourses', could not have been thinking of the recipients of these words as readers of written words, but only as listeners to spoken words. If the *Laws*, a late and very undramatic dialogue, was written or rather partly rewritten for delivery to Athenian listeners, *a fortiori* the same is likely to be true of the earlier and more dramatic dialogues.

(*g*) In the *Politicus* 286 B–287 A there is a queer digression. The Eleatic Stranger pauses to justify the length and tediousness of two stretches of the current discussion and one stretch of the previous discussion in the *Sophist*. He speaks of an 'impatience' with the length and irrelevance of these stretches and he concedes some justification for this impatience. He distinguishes those who wish to become better dialecticians and so will brook necessary *longueurs* from those who applaud and find fault on other scores. The latter 'we must ignore and pretend not even to hear them'. But neither in our *Sophist* nor in our *Politicus* has anyone so much as murmured. There are not even any non-philosophers dramatically present in the company.

It looks as if Plato has here inserted *post eventum* a partial apology, partial reproof to a real lay audience which had vocally expressed its understandable discontent with the difficult stretch about Non-Being in the *Sophist* and with the wearisome and seemingly pointless stretches in the *Politicus* about Weaving and the Backward Rotating Cosmos. Our own feeling that the *Sophist* and *Politicus* were badly designed for unacademic recipients is borne out by the way in which they appear to have been received by their actual lay audience. Plato has outlived his earlier genius in composing exoterically; but he is still irritated by his old public's new censoriousness. The passage from the *Parmenides* referred to above shows that Plato eventually learned the unpalatable lesson that what is suited to trained philosophers is unsuitable for Hoi Polloi. The general public has not kept abreast of the Academy. The dialectical mime has had its day.

(*h*) In the *Sophist* and *Politicus* Socrates is replaced as discussion-leader by the Eleatic Stranger. Why?

The main argument of the *Sophist* is anti-Eleatic in tenor; that of the *Politicus* has nothing Eleatic in it. The central problem of the *Sophist* is continuous with one major problem of the *Theaetetus*, in which Socrates is the discussion-leader. The analogy from Letters and Syllables used by Socrates in the *Cratylus*, *Theaetetus* and *Philebus* is used also by the Eleatic Stranger in the *Sophist* and *Politicus*. The Stranger is not a spokesman for any un-Socratic philosophical outlooks or methods. Even Platonic scholars sometimes forget that Socrates is not discussion-leader in these two dialogues.

On the theory that dialogues were recited to audiences, coupled with the rider that normally Plato himself took the speaking parts of his Socrates, a plausible explanation suggests itself of the replacement of Socrates by the Eleatic Stranger. The hypothesis is this. Plato, now pretty aged, was smitten by an illness which disabled him from dis-coursing to audiences. Dramatically, Socrates could no longer lead discussions. Plato had already completed his trilogy of the *Theaetetus*, *Sophist* and *Politicus*, all at this stage being normal Socrates-led dialogues; and just when the occasion for their oral delivery was close at hand 'Socrates' was incapacitated. What was to be done, given that no one else could be allowed to take over Plato's long-standing role as Socrates? The *Sophist* and *Politicus* needed only slight alterations in order to be deliverable. Plato was deputized for, in the new role of the Eleatic Stranger, by a friend or an actor, as Isocrates' public orations were de-livered from a substitute-throat. Nearly but not quite all that the text needed was the introduction of the Stranger at the beginning of the *Sophist* and the interpolation of a few Eleatic remarks (e.g. 237A, 241D, 242A).

The *Theaetetus*, however, needed and received a totally different treatment. The discussion contains a lot that is highly personal to Socrates, and anyhow Socrates has to say 'Farewell' to his devoted public. Very ingeniously Plato invents an unparalleled pattern of discussion-representation. For our *Theaetetus* is not in *oratio recta*, as are the *Sophist*, *Politicus*, *Philebus*, *Laws* and most of the earlier dialogues. But it is also not in *oratio obliqua*, as are the *Lysis*, *Charmides*, *Protagoras*, *Symposium*, *Phaedo*, *Euthydemus* and *Republic*. To his text of the original dialogue, which had been in *oratio recta* like the *Sophist* and *Politicus*, Plato added a new preamble in which after some conversation Euclides' slave reads out to Euclides, Terpsion and, dramatically, ourselves the *ipsissima verba* of a discussion that had been held between Socrates, Theodorus and Theaetetus thirty years before. The slave does not read out a reporter's story describing their conversation; he vocally re-enacts the conversation itself. The 'slave', presumably a trained actor, takes the vocal parts of each of the three speakers in turn.

We, the audience, are listening, dramatically in Megara in 369, just to the reciting-voice of the slave. But what he recites to us, like a delayed echo or a long-preserved gramophone record, is the actual words uttered by three different speakers thirty years ago in Athens. This is not *oratio recta*. It is relayed or echoed *oratio recta*. It is no wonder that this unique presentation-method is apologized for in the *Theaetetus* 143 C. It is a mistake to read this as an apology for direct speech. Direct speech needs no apology. The majority of Plato's dialogues are in direct speech. The apology is for using echoed direct speech to represent the utterances of absent speakers not by narrator's description, but by a single *diseur*'s multiple impersonation. Here and here only are we given, so to speak, a single human gramophone resurrecting the plural voices of departed speakers.

This novel literary expedient enabled the entire discussion to be orally delivered unaltered, without 'Socrates', i.e. Plato, being on the stage. Only 'Euclides', 'Terpsion' and 'the slave' are on the stage.

There remained one dramatic hurdle which Plato could not clear. Doubtless his hearers forgave it, if they noticed the matter at all. The chronological unity between the *Theaetetus* and the *Sophist* is now totally dislocated. Dramatically, we, the audience, are on our Monday in the company of Euclides and Terpsion in Megara in 369, while the middle-aged Theaetetus is dying and when Socrates has been dead for thirty years. But on our Tuesday we are, dramatically, in Athens in 399 in the lively company of Socrates, Theodorus, the Stranger and the promising lad Theaetetus. The *Sophist* and *Politicus* are not in echoed direct speech. The speakers' voices are not relayed by Euclides' slave. The yesterday of the *Sophist* is not our Monday in Megara but a Monday in Athens thirty years earlier. Dramatically, we, the audience, have grown thirty years younger between Monday and Tuesday, and the dying forty-eight-year-old Theaetetus has woken up after a night's sleep into the lad of eighteen that he had been in the year that Socrates was executed.

For this total hypothesis there exist some strong corroborations.

(*a*) In his *Letter* 58 to Lucilius Seneca says that Plato had a grave illness as the result of his journeys to Sicily. By adhering to a strict régime he was able to live and work for a long time afterwards. This illness would therefore have occurred a good number of years before 347 when Plato died, and after, but presumably not long after his return from Sicily in 360. An illness in the not very late 350's would tally well with the dating of the *Theaetetus*, *Sophist* and *Politicus* that is argued for partly on other grounds in Chapter VII.

(*b*) The inferred last-minute replacement of Socrates by the Eleatic Stranger would have necessitated one piece of very pervasive emendation of Plato's personal texts of the *Sophist* and *Politicus*. Wherever the interlocutors had originally used the vocative 'O Socrates', this would have either to be replaced between the lines by 'O Stranger' or else to be simply deleted. In fact what we find in these two dialogues is just seven or eight interlocutors' 'O Stranger' vocatives, whereas in the *Theaetetus*, *Cratylus* and *Philebus* there are respectively 90, 65 and 70 interlocutors' 'O Socrates' vocatives. Moreover, in the dialogues other than the *Sophist* and *Politicus* there always obtains a rough parity between the frequency of leaders' vocatives and that of interlocutors' vocatives. But in these two dialogues, while the Stranger addresses his interlocutors with the appropriate vocatives some three dozen times each, he receives in return only just over half a dozen 'O Stranger' vocatives, where the statistical expectation would be between two and four dozen.

These signs that Plato chose to dispense wholesale with the interlocutors' vocatives in just these two dialogues strongly confirm the idea that there had been a last-minute replacement of the discussion-leader. Erasure of vocatives was simpler and tidier than frequent interlinear insertion of new vocatives. Incidentally Plato has no dislike for the vocative 'O Stranger' in itself. It occurs reasonably often in the *Laws*, where the Athenian Stranger now and then actually addresses as 'O Stranger' one of his two interlocutors, though these have proper names of their own.

(*c*) This hypothesis would also give a simple explanation why in the *Politicus* 277 D the Stranger illegitimately refers to a bother that he had met with during the *Theaetetus* discussion—illegitimately since he had not been present; and why in the *Sophist* 248 B the Stranger, now on his first visit to Athens, unplausibly claims to be well acquainted with the champions of the Theory of Forms—unplausibly since this Theory did not have an Eleatic, but did have an Athenian habitat. Plato just forgot to eliminate these two originally Socratic remarks from the words to be spoken by the substitute discussion-leader.

These clues seem to establish beyond reasonable doubt the view that Plato normally composed his dialogues for oral delivery to audiences; that these audiences were general or lay audiences; and that Plato himself was normally the deliverer of his Socrates' words. To what sort or sorts of audiences were his dialogues thus recited? There is not an unique answer, but there is one answer the importance of which requires it to be stated at once.

3. GAMES-AUDIENCES

(*a*) If Plato's *Theaetetus*, *Sophist* and *Politicus* constituted a trilogy of which the three parts were to be delivered in three consecutive sessions; and if the account is accepted of the last-minute replacement of Socrates by the Eleatic Stranger, then we have to ask 'In what circumstances did there exist continuing three-session audiences, the time of whose assembly was so pre-ordained that Plato, in an emergency, could not get the time altered?' The answer is clear. The Games, which provided three- or four-day audiences for the dramatists, provided three- or four-day audiences for the dialogue-writers too. The dates of Games were rigidly calendared. A sophist like Hippias, offering an ordinary epideictic oration or lecture, could fix its place and time to suit himself (*Hippias Major* 286B). But if Hippias was to compete at the Olympic Games or one of the Athenian Games, he would have to be ready and present on the pre-appointed day.

(*b*) We know from Plato's own *Hippias Minor* 363–4 and 368 that there were at the Olympic Games competitions for discourses in prose as well as in verse; and Isocrates, who at the beginning of his *Panegyricus* complains that the original founders of the Games had initiated contests for athletes only, not for people who had trained minds, later praises Athens for providing contests not only of strength and speed, but also of eloquence, wisdom and all the other arts, λόγων καὶ γνώμης καὶ τῶν ἄλλων ἔργων ἁπάντων (45).

In [Aristotle's] *Problems* XXX 11 it is asked why the Games began without intellectual contests and the answer is suggested that here, though not in athletics, the judges must be as good as the competitors. In Diogenes Laertius' *Life of Theophrastus* 37 a letter from Theophrastus to Phanias seems to refer to *panegureis* as *venues* for philosophers' compositions.

(c) Diogenes Laertius in his *Plato* 56 reports Thrasyllus as saying that Plato published his dialogues in tetralogies in the way the tragedians competed with one another in the Games with dramatic tetralogies. It is not clear how closely Thrasyllus meant to assimilate the publication of dialogues to that of tragedies. His actual groupings of Platonic dialogues into fours are often ridiculous. He even treats the *Letters en bloc* as one dialogue.

But Thrasyllus did have something to go on. For the *Sophist, Politicus* and the unwritten *Philosopher* had been planned to form a sequence, and the *Theaetetus* is made, perhaps as an afterthought, dramatically the precursor to the *Sophist*. At the beginning of the *Timaeus* we hear of the planned trilogy of Socrates' discourse on the Ideal State, the *Critias* and the *Hermocrates*. The beginning and the end of the *Philebus* make it look like a torso, desiderating a prior Part I and a posterior Part III. It has a dangling 'tomorrow' at 50E. The *Cratylus* has one at 396E. However, a single instance of a trilogy of dialogues is enough for our purposes. Greece knew what trilogies were. They were sequences of three plays acted in successive sessions to continuing audiences. The 'yesterdays' and 'tomorrows' which dramatically link the discussions in the *Theaetetus, Sophist* and *Politicus* would have a live continuities-point for a three-day audience. They would have no live point for mere readers.

(d) Five of Plato's dialogues, namely the *Republic, Symposium, Ion, Timaeus* and *Parmenides*, allude to dramatically synchronous festivals. Conceivably some of these allusions were topical.

34

(e) In his *Oratio* 26 Themistius divides Aristotle's writings into three main groups, of which one consists of works composed πρὸς ἕνα ἀγῶνα, for a single contest (see p. 435 of Düring's *Aristotle in the Ancient Biographical Tradition*). Themistius has been taken to be referring to Aristotle's logical works, which do teach dialectical duelling. But this leaves 'single' unexplained. So Themistius might be referring to Aristotle's dialogues, which otherwise are omitted from his classification. Themistius certainly has Aristotle's exoteric compositions in mind, for in the next paragraph he describes their gracefulness and their suitability for the *demos* or the *plethos*—terms, incidentally, which could not denote the relatively few purchasers of books. A competition-piece at a festival, whether a play, an oration or, inferentially, a philosopher's dialogue, could compete only once. Thucydides presumably has some point in saying that his history is not an ἀγώνισμα εἰς τὸ παραχρῆμα ἀκούειν, a competition-piece to be listened to on a solitary occasion (Book I, ch. 22).

(f) The topic-titles of dialogues listed by Diogenes Laertius or known from other sources show a great number of recurrences. Dialogues 'On the Soul', 'On Whether Virtue is Teachable', 'On Beauty', 'On the Sophist', 'On the Statesman', 'On Justice' and so on were composed not only by Plato but also by Antisthenes, Crito, Simon, Aristotle, Xenocrates, Heracleides and others. It could be that competitors had to choose their dialogue-themes out of an authorized list, as we gather from Isocrates that competing orators chose their themes, ὑποθέσεις, out of such a list. Such lists would presumably be modified year by year.

3-2

The topic-title 'On Forms' could not have existed until the *Phaedo* had become well known. This might explain why Plato's *Phaedrus* is called 'About Love', when it is really about Rhetoric. The specimens of rhetoric introduced into the dialogue are indeed about Love, but they could have been about anything else without affecting the dialogue's argument. Perhaps 'About Rhetoric' happened not to be on the official list of topic-titles. It might also explain why Plato's *Sophist* has so artificially to safety-pin the philosophical theme of Non-Being or Negation on to the unphilosophical stretches about the Sophist. 'Non-Being' was not on the list; 'the Sophist' was. So Plato, who wanted to discuss Non-Being, ingeniously, though totally fallaciously, represented the notion of *non-being* as being specially closely related to the notion of *sophist*.

This idea of an official list of dialogue-themes might also provide an explanation of the fact that many dialogues, whether by Plato or by other writers, have two titles, namely a topic-title, for example 'About Friendship', and a proper-name title like 'Lysis'. If there were to be several competing dialogues about Friendship, these would need to be known by differentiating titles, and preferably differentiating titles which had not been used much or at all before. So the proper name of one of the *dramatis personae*, who sometimes was not a leading character in the dialogue, was used for the differentiating title of the dialogue. The pseudo-Platonic dialogue, *Hipparchus*, is named after a character who is not even dramatically present. He is only incidentally referred to by Socrates. No dialogue is recorded with the proper-name title 'Socrates'.

(g) Some of Plato's dialogues are in *oratio obliqua*. In the *Lysis, Charmides, Protagoras, Euthydemus* and *Republic* Socrates narrates stories about conversations that he himself had formerly had with Protagoras, say, or with Glaucon and Adeimantus. At the oral delivery of such dialogues we, the audience, would be listening all or almost all the time to the sole voice of 'Socrates', i.e. of Plato.

There remain three dialogues in *oratio obliqua*, namely the *Symposium, Phaedo* and *Parmenides*, Part I (only), in which the narrator is not Socrates but Apollodorus in the *Symposium*, Phaedo in the *Phaedo* and Cephalus in the *Parmenides*. These dialogues could have been recited to their audiences by speakers other than Plato. Why was Socrates off-staged in just these dialogues? Certainly, given that he was off-staged, stories could be told about him which he could not have told about himself. Phaedo can describe Socrates' death; and Apollodorus can describe the conversation at the dinner-table during the time when Socrates is in his meditative trance outside the house. But Plato may have employed this dramatic device of a narrator other than Socrates for another reason, merely taking advantage of the special opportunity that it gave him to tell things about Socrates that 'Socrates' could not have delivered. For these dialogues could be recited to Athenian audiences without Plato himself even being in Athens. Having appointed a friend or an actor to be 'Apollodorus' or 'Phaedo', Plato could, for example, go to Syracuse without leaving his Athenian public for some eighteen months unprovided with Platonic dialogues.

The suggestion is that the *Symposium* and *Phaedo* were

composed during the year or so before the April of 367 for delivery to the public at one or two of the Athenian festivals which would be taking place during the period when Plato was to be overseas. These two dialogues have been judged by scholars and stylometrists to be neighbours of one another in date of composition.

Now the *Symposium* 178 E–179 A contains an overlooked but unmistakable allusion to the defeat of Sparta at Leuctra by a much smaller Theban force, of which the Erastae were the spearhead. So the *Symposium* must date after the late summer of 371, which brings its composition very near to the inferred date 369–367. The *Thirteenth Letter*, no matter who wrote it, is internally datable to the winter-spring of 366–365, and it refers explicitly to the *Phaedo* as a dialogue which the Younger Dionysius 'probably' knows. Plato had just been the guest of Dionysius for over a year, so if the *Phaedo* had been published in book-form before Plato left Athens, he would have known that Dionysius had his copy. The letter proves that the book of the *Phaedo* had been published before early 365, and fairly strongly suggests that it had been published not long before this date. The mention of it is meant to be topical. So both dialogues do seem to have been composed during the two or three years before April 367, when Plato left Athens for Sicily.

Less surely the analogous thing holds of the *Parmenides*, Part I. It might well have been designed to be delivered in Athens in 361–360, while Plato would again be in Syracuse. This time, however, an alternative hypothesis needs to be considered. For if his illness in, say, 358–356 had damaged his physical strength or his voice but not his powers of composition, Plato might have designed the dialogue to be delivered from a substitute-throat, although he would himself be present in Athens at the time and merely *hors de combat*. However, the fact that the *Theaetetus* 183 E seems to refer back to the discussion between the youthful Socrates and the old Parmenides indicates, with other pointers, reasonably strongly that this dialogue-torso was composed before Plato's illness, and therefore that it was being composed with Plato's third visit to Sicily in prospect.

Any plausibility that belongs to this explanation of the non-Socratic narrators of the *Symposium*, *Phaedo* and *Parmenides*, Part I, is inherited by the general theory that Plato and the other writers of dialogues wrote for Games-audiences.

(*h*) This hypothesis might explain why we find a large cluster of Plato's middle-sized dialogues of so nearly exactly the same length. The *Protagoras*, *Symposium*, *Phaedo*, *Philebus*, *Phaedrus*, *Cratylus*, *Sophist* and *Politicus* are of the following lengths in Stephanus pages: 52, 51, 59, 55, 52, 57, 52 and 54. Even our *Phaedo* of only 59 pages seems after its public delivery in Athens in 367–366 to have received a five-page supplementation from 108C to 113C (see Chapter VII, 5). Perhaps Plato had found that 52–54 pages was the optimum length for audience enjoyment. Or perhaps the timetable of the Games imposed an upper limit. Aristotle in his *Poetics* VII 6 tells us that in some competitions the entries were regulated by the water-clock. He does not say what competitions these were, save that they were not for tragedies. Obviously they were not athletic contests. This suggestion should leave us wondering about the numerous very short dialogues like the *Ion*, of only twelve pages, or the *Laches*, of twenty-two pages. These seem too short to have kept a Games-audience entertained for long enough.

(i) When in 369–368 Dionysius I invited Isocrates, Aristippus, Aeschines, Plato and, for all we know, other distinguished persons to come from Athens to Syracuse in 367, to what was he inviting them? The visitors were to present new compositions to their host. Isocrates was to bring with him or send an advisory address; Plato composed for the visit his *Ideal State*, began to compose his *Critias* and planned to compose the *Hermocrates*. From the résumé of the first and the preamble to the second which incongruously preface our *Timaeus* it is clear that these contributions would have been presented on a 'today', a 'yesterday' and presumably a 'tomorrow'. The occasion for which Dionysius invited his distinguished guests was to have been at least a three-day occasion. Already it looks as if Dionysius had planned a festival of the regular pattern.

In his *Hiero* I. II Xenophon tells us that tyrants, debarred from attending the festivals of other states, have at great expense to organize their own festivals and to pay foreign competitors handsomely in order to induce or enable them to come.

At the beginning of his *Evagoras* we hear from Isocrates of a festival organized by the king of Cyprus in honour of his deceased father. Isocrates himself was lavishly rewarded for his three rhetorical contributions to it, namely, the

Evagoras, *To Nicocles* and *Nicocles*. Isocrates was also invited with Theodectes to compete in the Memorial Games organized by the widow of Mausolus of Halicarnassus. In his *To Nicocles* 13 and 54 Isocrates advises the new king to invite famous poets and sages from overseas as often as possible; in Plato's *Laws* 953 the Athenian Stranger lays down rules to facilitate such visits; and Xenophon in his *Hiero* makes Simonides give the same counsel to the tyrant of Syracuse. So Dionysius I, a constant patron of the arts, would have been doing quite a regular thing in organizing a Palace Festival and in inviting eminent literary persons to come from Athens to compete. Plato in accepting such an invitation would have been doing nothing *infra dignitatem*. His readiness to participate in a Syracusan festival demolishes any *a priori* presumption that he could not or would not have composed his dialogues for oral presentation in competitions at Athenian or Olympic Games. Rather, Plato was invited to compete in *panegureis* in Syracuse in 367–366 and 361–360 just because he was already famous for his contributions to such festivals in Athens and perhaps Olympia. In Chapter VII, 11, evidence is adduced for the idea that Plato's *Phaedrus* was composed for the Olympic Games of July 360.

(*j*) We cannot suppose that audiences for dialogues were very large ones. The debating techniques and even the topics debated could not have interested very many people who had never themselves taken part in such disputations. We could conjecture that it was especially for such un-dialectical minorities that Plato's myths catered.

The Boy-Love *motif*, strong in the *Lysis*, *Charmides*,

[*Alcibiades*], *Euthydemus*, *Gorgias*, *Meno*, *Symposium* and *Phaedrus*, suggests that the audience would consist largely of young men. It is the young men of whom Isocrates says in his *Panathenaicus* 26 that they are inordinately fond of the so-called eristic διάλογοι, though he may refer by this noun to disputations rather than to dialogues dramatically representing such disputations.

A clue of quite a different sort is provided by the *Meno*. When Socrates elicits geometrical truths from the slave-boy he employs a slightly intricate geometrical diagram. Now whether 'Socrates' displayed this diagram to the audience on a board or in the sand it would have been invisible to most of the audience if this had been a mass audience of many thousands. It must have consisted of a few hundreds at most.

If they were in this way side-shows, this might help to explain away the nagging fact that, with the possible exception of Theophrastus' letter to Phanias, extant Greek literature prior to Thrasyllus does not mention these inferred dialogue-competitions. But neither, apart from Plato's own *Hippias Minor*, does it mention as having their place in the Olympic Games any of the specific contests in which Hippias boasts of being always victorious. There was no perpetuation of the names of the prize-winners in these peripheral competitions.

(*k*) The alternative hypothesis is sometimes mooted that the audiences for which Plato composed his dialogues were private gatherings of students, colleagues and friends, that is, for the Academy and its guests. But most dialogue writers had no Academy, and anyhow Plato composed his elenctic dialogues before his Academy was founded. We have indeed good reason to think that the *Timaeus* and the *Parmenides*, Part II, were designed for Academic listeners only; but they were exceptional just in being non-exoteric —and in being totally undramatic. Moreover, this hypothesis would leave unexplained the apparent fact that the *Theaetetus*-trilogy and the dialogues narrated by Apollodorus, Phaedo and Cephalus were designed for oral publication at occasions the timing of which was not in Plato's control and the occurrence of which did not require Plato's presence.

There is an objection of quite a different sort to the idea that Plato composed his dialogues, as sophists sometimes composed their epideictic discourses, for *ad hoc* gatherings. First-rate works are not evoked by *claques*. They presuppose the existence of keen, practised and unindulgent critics. Their authors must match themselves and be matched by others against authors who are at least nearly as good. They must learn their art by considering the relative excellences and defects of their own and their rivals' compositions. The unpaced runner does not attain his best speed. We have lost all but a few specimens and fragments of the non-Platonic dialogues, but even if we did not possess these specimens and fragments, and even if history told us nothing about other dialogue writers, we could have inferred their existence just from the variegated excellences of Plato's dialogues. It was the Games that provided the judges, the rivals, the yawns and plaudits, the boos and the prizes for tragedies, comedies, mimes, rhapsodes' recitals and panegyric orations. It is inference that the Games pro-

43

vided them also for dialogues. If the inference is rejected, an alternative answer must exist to the question 'What competition did Plato know?'

4. THE MAMMOTH DIALOGUES

An entirely different account is needed of the mode of publication intended for the two mammoth dialogues, the *Republic* and the *Laws*. These two highly untypical dialogues would be much too long for even four-day audiences; and the *Laws* is both too much of a Blue Book to hold the attention of a general audience and too unargumentative to appeal to disputatious young men. After Book I there is nothing dramatic in the *Republic*; there is nothing dramatic in the *Laws* at all. Both works contain matter calculated to give the greatest possible offence to the Demos in general and to democratic politicians in particular. The revolting outburst in the *Republic* 495 B–496 A against philosophical aspirants of humble origins and callings was not designed for the ears of listeners of humble origins or callings. A maritime populace would bitterly resent the *Laws* IV 704–7. Yet the *Republic* and those parts of the *Laws* which before his death Plato had converted from monologue into conversation, however jejune, seem to be designed for Athenian listeners. Who were these listeners to be?

A passage in the *Laws* 634 E–635 A suggests that no young men are present in the audience; and much of Book II would provoke young men into unseemly ridicule of the elderly, if any young men were present. There are, besides, wearisomely many passages in the *Laws* where old men are mentioned as having special qualifications and as meriting special powers. It looks as if Plato expected his audience to consist entirely of mature or elderly men, like the members of his Nocturnal Council and like the three *dramatis personae* of the dialogue itself. No audience thus confined to one age group could have been provided by the Games or even by any *ad hoc* assembly open to the public at large. That our *Republic* too was planned to suit senior listeners is much more dubiously suggested by the opening conversation between Socrates and old Cephalus; by Book VII 538–9; and by the lurid descriptions in Books VIII and IX of the progressively degenerating young sons of the Timocratic, the Oligarchic and the Democratic Man. No lads are among the named *dramatis personae* of the dialogue. The Boy-Love *motif* is almost totally absent from the *Republic*. In the *Laws* Boy-Love is frowned on.

This point conceivably ties up with the one concession made to book-writing in Plato's *Phaedrus* 275–6 and 277 D–278 E. Socrates, after speaking scathingly of the training manuals or *Arts* which the sophists provide for would-be orators and others, goes on to allow that he 'who has knowledge of the just, the good and the beautiful will, for amusement, write to treasure up reminders for himself, when he comes to the forgetfulness of old age, and for others who follow the same path...When others engage in banquets and kindred entertainments, he will pass the time in such pleasures as I have suggested.' Phaedrus replies 'A noble pastime...the pastime of the man who can find amusement in discourse, telling stories about justice and the other subjects of which you speak.' In the later passage Socrates contrasts the silly man who writes a political composition and takes it seriously with the proper philosopher who, though he does compose written works, does so without great seriousness and purely as reminders of things known already. The *Phaedrus* thus gives us the picture of some elderly and cultivated gentlemen who are happier with books than in drinking parties; and the phrase 'telling stories...' suggests that their preferred entertainment is a companionable and not a solitary one. They foregather in intellectual symposia at which someone 'tells stories about justice...'. Since, lacking spectacles, most elderly Athenians could no more read manuscripts to themselves than most elderly Englishmen can read *The Times* without spectacles, it would be a natural thing for them to congregate in regularly meeting groups and have things read aloud to them.

Part of this seems to be implied by Isocrates' *Antidosis* 12. Isocrates advises his listeners not to try to go through the whole discourse in one sitting, but to call a halt for the time being before the audience wearies. Such a facility could not be enjoyed by a mass audience or by an *ad hoc* gathering of listeners who were strangers to one another. Delivery in instalments presupposes a continuing audience; the listeners' freedom to call a halt presupposes that they are on amicable terms with one another. Although a lot is said in the *Antidosis* about young men, nowhere are young men addressed as members of its audience. Isocrates' *Areopagiticus* also reads as if its intended audience would consist of elderly men, of right-wing political views.

It has been conjectured that Theophrastus composed his *Characters* for the post-prandial entertainment of regularly meeting dining clubs. In the *Republic* I 329 A old Cephalus talks of the frequent reunions of an old men's club to which he belongs; but he does not describe it as a book-reading club. Nor need we assume that the clubs or coteries to which the *Antidosis* was to be read aloud in instalments existed for this sole purpose. They might have been synchronously book-reading clubs, dining clubs, discussion clubs and even political clubs.

The [Platonic] *Letters* VII and VIII are explicitly addressed 'to the friends and connexions of Dion'. As the former of these *Letters* is of treatise length and as in many places their author writes as to an assembly of listeners, these *Letters* must have been meant to be imparted corporately and not individually to their addressees. The 'friends and connexions of Dion' must have been members of some kind of organized society or club in Sicily, and the *Letters* must have been designed to be delivered aloud, the *Seventh Letter* in instalments, at some of its meetings. This club was doubtless a Dionist political club. Political policies are recommended to it on the notional authority of Plato. But the recipients are nourished with moral, historical and philosophical matters as well. Since the *Letters* are forgeries, their concocter must have been able to rely on their being kept private to the club, else anti-Dionists would, though only after many months, have procured and published a repudiation of them by Plato. To ensure this privacy the deliverer of the *Letters* would need to prevent any copies of the *Letters* being circulated or, therefore, made. He would have the *Letters* read aloud, but he would not make his scripts available to the copyists. The idea of some scholars that these *Letters* were published to the world as pamphlets is anachronistic in itself. But anyhow multiplied copies could not both be kept private and be broadcast in writing to 'the friends and connexions of Dion'.

If there did exist in Athens the postulated literary or literary-cum-social-cum-political clubs, one of them could in the course, say, of a winter have gone through the whole of a mammoth dialogue like the *Republic* or the *Laws*. But so far it is little more than guesswork either that, apart from political clubs and dining clubs, such clubs even existed or that, if they did, the *Republic* and *Laws* were designed for consumption by them. The brief phrases in the *Phaedrus* 'the just, the good and the beautiful' (276 C, 277 D, 278 A), 'telling stories about justice' and 'political composition' do no more than suggest the *Republic*, in Books V and VI of which the trinity of the just, the good and the beautiful is mentioned half a dozen times. But we have another possible clue. Socrates speaks of the books which it is permissible for the true philosopher to write as 'reminders'. Reminders of what? Against forgetfulness of what? There was no danger of the contents of, say, the *Phaedo* or the *Euthydemus* going into oblivion. The copyists had provided the reading public with the texts of these dialogues soon after their oral delivery. There are, on the other hand, good reasons for thinking that our *Republic* was assembled out of separately composed discourses which, though they had for the most part long since been delivered to audiences, had not been allowed to appear as books.

The debate with Thrasymachus in Book I of our *Republic* seems on stylistic grounds to have been composed a good deal earlier than the other Books; and its argument, unlike that of the rest of the *Republic*, still exemplifies the Socratic Method in action. Thrasymachus is hardly mentioned in the last eight books of the *Republic*. This stretch should belong with the *Gorgias* to the period shortly before Plato abandoned the elenctic dialogue. Yet no *Thrasymachus* had come out as a separate book.

Plato had composed for delivery in Syracuse in 367–366 the *Ideal State*, that is the political gist of, roughly, Books II–V of our *Republic*. Owing to the death of the Elder Dionysius the *Ideal State* was not in fact delivered in Syracuse. Nor had it subsequently appeared as a separate book.

The attacks on Homer and the poets in Books II, III and X of our *Republic* are such massive interruptions to the arguments athwart which they lie that it looks as if we have here too something which had been separately composed but not made available to copyists.

Books VIII and IX were, it is to be hoped and conjectured, composed before Plato had experienced the hospitality, respect, friendship and perhaps munificence of a civilized and cultured young tyrant, that is, before 367. But there had appeared no separate book on the Decline of the State from the heaven of aristocracy into the hell of tyranny.

If all or some of this is so, then our *Republic* really is a preservation from oblivion of discourses otherwise unperpetuated. This idea that our *Republic* is a conflation of originally independent discourses is quite strongly borne out by the little heeded passage in Aristotle's *Politics* II 1264 b 39, where it is said that 'Socrates [*sic*]...has filled up the rest of [the *Republic*] with extraneous discourses....'.

Our *Laws* is partly in similar case. Apart from the embarrassingly silly digression 'On Drunkenness' in Books I and II, and the interesting but incongruous discourse 'On Impiety' in Book X, the work seems to have been composed as an address sequence giving Dionysius II a would-be practicable and unutopian *Code Napoléon* for the constitutional reconstruction of Syracuse. After the victory of Dion over Dionysius in 356 had reduced this working-model to a dead letter, Plato began the arduous task of recasting it into conversational form in order to make it palatable to Athenian listeners. This too was to have been a preservation from oblivion of something so far unpublished as a book. Not only does our *Laws* profess fairly explicitly to be intended for consumption by audiences to which no young men belong, but both it and the *Republic* seem to presuppose in their recipients total immunity from democratic sympathies. What circles restricted to conservative and senior listeners were there to provide protractedly continuing audiences?

In his *Politics* 1313 b 3 Aristotle cryptically mentions σύλλογοι σχολαστικοί; Isocrates mentions ἴδιοι σύλλογοι in his *Antidosis* 136 and 147; the *Second Letter* and the *Republic* 499 A talk of ἴδιαι συνουσίαι. If the societies or clubs here postulated did exist, they might have been known by titles like these. They would have been private societies. The members of such private clubs would have been familiar with the confidential co-optation rules of the Nocturnal Council (*Laws* 951 and 961) and would have felt cordial towards the idea of a studious coterie rather like their own constituting the Magnetes' Privy Council. It is

just such privacy that we need in order to explain how
Plato's presumably early denigration of the wicked and
miserable tyrant could be incorporated in our *Republic*
after Plato himself had been the year-long guest, friend and
philosopher-uncle of the intellectually eager young tyrant,
Dionysius, to whose virtues Plato pays his cordial, if also
diplomatic tribute in the *Laws* 710E–711. Only if our
Republic was to have its dissemination securely confined
inside some private clubs or coteries in Athens, could
Plato meet Dionysius or correspond with him without
fear of being accused of being double-faced, unless by his
own conscience.

There is one further, indirect argument for the idea that
our *Republic* was meant for some reliably private circles of
conservative consumers. If the conclusion of Chapter v is
true, that Plato had been penalized in the late 370's for the
defamation of politicians, orators, poets and artisans, and
if some of the discourses for which he was punished are resurrected in our *Republic*, then our *Republic* could not have
been given to the general public in book-form. There
would have been good prudential reasons why Plato
should have intended our *Republic* solely for like-minded
recipients, that is, for people who were or were likely to be
the victims of the Demos. As Athens might hear rumours
of the private delivery of the *Republic* to the postulated
coteries of its senior and conservative recipients, it could be
from these same prudential motives that in his *Phaedrus*
Plato seems both half to admit the existence of his 'political
composition' and to pass it off as an unserious piece, composed to give innocent pleasure to the aged.

4-2

The total conjecture is, then, this. There existed in Athens some private circles or clubs of which one function was to entertain and edify their middle-aged and elderly members with book-readings. A discourse like Isocrates' *Antidosis* or Plato's *Republic* would be read out in instalments through a plurality of sessions. The listeners would constitute a continuing audience. Each session might terminate with some discussion of the evening's instalment. Like the Nocturnal Council the circle would be a serious study group, holding its meetings after dark, while other citizens were enjoying themselves in their dining clubs. The *Laws* does not explain convincingly why its Nocturnal Council is nocturnal.

The reciter of the book would not be the author himself. Plato or Isocrates would have loaned to the club the scripts from which the club's reader would read aloud. Or perhaps the author would have presented the book for good as a κτῆμα ἐς ἀεί. It is this feature of the conjectured system which made Plato a 'book-writer'. He was the issuer of the text, not the oral deliverer of the words of a dialogue.

It is hard to swallow this speculation that Isocrates wrote his *Antidosis* or that Plato subjected himself to the huge literary tasks of assembling our *Republic* and reconstructing our *Laws* just for the benefit of the members of one or more private clubs or coteries, even if Plato also meant these compositions to exert some indirect and gradual political influence. It is all the harder that the very existence, until long after Plato's day, of such sedulous intellectual symposia is entirely inferential. It is small consolation that the tacitly assumed counter-theory, namely that Plato wrote these mammoth dialogues for individual readers of the written word, is just as speculative. We have no evidence that Athens yet contained many book-buyers other than those who purchased books for vocational purposes, like schoolmasters and the students for whom the sophists' *Arts* catered. Few elderly men could with their own eyes have read a long manuscript; and this would restrict the postulated book-buyers chiefly to those who could afford to possess educated slaves to read to them, like Euclides in the *Theaetetus*. So on this theory too Plato would have assembled his *Republic* and begun to rewrite his *Laws* mainly for a very limited class of Greek individuals, namely for those who were at once cultured, comfortably off, conservative, leisured and studious.

If these two dialogues were designed for, and strictly reserved to some private clubs or circles, it might explain the otherwise surprising fact that outside his *Politics* Aristotle very seldom alludes to or draws on the *Republic*. In the *Politics* the allusions are mostly to the political gist of Books II–V of our *Republic*, and to Book VIII. Aristotle here complains two or three times that Plato had left certain cardinal arrangements in his Ideal State inexplicit or unsettled. Neither Aristotle nor his colleagues seem to have asked Plato for his rulings on these points. On the present hypothesis Plato did not during his lifetime release his text of our *Republic* to the world at large, and therefore not even to members of the Academy. Aristotle and his pupils never heard or read our *Republic* until after Plato's death, though members of the postulated reading clubs had heard it, probably again and again, during the 350's and maybe the late 360's.

In the 420's there had been written a political treatise, nicknamed by historians 'The Old Oligarch'. This treatise is so acidulated against the Demos that scholars have inferred that it was designed to be delivered to the members of an anti-democratic political club. We could well imagine that as such clubs became less and less politically effectual, their anti-democratic pugnacities became more and more literary. They would have relished Books VIII and IX of the *Republic*. The surprising fact that Thucydides' *History* is never mentioned or cited by Isocrates, Plato, Aristotle, Demosthenes or Xenophon, though Xenophon certainly knew it, suggests the idea that it too was written for a society the meetings of which were private. The penultimate sentence of its I, 22 shows that it was intended for listeners. Thucydides must have expected them to remain constant through many, many sessions.

CHAPTER III

PLATO AND SICILY

I. WHO INVITED PLATO TO COME TO SYRACUSE IN 367?

The answer to this question that has been generally accepted is that shortly after his accession to the tyranny the Younger Dionysius, jointly with Dion, wrote to Plato urging him to come during that same year. After some hesitation Plato took ship for Syracuse and got there in the early summer of 367.

This accepted story, however, is chronologically impossible. The accession of the Younger Dionysius came soon after the death of the Elder Dionysius. Now this aged tyrant was not only alive at the beginning of the winter of 368–367 but, as Diodorus Siculus tells us in Book xv, 74 of his *Bibliotheke*, he lived to receive the glad tidings of the victory of his Tragedy at the Lenean Games, which were held in Athens at the end of January or at the very beginning of February. He died shortly but apparently not immediately after his receipt of these tidings. So he was alive at least some way on into February 367.

On the supposition that the member of his choir who brought the good news from Athens made his journey immediately after the Lenean Games, he could not with the best possible luck have got to Syracuse in less than a week or ten days after the beginning of February. The mileage is too great. So old Dionysius must, even on this assumption, have been alive fairly well on in February, with the accession of his son a little later still; and this would already render suspect the story of Plato reaching Syracuse in April or May in response to a letter dispatched from Syracuse to Athens by the new tyrant after his accession.

But the supposition just made is untenable in itself. For the sailing season did not open until after the Dionysia, that is after the first three or four days of April. For very good reasons no merchant ships put to sea until the hurricane season was over at the very end of March. *Letter* VII 347 C tells us that there was no winter sailing, as in effect the *Laws* 952 E does also. In wartime warships and transports, though not the big convoys, did have to make the long and dangerous journey between Athens and Syracuse during the winter season. Sometimes they were lucky, sometimes they were unlucky. But the risks were much too great for any shipowner or merchant to run. The crossing of the Adriatic in particular was a terror to sailors. There was no ship for the messenger to take until the time that Plato also set sail. True, Diodorus Siculus tells us that the messenger took ship from Corinth and went by the short and initially sheltered route through the gulf of Corinth. Plato had to go round the Peloponnese. So the messenger would certainly have gained many days over Plato by taking this short route. We are told that he was favoured by the weather. But by the time he reached Syracuse Plato had already got part of the way to Syracuse.

The Elder Dionysius must have lived until, at the earliest, the mid-April of 367. We could have been sure *a priori* that Plato's ship left Athens at the opening of the sailing season at the beginning of April, but the *Seventh Letter* 329 C–E itself tells us that Plato had been in Syracuse for three months and a bit before Dion was banished; and that even then there would have been time for Plato to get a passage back to Athens before the close of the sailing season. As the homeward-bound ships must have left Syracuse by the beginning of September in order to make sure of reaching Athens while sailing was still possible, Plato must have reached Syracuse at latest in May 367 and more likely in late April. Plato was already at sea before the Younger Dionysius acceded to the tyranny.

So the *Letters* III, VII and XIII, which are the sources of the generally accepted account, cannot be telling the truth about Plato's invitation. They cannot therefore be by Plato. The Younger Dionysius did indeed, after his accession, give protracted hospitality to Plato; and the knowledge of this fact may well have led, if not the author, at least the recipients of these *Letters* to believe that Plato's actual host had been Plato's inviter. Considerations of the type with which Freeman Wills Croft has familiarized us were not familiar to fourth-century Greeks.

The conclusion is that Plato left Athens for Syracuse in early April 367 on an invitation that he had received during 368 or perhaps late 369 from the Elder Dionysius. This conclusion can be avoided and therewith the credit of these three *Letters* be temporarily protected only by one of two *ad hoc* hypotheses. Either by the courageous, conjunctive hypothesis that not only did the member of the choir manage to get a ship's captain to carry him from Corinth to Syracuse during February, but also that after the messenger's arrival in Syracuse, and after the Elder Dionysius' death, the new tyrant managed to get a letter back from Syracuse to Athens between, say, late February and, say, late March in time for Plato in hurried response to take ship from Athens at the beginning of April. Or else by the hypothesis that Plato's second visit to Sicily occurred not in 367 at all, but in 366; with the corollary that the story is false that when Aristotle joined the Academy in 367 Plato was in Sicily and Eudoxus was acting as his deputy as Head of the Academy.

We happen to be in possession of corroborations for the idea that Plato had been invited by the Elder Dionysius:

(*a*) Though they are usually forgotten, the philosophers Aristippus and Aeschines were with Plato in Syracuse. Someone must have invited them, yet no story survives or would be welcomed to the effect that Dion had prevailed on the young tyrant to invite all three philosophers from Athens to establish, jointly or severally, a New Jerusalem in Sicily.

(*b*) We possess his *Letter* I to Dionysius I, written in 368, in which the Athenian orator, Isocrates, laments that he is too old to make the journey to Syracuse. He sketches the advisory address which he is sending for a deputy-throat to deliver, and he warns the Elder Dionysius against some unpractical politicians, named, we may guess, 'Plato', of whom Isocrates speaks in similar terms elsewhere.

(*c*) In 369 a Triple Alliance had been formed between the Elder Dionysius, Sparta and Athens. This Triple Alliance had been consummated in Athens by the election of the tyrant's two sons to honorary citizenship of Athens. Cynics ascribed the victory of Dionysius' tragedy at the Lenean Games of 367 to diplomatic rather than to aesthetic enthusiasms.

(*d*) Not only was Dionysius I a constant patron of the arts and of artists but the organization by tyrants and monarchs of festivals modelled on those celebrated at Olympia, Athens and the isthmus of Corinth was quite a common thing. Xenophon mentions the practice in his *Hiero* I 11–13; Isocrates' contributions to a festival in Cyprus in memory of Evagoras brought him handsome rewards; Philip held rival Olympic Games at Dium; and the widow of Mausolus organized an Obituary Festival at Halicarnassus. In 361–360 the Younger Dionysius was to hold an analogous gathering in Syracuse. The Elder Dionysius would have been doing something quite normal and also diplomatically timely if he had in 369–368 invited Isocrates, Aeschines, Aristippus, Plato, and presumably plenty of other luminaries and champions to come to what in hypothetical retrospect we could call his projected 'Triple Alliance Festival' of 367–366. Isocrates seems to allude to this alliance in his *Letter* to Dionysius. The fact that old Dionysius certainly did invite Isocrates and almost certainly did invite Aristippus and Aeschines would by itself make it probable that he also invited Plato. Why would he have passed Plato over?

2. WHAT WERE ISOCRATES, PLATO, ETC., INVITED FOR?

If Dionysius I invited a plurality of philosophers and other luminaries all together, then the presumption is that he invited them all to deliver new compositions in Syracuse.

This presumption is borne out by Isocrates' *Letter* to Dionysius which shows that he was going to send an advisory address counselling Dionysius to lead and thereby to unite Hellas in a Holy War against the barbarians, that is against the currently menacing Carthaginians. If so, then Plato would have sailed to Syracuse with his own discourses composed for the same occasion; and the unsporting Isocrates would have been warning Dionysius against a contributor of compositions competing with his own. Can any such Platonic compositions be identified?

Plato's unfinished *Critias* gives us the beginning of a mythical history of an antediluvian war between Hellas, heroically led by Athens, and Atlantis. Plato's description of Atlantis tallies in so many dozens of particulars with Carthage that no Greek and *a fortiori* no Sicilian could have failed to take the name 'Atlantis' to be Plato's myth-name for Carthage. These parallels are assembled in the section on the *Critias* in Chapter VII, 6. If so, then the *Critias* would be likely to have been designed for delivery to Sicilians, to whom the Carthaginian threat was a constant and growing anxiety, and not to Athenians, to whom it was not. The *Critias* was an advisory address, thinly disguised as a piece of imaginary history, counselling Dionysius I to lead and so unify Hellas in a Holy War against Carthage. Plato's idea was just the same as Isocrates' idea.

A simple explanation now offers itself of the fact that the *Critias* is unfinished. Plato had begun the *Critias* in Athens, meaning to complete it after reaching Sicily. But he arrived to find that the Elder Dionysius had just died. His proposed Winston Churchill had been succeeded by a rather unexecutive young man; and the Palace Festival had been cancelled at which Plato was to have delivered his message.

From the ill-fitting opening of our *Timaeus* and the limp opening of our *Critias* it is clear that the *Critias* was to have been the second of three discourses. The third, the *Hermocrates*, was left unwritten. Of the first, namely Socrates' discourse on the *Ideal State*, we get a résumé which covers the political gist of Books ii–v of our *Republic*. As we get parallel résumés of just this political gist both at the beginning of Book viii of our *Republic* and in Aristotle's *Politics* ii; and as the *dramatis personae* mentioned in the *Timaeus* and the *Critias* are not those of our *Republic* but include a Sicilian and an Italian; and as Socrates' discourse on the Ideal State seems to have been, what the *Critias* is and the *Hermocrates* would have been, an address in monologue and not, like our *Republic*, a conversation, we have to conclude that Socrates' discourse was not, what scholars have supposed, our *Republic*, but a much shorter piece which, recast into conversational form and provided with new Athenian *dramatis personae*, was later amalgamated with much other material into our *Republic*. Like the *Critias* the original *Ideal State* or *Proto-Republic* was composed for delivery in Syracuse in 367–366.

Like the *Critias* the original *Ideal State* is a thinly disguised advisory address. It counsels the Elder Dionysius to cure the political and social maladies of Syracuse by converting the members of the governing class of Syracuse into property-less Guardians, and by abolishing, for the governing class only, all family ties. However utopian, both of these prescriptions were based on a correct diagnosis of ills that really were of the utmost gravity in Sicily, though they did not obtain in fourth-century Athens. Dynastic rivalries and the concentration of wealth in a few hands did keep Syracuse on the edge of a political volcano. In 357 the volcano erupted. Propertied 'barons' led by Dion joined forces with Carthage. Sheepdogs and wolves united. Some of the opulent Sicilian families hated their rival families and the Syracusan Demos worse than they hated the Carthaginians. Plato had meant to tell old Dionysius how to prevent this eruption. We need not speculate whether the old tyrant would or could or should have tried to take Plato's political advice if he had lived longer.

This idea that by April 367 Plato had composed for delivery in Sicily his original *Ideal State* and had begun to compose his *Critias* is strongly confirmed by the otherwise inexplicable ties between the *Timaeus* and these two discourses. For our *Timaeus* begins with Socrates' résumé of his *Ideal State* and goes on with Critias' preamble to his story of Atlantis and with the opening of this story itself. Only a weak pretence is made in the *Timaeus* at 20A and 27A that this cosmological and physiological discourse is, alongside of the *Critias* and the *Hermocrates*, a response to Socrates' request for discourses supplementary to his own. Not even a weak reason is offered for Timaeus discoursing on the *Origin of the World and of Man* after the beginning of Critias' story of Atlantis and before its completion. Neither discourse has the slightest relevance to the other; and the *Timaeus* has none to the *Ideal State*. The *Timaeus* is not an advisory address. It was composed in Sicily for the pedagogic benefit of the Academy and not for the political edification of Sicily.

It has long been realized by scholars that much of the cosmology and much, if not all, of the anatomy, physiology and pathology of the *Timaeus* derives from Archytas of Tarentum and from Philistion of Locri and Syracuse. This derivation already makes it likely that Plato gathered these scientific harvests during one of his last two visits to Sicily. Archytas' chief disciple, Archedemus, who lived in Syracuse, was on friendly terms with Plato, and Plato dwelt in his house for a part of his third visit. The forged *Second Letter* embodies an invitation from Plato to Philistion to come to Athens, an invitation which the forger, if contemporary, would have been imprudent to fabricate.

The author of the *Seventh Letter* makes Plato speak of a discourse that he had delivered before the Younger Dionysius. It is twice described as being about Nature. No Platonic dialogue other than the *Timaeus* could be so described. We are told two or three times that this was the solitary discourse that Plato delivered to Dionysius, as if he might have been expected to deliver other discourses as well. Now Plato in 367 did have with him his *Ideal State* and his unfinished *Critias*, but owing to the cancellation of the Elder Dionysius' planned festival he did not deliver them. This makes it plausible to suggest that before leaving for home in the late summer of 366 Plato did deliver his newly completed *Timaeus* to Dionysius, but prefaced it with a résumé of his undelivered *Ideal State* and with the preamble and beginning of his undelivered and uncom-

pleted *Critias*. He thus contrived, somewhat clumsily, still
to convey the gists of his two planned messages to Sicily,
hoping, perhaps, that even these message-extracts might
do some good or at least arouse some interest in Sicily.

This reconstruction of Plato's second visit to Sicily lacks
the romantic interest of the account yielded by the
[Platonic] *Letters*. So far from having come to Syracuse to
found his Ideal State on Sicilian soil, Plato came with other
luminaries bringing with him a dialogue and a half to present at a Court Festival. His *Ideal State* and his *Critias* were
indeed advisory addresses, as the contribution of Isocrates was to have been. But as the intended recipient of
the advice was the aged Dionysius, the writers' hopes that
any of their doubtless variegated counsels would be really
put into practice were presumably fairly modest. Advisory addresses formed a regular part of the oratory delivered at *panegureis*, and their actual influence on the
courses of events was of the same minor, though not
negligible order of magnitude as that of the influence that
leading articles used to have in the days when newspapers
published thoughts. Isocrates, who wrote plenty, speaks
without illusions about the inefficaciousness of panegyric
orations in his *Letter to Dionysius* 5–6 and in his address
To Philip 12–13 (cf. Plutarch's *Timoleon* xxxvii 3).

The orthodox notion that Plato left Sicily in 366 dis-
heartened by his failure to found his darling Ideal State has
pathos in it, but no truth. The truth is that he left Sicily in
excited possession of a mass of new natural science.
Archytas and Philistion had given him a wealth of systematized knowledge of Nature. No longer has the Other

World to monopolize the Sunlight. The philosopher's Here is no longer his prison.

Even the heartbreak caused in about 371 by the shattering of Plato's dreams of political influence in Athens was now, or was quite soon to be partly mended. For the young Dionysius must have encouraged Plato to draw up his relatively unutopian *Code Napoléon* for Sicily, which we read, still partly in address-style, in our *Laws* III–XII. The first half of this Code was presented in Syracuse in 361–360. The second half must have been composed before 356, when the expulsion of Dionysius by Dion shattered this dream too. Still Plato had worked for up to half a dozen years knowing that the products of his concrete political thinking were desired by the head of the wealthiest and most powerful state in the Greek world.

In two quite different ways Sicily rescued Plato from his utopianisms by curing him of the despairs that had engendered them. Archytas, Philistion and the Younger Dionysius brought Plato both down to Mother Earth and up to Mother Earth. The World is no longer sundered into a Cave and a Sun; and for the philosopher Heaven's veto on suicide is no longer a cruel impediment to a desiderated release. When Protarchus says in the *Philebus* 62 'we call that a ridiculous state of intellect in a man, Socrates, which is concerned only with divine knowledge' and 'I do not know, Socrates, what harm it can do a man to take in all the other kinds of knowledge (*epistemas*) if he has the first', Plato's tone of voice is quite other than that of the *Phaedo* and the *Republic*. His new tone of voice reminds us forcibly of the eloquent passage at the beginning of Aristotle's

De Partibus Animalium I. 5. Plato's doctrine in his *Philebus* of the limit and the limitable, for which he is in debt to Archytas, is a theory not of two discordant worlds but of two concordant factors. He is now operating with a new pair of polar opposites, a pair, this time, with which Aristotle also unreservedly operates.

Sicily may at some time have rolled back from Plato a third, more domestic cloud. In his *Life of Plato* 9 Diogenes Laertius transmits the counter-fashionable story that Dionysius bestowed over eighty talents upon Plato. We may doubt the scale, but not easily the existence of this bounty. Some such largesse must have become public knowledge or belief before 353, since the *Letters* (321 C, 318 E, 353 D and perhaps 328 C and 352 A) are at pains to make their Plato deny such grounds for gratitude. Dionysius could, like Nicocles and other culture-patronizing despots, have been munificent without Plato having been a mendicant. Maybe Plato earned his honorarium with his *Proto-Laws* (cf. *Laws*, 953 D, with Isocrates' *To Nicocles*, 13, 22 and 53. Nicocles rewarded Isocrates very handsomely).

If Dionysius had been conspicuously munificent in 361–360, it would explain the otherwise oddly financial tone of Socrates' prayer to Pan at the end of the *Phaedrus*. The real Socrates never became rich. Plato, after having been well off, does seem to have been relatively poor during the 360's. Perhaps Dionysius rescued him during his last visit to Syracuse. If so, Plato in his *Phaedrus* is publishing his 'thank you', possibly to the ears of Greece at the Olympic Games of 360 which he attended on his way back from Syracuse to Athens.

As Phaedrus responds with the maxim of the Pythagorean brotherhood, 'friends have all things in common', it may not be too far-fetched to guess that Dionysius' bounty or, more likely, Plato's disposal of part of it took the provident form of an unconfiscatable endowment-trust for the Academy. The Academy is unmentioned in Plato's modest will, so presumably it had already acquired the status of an endowed religious foundation, like that of the Lyceum according to Theophrastus' will (Diogenes Laertius' *Life of Theophrastus*; and cf. his *Epicurus*, 11).

The *Laws* 744 E requires a man who comes into a fortune by finding, gift, profit or luck to donate to the State and to its patron Gods what exceeds his proper allowance. He then incurs no penalty or discredit. Perhaps Plato acted on this idea and so mollified his political ill-wishers. The State got its cut; for the Gods' share the Academy became an endowed religious foundation; and, on the hypothesis of Plato's downfall that is argued in Chapter v, Plato himself not only emerged from poverty and disgrace but could again teach the young men dialectic. His *Parmenides* would then spell neither defiance of an old court-order nor breach of an extorted undertaking. The young man is now advised to study dialectic, not sternly forbidden to touch it. The *Republic*'s veto has been lifted.

This speculation would tally nicely with Socrates' prayer at the end of the *Phaedrus* that only so much wealth might be his as the reasonable man could do with. 'Socrates' was now justifiably scared of provocative personal wealth. On this fairly conjectural account Plato was, in the 350's, a rehabilitated citizen, thanks to

Dionysius; and the Academy was a self-supporting college, thanks to Dionysius.

All this would help to explain the *Seventh Letter*'s total silence about the Academy. Its Dionist addressees should not be reminded of any gratitudes of Plato towards Dionysius.

Two or three generations after Plato's death it was alleged that Epicurus had called Plato's entourage 'toadies of Dionysius', and Plato himself 'golden' in some pejorative sense (Diogenes Laertius' *Life of Epicurus* 8). This allegation against Epicurus, true or false, proves that there were at that time still current some stories about Dionysius, Plato and the Academy of a tenor totally disparate from that of the *Seventh Letter*. The close of the *Seventh Letter* itself shows that un-Dionist stories were already rife six years before Plato died.

In his *Life of Speusippus* 2 Diogenes Laertius cites a letter, of questioned authenticity, from Dionysius to Speusippus reproaching him for departing from Plato's practice by charging fees to students, whether they were willing or not. If it was his benefaction that had enabled Plato's Academy to remit fees, Dionysius would have had a personal grievance against Plato's successor for exacting them.

3. THE REAL DION

Chronology by itself proves that *Letters* III, VII and XIII were not written by Plato; and *Letter* VII carries *Letter* VIII with it. Plutarch, Diodorus Siculus, Diogenes Laertius and later historians and scholars have relied on these *Letters* for their accounts of Dion's virtues and of the young

Dionysius' vices. If the *Letters* are forgeries, then the traditional story about Dion is without any authority. We have no independent reasons for thinking that Plato set any store at all by Dion. Nor even with the aid of the *Letters* is it easy to specify what was the supposedly horrific wickedness of the young Dionysius. He did not have his opponents executed or assassinated but merely transplanted to the Peloponnese, where they retained the income from their Sicilian estates. He was reproached for being too generous to the Demos but it is unlikely that the Demos itself resented this partiality. He did not sell the fort to the Carthaginians, though he did lack the Napoleonic qualities of his father. There is likely to be some truth in the allegation that he over-indulged in wine, though this is a standard allegation for political opponents to make against the inmates of palaces. On the other side he like his father was a keen and seemingly munificent patron of culture. We have independent reasons for thinking that from 367 he was and remained on very good terms with Plato.

Worse still. Since these *Letters* were contemporary forgeries and not later concoctions composed for sale to libraries, then this fact together with their contents strongly suggests that they were forged as propaganda weapons against Dionysius and on behalf of Dion and Dion's faction. *Letters* VII and VIII are expressly addressed to Dion's 'associates and friends'. So they are likely to be systematically tendencious, designed to make people believe things to the credit of Dion and to the discredit of Dionysius that they would not otherwise believe.

We should try, then, to hold in suspense the traditional

story of Dion's virtues and ideals and see if we can glean something of the real story also from the incidental admissions, apologies and reticences of the *Letters* and of Plutarch's *Dion* and *Timoleon*. The fact that Dion is one of his heroes lends a lot of weight to the ample evidence that Plutarch offers for a very unfavourable verdict. Some of his history of Dion is based directly on reports written by Dion's Athenian lieutenant, Timonides, to his Academic friend, Speusippus. Timonides held a responsible position in Dion's expeditionary force.

Dion in 367 was a middle-aged man of enormous wealth. Whatever his principles may have been, he had served the Elder Dionysius unremittingly until that despot's death. He had on some earlier occasion gone to Carthage as Dionysius' envoy. On a later occasion he let it be known in Syracuse that if the young Dionysius wanted war with Carthage, he, Dion, would provide and maintain a fleet of 50 triremes; but if peace was wanted, he would sail to Africa and put a stop to the war on the best terms possible. He remained, apparently, a *persona grata* in Carthage.

In the summer of 367, three months and a bit after Plato's arrival in Syracuse, the young Dionysius banished Dion from Sicily because a letter from Dion to some Carthaginian officials had been intercepted in which Dion urged the Carthaginians, when negotiating with Dionysius for peace, to insist on the presence of himself, Dion, at the parleys since he would help them to arrange everything securely. The *Seventh Letter* is significantly silent about this very solid justification for the banishment.

Dionysius allowed the exile to draw the income from his large Sicilian estates but refused to let him realize and take out his capital. He allowed him, however, to have two shiploads of property and servants. 'For Dion had great riches and an almost princely splendour of appointment in his way of living, and this his friends got together and conveyed to him.' '...as far as wealth and riches went, he was a brilliant figure among the Greeks, to whom the affluence of the exile gave some idea of the power of the tyrant' (Plutarch, *Dion* xv). The Dion of the *Letters* seemed more monastic than this.

We need not doubt the stories of Dion's munificences to the Academy, and especially to Plato's nephew, Speusippus. Speusippus was a partisan, if not a confidential agent of Dion and the correspondent of Timonides, Dion's Master of the Horse.

Ten years after his banishment Dion assembled at Zacynthus his expeditionary force against Dionysius. The story that it was his high-minded object to rescue Syracuse from the merciless tyranny of Dionysius and to give it free institutions loses some of its plausibility when we hear that of the thousand Sicilian exiles in the Peloponnese only twenty-five would join Dion's army. Nor do we hear of any support for his expedition coming from Corinth, the mother-city of Syracuse. Dion's force consisted almost entirely of mercenaries. *Letter* VII 346 B–C and Plutarch's *Dion* XVI 3 make it apparent that Dionysius' refusal to let Dion have more than the income from his vast Sicilian fortune was due to his expectation that Dion would employ his capital, if he got it, to hire and equip such an army. If so,

Dionysius' action seems politic rather than unprincipled. Although his capital was thus frozen in Sicily, Dion still contrived to get the money to hire a private army. Plutarch tells an anecdote which may be pertinent. Before his little army left Zacynthus Dion gave it a sumptuous banquet in the stadium. 'The mercenaries were amazed at the splendour of the gold and silver beakers and of the tables, for it passed the limits set by a private man's fortune; they reasoned too that a man who...was master of such affluence would not engage in hazardous enterprises unless he had solid hopes of success and friends over there who offered him unbounded resources' (*Dion* XXIII). We are left to guess whether his backers 'over there' were moneyed Sicilians or Carthaginians.

The story of the voyage of the expeditionary force from Zacynthus to the south coast of Sicily contains one very revealing episode. The force landed over 100 miles west of Syracuse at Minoa, the port of Acragas, which was in Carthaginian hands. It 'happened' that its Carthaginian commander, Synalus, was an old guest-friend of Dion. No one was killed when Dion's mercenaries dashed into Minoa and occupied it. Dion restored the city to Synalus without doing it any harm, and Synalus entertained the soldiers and supplied Dion with what he wanted. Later on he transported Dion's munitions for him to Syracuse on wagons which he provided. This incident is hardly susceptible of an innocent interpretation. The *Seventh Letter* does not refer to it.

There had been an earlier incident which points in the same direction. When his little convoy had reached Pachynus, the south-eastern headland of Sicily, Dion would not do as his pilot, Protus, insisted, namely make an immediate landing on the Sicilian coast. Instead he sailed further south. It looks as if Dion was determined, despite the extra distance from his objective, to land his army nowhere else in Sicily than Minoa, that is, as if he had already made his transport arrangements with Synalus, and maybe other arrangements too. But he had kept this dark even from his pilot.

In a remarkably few days Dion's army had marched from Minoa to Syracuse, where it was ceremonially greeted by the 'men of note and cultivation', that is 'the gentry' or 'élite', as Dion's partisans are called by Plutarch. At first all went well. Dionysius with his fleet had been several days' journey away and by the time he returned Dion was in possession of Syracuse, apart from the Acropolis.

But now a surprising thing happened. The Syracusan populace was, not long after Dion's arrival, voting for the appointment of a board of generals to displace their professed liberator. For some reason they wanted to see the backs of Dion and his mercenaries. Without having lost a battle Dion and his mercenaries had to remove themselves to Leontini. What had gone wrong?

Certainly Dion was elderly, stout and haughty in manner. But it is unlikely that a people which had supposedly been groaning for half a century under an iniquitous tyranny would after a few days have rejected its Garibaldi for such reasons alone. Plutarch has to admit that his idealist hero was suspected by many of aiming at the tyranny himself, but even this seems hardly to explain the promptness of the rejection. Presumably Dion did not blurt out to the world these hypothetical personal ambitions while Dionysius or his son was still occupying the Acropolis. From Plutarch's account it appears that it was Dion's mercenaries whom the Syracusans could not stomach. Yet all generals, including the young Dionysius, employed mercenary troops. Why should Syracuse spurn a mercenary Freedom Army before it had finished its mission of liberation?

Dion's original force had consisted of some 800 Greek mercenaries, mostly from the Peloponnese. Between Minoa and Syracuse he had then in a very short time recruited and organized at least 5,000 more mercenaries from southern Sicily. Some of these were Sicanians and Sikels from the rural areas; many of them were recruited in Acragas, Gela and Camarina. Acragas, Gela and Camarina had ceased to be predominantly Greek cities with their capture and sack by the Carthaginians fifty years before. So the mercenaries whom Dion recruited here must have been largely 'barbarians'; that is, non-Greek Sicilians. Moreover, since at least Acragas was presumably under Carthaginian control, the mercenaries recruited here must have been allowed and may have been induced by the Carthaginians to join Dion. So swift was Dion's recruitment, arming and mobilization of his 5,000 largely non-Greek mercenaries that we may suspect that the Carthaginians had got his local reinforcements, as well as his transport, ready for him before he arrived. Dion is said to have told his Greek mercenaries before leaving Zacynthus that they were to be the officers in the army which he would collect in Sicily. Though he had been out of Sicily for ten years, he was already sure that there was going to be such an army; one which would require Greek officers; and one which he would recruit between Minoa and Syracuse.

Conceivably, then, the Syracusans wanted to be rid of Dion's mercenaries because many of them were Sicilian 'barbarians', who were traditionally hostile to Syracuse, and perhaps also because they were thought to be virtually a Carthaginian loan to Dion's army, like his transport that Synalus provided for him.

After a confusing chapter of incidents in which there bulked large acts and gestures of hostility towards Dion on the part of the citizen-sailors of Syracuse, Dion became master of the city. When the motion was proposed to the assembly that Dion should be made generalissimo, the aristocracy approved of the motion and urged the appointment, but the mob of sailors and day-labourers tumultuously opposed it. There was one important point of policy over which Dion was in irreconcilable opposition to the democratic faction. Uninfluenced by the Platonic ideal of unpropertied Guardians he refused a redistribution of land and houses, that is, a break-up of the gentry's landed estates and mansions (Plutarch, *Dion* XXXVII 3 and XLVIII 3). In *Letter* VII 351 B the notional Plato duly disapproves of such redistributions. Later on Timoleon did carry through a redistribution of land and houses (Plutarch, *Timoleon* XXIII 4). It looks as if Dion's faction in Syracuse consisted of propertied gentry who lacked communistic aspirations. Perhaps it was some apprehension of property redistribution

75

which united them against Dionysius and reconciled them to collaboration with Carthage. Was Dionysius' real enormity the sin of favouring the Demos? (see Plutarch, *Dion* VII 3, XII 1 and XIII). According to Plutarch (*Dion* LIII 2) Dion had it in mind to establish, with Corinthian help, 'a mixture of democracy and royalty...wherein an aristocracy should preside and administer the most important affairs...'.

Syracuse, governed by Dion, then abolished its navy, just as the Thirty had abolished the Athenian navy. The grounds for this remarkable step, which gets no mention in the *Letters*, are only sketchily indicated by Plutarch, namely that a fleet is of no use, that sailors are political trouble-makers and that triremes involve their crews in expenses. Whatever Dion's motives may have been, his step must have seemed like the answer to Carthaginian prayers—or else like compliance with Carthaginian instructions. We hear no more of naval opposition to Carthage from Syracusan warships, and a dozen years later Carthaginian warships are in control of Sicilian waters right up to Messina and Rhegium. Timoleon has to run a Carthaginian blockade in order to get his little expeditionary force into Sicily. For a short time Syracuse itself and its harbour are in Carthaginian hands.

At some stage Dion had Heracleides assassinated. Heracleides was an admiral, beloved by the sailor-citizens and in favour of property distribution. Yet, obscurely, he was an ambivalent co-revolutionary with Dion. Plutarch assures us that his high-principled hero greatly regretted the necessity for this liquidation. It certainly compares unfavourably with Dionysius' treatment of his political opponents. It is tempting to conjecture that Heracleides had objected to the abolition of his fleet and the consequential presentation to Carthage of control of the Mediterranean.

Dion's rule was brief. His Athenian friend and captain of mercenary troops, Callippus, got him murdered by some dissident Peloponnesian mercenaries. The only reason mentioned for this history-shaping act is that Callippus disapproved of tyranny. Despite his principles he himself then became tyrant of Syracuse, but did not last long.

In 346 Dionysius, whose bad record and unpopularity in Syracuse seem to have been exaggerated, was apparently without turmoil restored to his post at Syracuse. He ruled again for a short spell before voluntarily resigning his command to the more potent Corinthian general, Timoleon. His retirement to private life in Corinth, the mother-city of Syracuse and the home of Timoleon, may indicate that his record as governor of Syracuse had not been indelibly black.

The Dionists had at some stage after Dion's death betaken themselves once more to Leontini, where the tyrant, Hicetas, a friend of Dion, became their new leader. His policy was perfectly clear. In open co-operation with the Carthaginian fleet he would conquer Sicily and split the control of it between himself and Carthage. He himself would be ruler of Syracuse; the Carthaginians would rule the bulk of the rest of the island. This overt policy of Hicetas and the ex-Dionists in the 340's need not have been the continuation of a covert policy of Dion and the Dionists in the 350's. But *Letters* III, VII and VIII do give us a little evidence in favour of the idea that it was such a continuation.

In these *Letters* (315 D, 316 B, 319 B–C, 331 E, 336 A, 336 C–D, 357 A–B) the notional Plato again and again says that Dion 'would have' repopulated with Greek colonists the Sicilian cities which had been extinguished by the Carthaginians. This is the policy which Timoleon later on successfully carried out. 'Plato' does not venture to deny that this had also been the plan of young Dionysius, but he chides Dionysius for claiming priority in the plan over Dion and himself, 'Plato'. If these *Letters* are Dionist propaganda letters, then we can be sure that Dionysius was so well known to have had this policy that it would have been folly for the *Letters* not to admit it. But we can also be fairly sure that the Syracusans did not know or believe that Dion had had this policy, else there would have been no point in 'Plato' averring so often that it was from his personal knowledge of Dion that he could say that Dion had had it in mind. On this matter the *Letters* were trying to divert the credit for a popular policy from Dionysius, who deserved it, to the Dionist party, which was not known or believed to deserve it. But if Dion had not intended to re-hellenize the former Greek cities of Sicily and thus to hem in or even extrude the Carthaginians, what had he really intended? He had intended to split Sicily between the Carthaginians and himself in just the way in which Hicetas later intended to do so. *Letters* III, VII and VIII had to be concocted largely because it was widely believed that Dion had made such a deal with Carthage. 'Plato's' retrospective testimony to Dion's reticent Hellenism was urgently needed just in order to counter this otherwise insuperable objection to the Dionist party. The fact that *Letters* VII and VIII seem to be trying to persuade the Dionists, even at this late hour, to adopt the anti-Carthaginian policy of re-hellenization strongly indicates that hitherto they had not adopted it.

In *Letter* VIII 357 A–B 'Plato' represents Dion as having planned to resettle with Greek citizens the barbarized parts of Sicily 'by depriving the barbarians of the land they now hold—excepting those who fought in defence of the common liberty against tyranny'. This reservation for the non-Greeks who had fought in Dion's army might be of great significance. For at least Acragas, Gela and Camarina had supplied him with troops. So apparently Dion did not intend to re-hellenize these three cities, though the largest of them, Acragas, was, presumably, at the moment of Dion's landing under Carthaginian control. Possibly Gela and Camarina were also at that time under Carthaginian control. After his great victory over the Carthaginians Timoleon did re-hellenize Acragas and Gela, among other cities. So Dion's implied reservation of Acragas, Gela and Camarina from re-hellenization was surely a major concession to Carthage. It was, we may infer, part of the deal that the whole south coast of Sicily should be a Carthaginian sphere of influence. Dion's 'excepting those [barbarians] who fought in defence of the common liberty' ostensibly safeguarded the interests of the Sicanians and Sikels of the Sicilian south coast, but really safeguarded those of their Carthaginian protectors.

We can, then, without going far beyond the *Letters* and

Plutarch's *Dion* and *Timoleon* make out a good case for Dion having been the champion of the Sicilian property owners and the Major Quisling of the Carthaginians. Timoleon rescued Sicily and Italy jointly from Carthage and from her Dionist collaborators. Dion's party, which narrowly failed of its short-term aims, did, however, achieve one long-term success. By means of a few forged letters it attached to Dion for two thousand years the glory of having tried to realize in Syracuse the Ideal State of Plato.

A major difficulty had confronted the composer of *Letters* III, VII and VIII, which had not confronted him when he wrote *Letter* XIII. He had now to present Plato as having been since 367 wholeheartedly on Dion's side and so completely in his confidence as to be able to give his impressive personal authority for what had been in Dion's mind, when this had not been revealed to anyone else. Yet every Syracusan knew that Plato continued to stay on as Dionysius' honoured personal guest for a year after Dion's expulsion in 367. They knew, too, that Plato came back to Syracuse only five years later, this time with a number of his colleagues from the Academy, and was again the personal guest of Dionysius for a full year; and 'to the whole of Sicily we appeared to be friends' (*Letter* VII 348 A). To explain away these awkward facts it was necessary to make out that it was in order to help Dion that Plato remained Dionysius' guest from the summer of 367 until the summer of 366, and that he returned in 361 to be his guest again for another year. This required concocting a story according to which Dionysius both wanted to have Plato for his guest and wanted to frustrate Plato's aim in visiting him. As it was known that Dionysius at least patronized and possibly was fascinated by philosophy, the ingenious solution was found of making Dionysius' philosophical ardours and vanities the motive for his clinging to Plato's society, while his political vendetta gave him his motive for frustrating Plato's aims.

The *Seventh Letter* says that Plato returned to Sicily in 361 partly in order to get restored to the exiled Dion his sequestered capital. This story has one awkward implication. Dionysius rightly suspected, and the author of the *Letter* knew that he rightly suspected that Dion required this huge capital sum in order to hire a mercenary army. So either Plato in dunning Dionysius for the restoration of this capital sum to Dion would have been plotting against his host; or else he would have been acting as the unwitting catspaw of Dion. Either Plato was trying without success to gull Dionysius, or Dion was succeeding in gulling Plato. Neither option would leave us with two high-minded heroes. The alternative suggestion that Plato wanted to relieve Dion's personal financial embarrassments would not stand inspection.

In dull fact Plato's second and third visits to Syracuse had nothing whatsoever to do with Dion, and only theoretically had they anything to do with Sicilian politics. Our evidence, outside *Letters* III, VII and VIII, suggests that Plato remained on excellent terms with Dionysius II. *Letter* XIII indicates this. The *Laws* 710–11 does so too. Some malicious stories against Plato in Diogenes Laertius'

Life of Diogenes would have been pointless unless Plato had been generally known to be in close liaison with Dionysius. The picture of the intimate alliance between the two idealists, Plato and Dion, was fabricated by the author of the *Letters*. Probably Speusippus was not very strenuous in criticism of this picture.

4. THE FORGER

If one man concocted *Letters* III, VII, VIII and XIII, and if he did so at their ostensible dates, then *Letter* XIII shows that he was in Athens in the winter of 366–365. He was almost certainly in Syracuse in 361–360, since, although Plato's *Laws* was not issued in book-form until after Plato's death, yet several years before Plato's death the author of *Letters* III, VII and especially VIII makes Plato prescribe for Sicily a number of the political and social recommendations of Books III–VII of our *Laws*. So the writer presumably heard Plato's oral delivery of the *Proto-Laws* in Syracuse in 361–360.

The author of the *Thirteenth Letter* knew a lot about Plato's domestic circumstances and even about the gifts that Plato was dispatching to Dionysius, his wife and children. He must have been intimate either with Plato or with some relative or intimate of Plato. The composer of these *Letters* was a highly educated man with considerable literary gifts. There are some Isocratean phrases and sentiments in the *Letters*, and structural parallels between the *Seventh Letter* and Isocrates' *Antidosis* have been conjectured to be unfortuitous. Opinions are divided about the writer's philosophical abilities. His exposition of the

Theory of Forms is thought by some to be of high Platonic quality. To others it seems not only to be grossly anachronistic, since it was written later than Plato's *Parmenides*, Part I, but also to give off a second-hand and even Speusippan smell.

There is one known person whom much of this complex description fits. Helicon was a pupil of Eudoxus, with mathematical and astronomical talents of his own. According to the *Thirteenth Letter* he was associated with, or else a pupil of one of Isocrates' pupils. This *Letter* shows that Helicon was still in Athens in the winter–spring of 366–365, but was about to sail to Syracuse. Plutarch's *Dion* XIX tells us that Helicon was in Syracuse in 361–360. Since the *Thirteenth Letter* is a forgery, its author must have had some special motive for introducing into the *Letter* so careful a testimonial to Helicon's trustworthiness.

The author of the *Seventh Letter* seems to be quite ignorant of the contents of Plato's *Timaeus*, if this is identical with the solitary συνουσία that Plato delivered in Syracuse in 366. Helicon was in Athens at that time and so could not have been present at its delivery. The *Timaeus* was not issued to the world in book-form until after Plato's death. It was reserved for the instruction of students in the Academy. So Helicon, who was in Sicily from early 365, was without access to the text of the *Timaeus* and without access to the oral reports of its Academic recipients.

All this, however, amounts only to a fairly thin circumstantial case for the identity of Helicon with the composer of these *Letters*. We have no other evidence that Helicon was a partisan or agent of Dion and his faction, or that he was in with the Academics, Speusippus, Timonides, Eudemus and Miltas, who according to Plutarch's *Dion* XXII were all Dionists.

The purposes of the forger of the *Thirteenth Letter* are obscure. It is written as to Dionysius, and its wary testimonial to Helicon seems to have been meant to insert Helicon into Dionysius' entourage.

On the other hand its chidings of Dionysius for his financial unreliabilities would seem to have been meant not for Dionysius' eyes but to damage his credit in Athens; and its representation of Plato as financially dependent on Dionysius even for domestic expenses is likely to have been meant to persuade some people in Athens to attribute Plato's backing of Dionysius to stipendiary motives. The idea of representing Plato as the authoritative sponsor of an idealistic Dion has not yet been thought of; nor its corollary that Plato had split with Dionysius by 366.

Parts of the *Letter*, for example 361 A–B, 363 A and E, have so natural a ring that one is tempted to speculate that the forger had access, perhaps *via* the ship's captain, Terillus (363 C), to a genuine letter from Plato to his Syracusan host, and that he composed a doctored version of this *Letter* for the benefit of some select Athenian recipients. The *Letter* read by Dionysius had received some but not all of this doctoring. But this is an unpalatably intricate hypothesis.

5. PLATO'S THIRD VISIT TO SICILY

The *Seventh Letter* has persuaded the world that Plato reluctantly came back to Sicily in 361 partly in the remote hope that he might yet capture the heart of Dionysius for philosophy, thereby, somehow, cementing good relations between Syracuse and Tarentum (339 D–E); and partly with the more mundane mission of trying to induce the young tyrant to release the exiled Dion's sequestered capital (346–7).

Even if the authenticity of this *Letter* was not disproved by the timing of Plato's second voyage to Sicily and of Dionysius' accession to the tyranny, both in April 367, it would be almost as conclusively disproved by the following fact. Plato came to Sicily in 361 together with Speusippus, Aeschines, Aristippus, Xenocrates, probably Eudoxus and possibly the young Aristotle. But the *Letter* is silent about this cortège of Athenian intellectuals. It lets us think that Plato came from Athens alone and on a mission that was personal to him. The author of the *Letter* has to hush up the delegation since he could not plausibly pretend that all its members came to dun Dionysius for Dion's capital, or even that they all came in order to win the young tyrant for philosophy. On the other hand, he could not admit the truth that they had been invited to Syracuse to make their several contributions to a Palace Festival without admitting that Plato too might have been invited for the same cultural reason, an admission which would have exploded the *Letter*'s central theme, namely that Plato made his second and third visits to Syracuse in support of his and Dion's shared ideals.

The author of the *Letter* glosses over, but does not extricate himself out of the embarrassing quandary that was mentioned earlier. He knows, and knows that Dionysius knew that Dion required control of his capital in order to

hire a mercenary army with which to make himself master
of Syracuse. By the time of the writing of the *Letter* in
about 353 his notional Plato too knows these facts, yet he
is allowed to confess neither that his pressure on Dionysius
to let Dion have the money had been disingenuous, nor
that it had been ingenuous.

The *Seventh Letter*'s account of Plato's second and third
visits to Sicily has to be discarded *in toto*. Plato's third visit
had nothing to do with Dion's grievances or policies.
Plato and the other Athenians came to contribute to a
festival that had been organized by the Younger Dionysius
in concert with Archytas. Can any of the literary contributions of any of the visitors still be identified?

(*a*) In the last section of this chapter some tenuous arguments are assembled for the idea both that Xenophon presented his dialogue, the *Hiero*, to the young Dionysius at
the Syracusan Festival of 361–360, and, in connexion with
Xenophon's conjectured attendance at this festival, that
Speusippus, Aristotle and many others presented their
encomia on Xenophon's dead son, Gryllus, at the same
festival, partly in order to gratify Xenophon in person.
Some festival at about this moment must have been the
venue for the delivery of these encomia; Speusippus is recorded as the author of such an encomium; and Speusippus was certainly in Syracuse in 361–360. Aristotle knew
that these encomia were composed 'partly to gratify'
Gryllus' father, who would presumably have to hear the
encomia in order to be gratified by them.

Independent reasons, none of them by itself conclusive,
for thinking that Aristotle came with the Athenian delega-

tion to Syracuse in 361 would, together with the known
fact that he too composed a *Gryllus*, be reasons for identifying the Syracusan Festival with the *paneguris* for which
the encomia on Gryllus were intended. Conversely, other
reasons for identifying this festival with the one for which
these encomia were intended would be reasons for thinking that Aristotle belonged to the Athenian delegation.

(*b*) In his *Plato und die sogenannten Pythagoreer* (pp. 142–3,
307, 332–3 and 384), E. Frank attributes to Speusippus and
to Xenocrates quasi-Pythagorean compositions, written in
amateurish Doric. According to Diogenes Laertius
Aristippus, a *persona grata* in Syracuse, presented to Dionysius, on some occasion or other, things that he had composed; and some of his compositions were in Doric. As
Doric was the dialect of Syracuse and Tarentum, it seems
likely that visitors sometimes doricized just as a compli-
ment to their hosts. Perhaps, then, the crudely doricized
compositions of Speusippus and Xenocrates were meant
for Sicilian recipients, and perhaps their contents tried to be
Pythagorean in topic for the same amiable reason.

The less charitable view would be that Speusippus and
Xenocrates wished to pass off on a gullible world as
genuine Pythagorean relics compositions of their own.
When Speusippus put into the mouth of Philolaus views
excogitated by Speusippus himself, he meant to cheat.
If we would rather ascribe courtesy than fraudulence to
Plato's colleagues, we must give hospitality to the idea that
on their one known visit to Sicily Speusippus and Xenocrates presented philosophical compositions that were
courteously meant to be Italian in both topic and diction.

Such compositions would no more have been fraudulent than Plato's own *Timaeus* had been fraudulent in putting into the mouth of a notional Locrian coeval of Socrates the much later cosmological and physiological doctrines that Plato had gratefully absorbed from Archytas and Philistion in 367–366. Indeed Speusippus and Xenocrates could have been modelling their compositions on the general pattern of the *Timaeus*, with the difference that Plato had designed his *Timaeus* for the Academy and not for a Syracusan festival.

That later generations should have fathered the compositions of Speusippus and Xenocrates on to real Pythagoreans would be quite unsurprising. Comparable *provenances* were credulously ascribed to Plato's *Timaeus* too. For dramatic purposes Plato's dialogues are all somewhat archaized, the *Parmenides* very considerably so. But no one was deceived by this dramatic practice until later ages hankered to credit everything to a pleasingly mysterious Long, Long Ago. It should be noticed that the anonymous *Timaeus Locrus* is also written in amateurish Doric. It too was glorified with a pre-Platonic genesis.

(*c*) With much greater confidence we can nominate as Plato's own contribution to this festival his *Laws*, or rather the first version of Books III–VII of our *Laws*, in the original monologue style or address style in which long stretches of our *Laws* remain.

Here we get Plato's *Code Napoléon* for Syracuse with, at 710–11, its startling postulation of a state governed by a young, teachable, courageous and self-controlled tyrant in fortunate conjunction with a great legislator. We have to supply for ourselves their names, 'Dionysius' and 'Plato'. The notional Cretan colony for which the Athenian Stranger legislates is, like Syracuse, a Dorian one. The idea that the original *Laws* was actually presented by Plato to Dionysius on some public occasion as a practicable political blue print for Sicily is confirmed by this fact. Although our *Laws* was not published in book-form until after Plato's death in 347, yet the fabricator of *Letters* III, VII and especially VIII makes his 'Plato' put forward, explicitly for Sicily's benefit, a considerable number of practical political recommendations tallying with some of the contents of what are now Books III–VII of our *Laws*. Since he could not have got this knowledge from their not-yet-issued text, the fabricator must have got it some time before 353 from hearing an oral delivery of it by Plato himself. As the *Letters* have a Sicilian *provenance*, their fabricator is likely to have heard this delivery in Syracuse; and if so, he must have heard it before 357, when Dion invaded Sicily. Aristotle tells us that the *Laws* was written later than the *Republic*. So Plato's oral delivery of his *Proto-Laws* must have taken place on his third and last visit to Syracuse.

In his contribution to *Aristotle and Plato in the Mid-Fourth Century*, Glenn Morrow shows that Aristotle in his account in his *Politics* II of Plato's *Laws* is unacquainted with parts of the *Laws* outside Books III–VII. Morrow argues that this stretch must have existed and been known to Aristotle separately before Plato completed our *Laws*. Aristotle himself gives us a further pointer to the existence of a *Proto-Laws* when in his *Politics* he makes not the Athenian Stranger but Socrates the spokesman of the *Laws*.

6. ARISTOTLE AND SICILY

In 361 a delegation of philosophers from Athens and the Academy went to Syracuse on the invitation of the Younger Dionysius and probably of Archytas of Tarentum. The delegation included Plato, Speusippus, Aeschines, Aristippus, probably Eudoxus, almost certainly Xenocrates, and doubtless plenty of other notables. But if the youngish Xenocrates, then why not also the young Aristotle? Scholars and historians would have raised this question before had they not assumed the truth of the *Seventh Letter*'s story of Plato's third visit to Syracuse.

Certainly Aristotle nowhere mentions this conjectured journey; but then he nowhere mentions a single event in his own life of any biographical interest. Certainly, too, no other authority tells us of such a visit; but then no authority, including the *Seventh Letter*, mentions the Athenian delegation as such. We have to piece its existence together out of references made separately to Plato, Speusippus, Xenocrates, Aeschines, Aristippus and Eudoxus by the *Seventh* and *Third Letters*, by Plutarch in his *Dion*, by Diogenes Laertius in his *Lives*, and by Aelian in his *Varia Historia* VII 17, together with the story that the deputy-Head of the Academy during Plato's absence in 361–360 was none of these colleagues of Plato but the relatively junior Heracleides Ponticus.

(*a*) Aristotle wrote a book about the Pythagoreans, and we know that this was at a quite early stage in his life. The fragments that we possess from this book give the strong impression that the stories which he retails had been culled not from other books—what other books were there?—but orally from legends and traditions still current in southern Italy. The phrase 'they say' is frequent in Aristotle's remarks. The Pythagorean philosophical doctrines which Aristotle here cites seem likely also to have been collected orally from Italian thinkers like Archytas of Tarentum and his chief disciple, Archedemus, then resident in Syracuse. For if they had been available in books we should have heard of these books; and Plato, Speusippus, Xenocrates and Theophrastus could have drawn on them too, which they seem not to have done. In his *Metaphysics* XIV 1092b11 Aristotle tells us something about Eurytus which, according to Theophrastus (*Metaphysics* 6a19), came from something that Archytas *said* (ἔφη).

(*b*) In his *Politics* Aristotle draws a surprising number of his political illustrations from the Mediterranean, the Adriatic, Sicily and Italy, particularly southern Italy. In Book VII, 1329b8–22, a passage refers to practices current in Italy 'at the present time'. As it includes a piece of gratuitous local topography it is likely to derive from someone who had quite recently visited the locality in person. At 1320b10 (and compare 1263a35) Aristotle describes with approbation contemporary political practices at Tarentum, and, at 1269a2, with disapprobation a contemporary law at Cyme.

(*c*) The *De Mirabilibus Auscultationibus* is an album of travellers' yarns. As in other such class-albums, like the *Problems* and the so-called *Platonic Definitions*, the items come from many contributors, including, apparently, juveniles. Lots of these yarns are certainly not by the critical Aristotle. Many are from parts of the world which Aristotle never saw. Some are drawn from Hanno, Callisthenes, Polycritus, Xenophanes and 'Phoenician histories'. One (173) derives explicitly from Eudoxus, so possibly some others do too. Over a score of its zoological items occur also, sometimes with reduced credulity, in Aristotle's *Historia Animalium*, especially Book IX, and two or three of them occur in his *De Partibus Animalium*. So at least a good many of the travellers' tales had already been recorded, if not yet collected in an album, when Aristotle was not very old. Some of the stories, to judge from their vocabulary, style, attention to detail and ungullibility, might well be extracts from travel diaries of Aristotle himself. There are plenty of travellers' stories, mostly sensible ones, about Sicily, the Straits of Messina, the Lipari islands, and the 'boot' of Italy, including places associated with Pythagoras. A novelist could retrospectively concoct for Aristotle, perhaps accompanying Eudoxus, an instructive overland journey between Syracuse and the palace of Archytas in Tarentum through places mentioned either in this album or in the fragments of Aristotle's book *On the Pythagoreans* or in Aristotle's *Politics*. The journey would include a visit to the volcanic Lipari islands (cf. *Meteor.* 367a with *De Mirabilibus Auscultationibus* 34, 37, 38, especially 101, 132).

(*d*) In his *Historia Animalium* Aristotle gives us a wealth of first-rate information about fishes and shellfish. Not only are a lot of the species that he describes identifiable with known Mediterranean and Adriatic species, but nearly two dozen times he gives them names which, not much altered, are still used by the fishermen of Naples, Genoa, Venice and Taranto. Several of the fishing methods which he describes are still practised by Adriatic fishermen. If Aristotle had not himself examined the creatures caught by Sicilian, Italian and perhaps especially Tarantine fishermen, and discussed with them the life histories, habitats and spawnings of these creatures, then he must have drawn on the knowledge of some zoologist who had done so, as observant, systematic and anatomically-minded as himself. Who? Aristotle occasionally refers explicitly to Sicily and the Adriatic, and once to Tarentum. In his *Politics* 1291 b he mentions the large population of fishing-folk at Tarentum.

D'Arcy Wentworth Thompson in his Oxford translation of the *Historia Animalium* gives due attention to the sources in the eastern Aegean of much of Aristotle's marine lore. Yet, though he himself provides the evidence, he does not give particular notice to the Sicilian-Italian source of a good deal of the rest of Aristotle's marine lore. This evidence points to Aristotle having visited Sicily and Italy at some time. It does not point to any specific period in his life. But thanks to Dion Sicily was no place for visitors after 357; and Sicilian and Italian waters were unprotected from pirates and from Carthaginian warships after about 355 when Dion abolished the Syracusan navy. As the *Historia Animalium* gives careful eyewitness accounts of the spawnings of numerous species of fish and shellfish, it is natural to infer that the eyewitness visited Italian waters in springtime. The suggested overland journey of Aristotle and Eudoxus from Syracuse to Tarentum would have been in, say, February–April 360.

It is, however, an objection to this argument that the anatomical knowledge of fishes and shellfishes shown by Aristotle in the *Historia Animalium* is of too high an order for him to have possessed it by the age of twenty-four, however well he had been coached by Speusippus and Philistion.

(*e*) Aristotle is credited by Diogenes Laertius with three books on the philosophy of Archytas, as well as with one book called *Extracts from the 'Timaeus' and the Works of Archytas*. It is sometimes assumed that Aristotle got his interest in, and his knowledge of the doctrines of Archytas from books written by Archytas that were available in Athens. Yet, so far as we can tell, no other Athenian philosopher of Aristotle's time was acquainted with such books, and though Aristotle frequently refers to the contemporary doctrines of 'so-called Pythagorean' or Italian philosophers, and occasionally refers to Archytas by name, he never names or claims to cite from their books. Simplicius, who says that the young Aristotle was powerfully influenced by Archytas, does cite a lot of things allegedly written by Archytas. But the bulk of these extracts can be proved not to be by Archytas. We have no reason to suppose that Archytas did issue much in writing, still less that many, if any, such writings were accessible in Athens when Aristotle was a young man. But if not, then Aristotle must have learned the doctrines of Archytas orally, either in Tarentum from Archytas himself or else from his chief disciple, Archedemus, or from Philistion, if, which we do not know, Philistion knew these doctrines. Archedemus almost certainly did visit the Academy more than once. For, though the [Platonic] *Letters* which tell us so are forgeries, their author would not have told lies about things which were common knowledge in Syracuse. But if Archedemus, Philistion or both orally imparted the doctrines of Archytas to the Academy, why, so far as we can tell, is Aristotle, after Plato's *Timaeus*, the sole Academic authority on these doctrines? It is argued in this chapter (Section 2), and in Chapter VII, 7, that the ideas of Archytas and Philistion which form the scientific content of the *Timaeus* had been acquired by Plato during his second visit to Sicily in 367–366. They were not at that time, when Aristotle was eighteen, available in Athens in book-shape, else it would have been otiose for Plato to write his *Timaeus*. Aristotle knows much more about the doctrines of Archytas and Philistion than he could have gleaned from the *Timaeus*.

(*f*) C. Albutt's *Greek Medicine in Rome* and W. Jaeger's *Diokles von Carystos* make it clear that Aristotle's physiology is so heavily indebted to the teachings of the Syracusan doctor, Philistion, that the young Aristotle must have sat at Philistion's feet for quite a long spell. Where? From the invitation to Philistion to come to Athens given in the forged *Second Letter*, and from the mention of the unnamed Sicilian doctor in the famous fragment of Epicrates, Jaeger infers that Philistion taught Aristotle in Athens. He also adduces a remark from Diogenes Laertius' *Eudoxus* to show that Eudoxus studied under Philistion in Athens. But Jaeger does not give weight to the fact that according to this remark Eudoxus studied not only under Philistion but also under Archytas; or that Aelian says that Eudoxus was with Plato in Syracuse (*Var. Hist.* VII 17); or that Eudoxus did not in 361–360, as in 367–366, deputize for Plato as Head of the Academy. Whether or when Philistion visited Athens, and whether, if he did so, he stayed long enough to teach physiology, we cannot tell. But the alternative hypothesis remains, namely that Aristotle visited Sicily for over a year, and that it was while there that he studied under both Archytas and Philistion, perhaps side by side with his own teacher, Eudoxus. In default of this unifying hypothesis we should require two independent explanations: one to explain Aristotle's knowledge of the doctrines of Archytas, the other to explain his knowledge of the doctrines of Philistion. Indeed we should need a third explanation as well, to account for Aristotle's acquaintance with the Pythagorean legends and the political practices that were current in the 'boot' of Italy; and maybe a fourth to account for his knowledge about the Lipari islands and about marine fauna and fishing devices in the Mediterranean and Adriatic.

(*g*) If, what is not argued here, the *Timaeus Locrus* is identical with Aristotle's *Extracts from the 'Timaeus' and the Works of Archytas*, then the fact that the *Timaeus Locrus* is written in amateurish Doric strongly suggests that Aristotle composed the work for delivery to a Sicilian audience.

(*h*) It is argued in Chapter VII that Plato composed the *Phaedrus* during his sojourn in Syracuse in 361–360, and that he delivered it at the Olympic Games in July 360. The

Phaedrus announces to Hellas that the Academy is now going to teach rhetoric. Aristotle did inaugurate the teaching of rhetoric in the Academy in considerable accordance with the curriculum laid down in the *Phaedrus*, and this inauguration must have followed very soon after Plato's return to Athens in the late summer of 360, when Aristotle was twenty-four or twenty-five. Plato had presumably drawn up the new course of instruction that is outlined in his *Phaedrus* in confabulation somewhere with the young man who was to conduct it. If so, then maybe Aristotle got his *licentia docendi* from Plato while both were in Syracuse; and maybe he heard the author of the *Phaedrus* announcing his *licentia docendi* to Hellas while both were at the Olympic Games when *en route* from Sicily to Athens. Did the young Aristotle take the speaking part of the young Phaedrus at these Games? The rhetorical voracity of Phaedrus, marvelled at in the *Phaedrus* 242, might be the literary voracity of the young Aristotle who was nicknamed 'the Reader' by the Academy.

In the *Phaedrus* 279 Socrates prophesies for the youthful Isocrates eminence both in rhetoric and in philosophy. Yet when Plato wrote this dialogue the aged Isocrates, who had attained eminence as a teacher of rhetoric, had become nothing of a philosopher—as is declared in the *Euthydemus* 305. Why does Plato make Socrates give this glowing mis-prognosis? Perhaps Plato is referring, under dramatic cover, to the Academy's youthful teacher-elect of rhetoric, in whom Plato discerns the philosopher-to-be. 'Socrates' is Plato, and his 'Isocrates' is Aristotle.

(*i*) In 362–361 Xenophon's son, Gryllus, died in battle.

According to Diogenes Laertius' *Xenophon* a lot of people are said by Aristotle to have written encomia and funeral orations upon Gryllus, partly to please his father. Speusippus and Isocrates are said to have composed such orations. Aristotle himself certainly wrote a *Gryllus*. We are not told for what occasion these rhetorical tributes were composed. Funeral orations on Gryllus would naturally be delivered quite soon after the heroic death of their subject in 362–361. *Panegureis* were *ex vi termini* the *venues* for panegyric orations.

According to Athenaeus' *Deipnosophistae* x 427 Xenophon attended a banquet given by Dionysius in Syracuse; we are not told whether his host was the Elder or the Younger Dionysius. Xenophon's dialogue, the *Hiero*, on 'How to be happy though a Tyrant', reads like a tactful homily meant for the ears of a live and still receptive tyrant. The dialogue does not bespatter the tyrant with the regulation douches of vitriol. As it has a Sicilian title and setting, the *paneguris* for which it was presumably composed is likely to have been a Syracusan one. A just possible allusion to Dion in *Hiero* I, 9 would date the dialogue after 367 and before 357. So Xenophon, who died in about 354, may have presented this dialogue at the festival in Syracuse in 361–360. Its text was certainly available in Athens before 355, since in his *On the Peace* 113 of that year Isocrates virtually borrows a passage from the *Hiero* III, 8.

As we have seen, Xenophon, in the *Hiero* I, 11–13, tells us that tyrants cannot attend foreign festivals. They have therefore to hold their own festivals, and they pay heavily in order to get contestants to come to them from abroad.

This remark, with another at XI, 10, might have a topical point.

So perhaps the numerous encomia upon Gryllus were all presented at this Syracusan Festival, partly to gratify his father who was to be present in person. In the absence of newspapers, encomia on Gryllus would gratify his father only if he were there to hear them. The theme may have been a competition theme set in honour of Xenophon, who was at this time resident in Corinth, the mother-city of Syracuse. Speusippus' *Gryllus* and Aristotle's *Gryllus* would then be almost certain to have been composed as competition pieces for this same occasion; Speusippus and Aristotle would both have come with the delegation from Athens in the capacity of competitors at this festival; and old Xenophon would have heard young Aristotle's first public discourse. Of Speusippus we do know independently that he was in Syracuse in 361–360. Wherever the *paneguris* was for which he composed his *Gryllus*, it must have taken place at about this time. But if not in Syracuse in 361–360, or else at Olympia in July 360, then where and when? Was Aristotle there too with his *Gryllus*? Was Xenophon there?

(*j*) Plato's *Laws* was published only after Plato's death. Yet some half a dozen years before Plato's death the forger of *Letters* III, VII and especially VIII had made his 'Plato' recommend as the cure for Sicilian troubles many of the ideas which we find in Books III–VII of our *Laws*. The forger or an informant of the forger must have heard Plato deliver these ideas. Plato's cordial and optimistic reference in the *Laws* 710–11 to the teachable young tyrant in close collaboration with the great legislator shouts to us that originally the *Laws* was an advisory address-sequence presented by Plato to young Dionysius. It had been composed for Plato's third visit to Syracuse and was actually delivered there in 361 or 360.

In his *Politics* Book II Aristotle discusses in some detail the contents of the *Laws*. But, as Glenn Morrow has shown, Aristotle seems here to be unacquainted with any parts of our *Laws* outside the same books, III–VII. Apparently what Aristotle knew was an early version of this part only of our *Laws*. Aristotle knew just what the forger of the *Letters* knew. Yet no book of this early version was published, else we should possess both our *Laws* and this earlier version of its Books III–VII, still in its original address-style.

That what Aristotle knew was not just a part of our *Laws*, as this stands, is confirmed by the fact that Aristotle makes Socrates the mouthpiece of its ideas. The discussion-leader in our *Laws* is the Athenian Stranger. Even if Aristotle had blundered, his students would have corrected him if the text of our *Laws* had been available to them. As they did not correct him, Aristotle must have written his exposition of the *Laws* Books III–VII without yet having had access to our *Laws*; and Socrates must have been the spokesman of the original *Sicilian Laws* as he had been, six years earlier, of the *Proto-Republic*.

How did Aristotle know this first version of the *Laws*, if its text had not been issued? More answers than one are thinkable. One answer is that like the forger of the *Letters* Aristotle heard Plato delivering it in Syracuse in 361–360 and made full notes of what he had heard. Aristotle and the concocter of the *Letters* were sitting and taking notes on adjacent benches. Some of Aristotle's defective exegeses would be explained by the hypothesis that he had to work, not on the text of the *Sicilian Laws*, and *a fortiori* not of our *Laws*, but only on his and his colleagues' memories and memoranda of what Plato had delivered orally in Syracuse in 361–360, when Aristotle was twenty-four.

This assemblage of straws does not prove that Aristotle was with the Athenian delegation in Sicily in 361–360; but it amounts to a circumstantial case for it better than the case against it that rests on the silences of taciturn history.

CHAPTER IV

DIALECTIC

I. FOREWORD

From the beginning to the end of his writing days, from his *Lysis*, say, to the second part of his *Parmenides*, Plato's heart was wrapped up in the practice and the propagation of dialectic. His captivation by the Theory of Forms was of relatively short duration, lasting, perhaps, for about the half-dozen years from, say, 370 to 364; but anyhow this captivation was itself in part derivative from his devotion to dialectic. The tracker of Plato's intellectual development needs to keep one finger all the time on the clue of dialectic.

Unhappily most historians of Plato's thought either glorify dialectic into something too rarefied to be anything actually practised on a Monday morning; or they downgrade it into something too pettifogging to be permitted to blinker their seer. Yet for the understanding of Plato, as for the understanding of any other original philosopher, what is essential is the appreciation of the style and the structure of his heartfelt arguments.

Another scholarly tradition still throws across the terrain its separate beams of darkness. It is often assumed that admiration for Plato requires contempt for Aristotle, and admiration for Aristotle requires contempt for Plato. One must vote with one party or the other. Yet the dialectic that Plato taught and practised is the dialectic that Aristotle taught and practised. It is in Aristotle's *Art of Dialectic* that we find the technology of the Socratic Method. The transition from Plato's *Euthydemus* to Aristotle's *Topics* is the progress from craft to Art. In his *Peri Ideon* Aristotle dissects the Theory of Forms according to the procedures of *pro* and *contra* dialectic, though not, as we have it, in question-answer style. Plato's *Parmenides*, Part II, conforms to the same pattern, though it is nominally in question-answer style. What, then, is dialectic on a Monday morning?

2. ARISTOTLE'S 'ART OF DIALECTIC'

A treatise called *The Art of So and So* is a body of general rules, explanations, examples, warnings and recommendations, the study of which is calculated to help the student to become proficient in the practice in question. It is a training manual. Protagoras is said to have written an *Art of Wrestling*. Some people may learn to wrestle well from mere flair, habituation and imitation; but there is much to be learned also from the technical theory of wrestling. The same thing is true of medicine and navigation. Rule of thumb is not enough.

Between the time of Protagoras and that of Aristotle in his early teaching years there had appeared a considerable number of *Arts of Rhetoric*. Intelligent and ambitious young Greeks who looked forward to careers in public life needed to be taught how to compose forensic, political and panegyric orations. Nor, save for a few specialists like mathematicians, astronomers and doctors, was any other higher education provided until the Academy began. Not all, but many of the sophists of whom anything is known were teachers of rhetoric. The training manuals of rhetoric that Plato mentions in his *Phaedrus*, especially 266–7, were all composed by sophists. Some *Arts* were versified to aid memorization by students. Aristotle too wrote an *Art of Rhetoric*, which we possess. But what concerns us is something different. He also wrote an *Art of Dialectic*, known to us as his *Topics*. What was the practice of dialectic of which Aristotle's *Topics* is the *Art*? We know what the practitioners of rhetoric practised, in what circumstances and for what professions or careers. We are not so sure what a student of the art of dialectic hoped to become a practitioner of. We know the kind of career that a Demosthenes had. Was there a corresponding kind of career for a dialectician? If not, then for whom was Aristotle providing a training manual, and for what vocation?

Aristotle's *Art of Rhetoric* is mentioned alongside his *Art of Dialectic* partly because Aristotle himself closely associates the two practices (e.g. *De Arte Rhet.* Book I i 11–14; ii 7–9, etc.; *Topics* 164 a 5, 167 b 8, 174 b 19). Moreover, as we shall see, the exercise which Aristotle calls 'dialectic' had been taught for a long time before Aristotle, generally as an ancillary to rhetoric. Rhetoric and dialectic were the two limbs of the Art of Discourse.

The *Topics* is a training manual for a special pattern of disputation, governed by strict rules, which takes the following shape. Two persons agree to have a battle. One is to be questioner, the other answerer. The questioner can, with certain qualifications, only ask questions; and the answerer can, with certain qualifications, only answer 'yes' or 'no'. So the questioner's questions have to be properly constructed for 'yes' or 'no' answers. This automatically rules out a lot of types of questions, like factual questions, arithmetical questions and technical questions. Roughly, it leaves only conceptual questions, whatever these may be. The answerer begins by undertaking to uphold a certain 'thesis', for example that *justice is the interest of the stronger*, or that *knowledge is sense-perception*. The questioner has to try to extract from the answerer by a series of questions an answer or conjunction of answers inconsistent with the original thesis, and so drive him into an 'elenchus'. The questioner has won the duel if he succeeds in getting the answerer to contradict his original thesis, or else in forcing him to resign, or in reducing him to silence, to an infinite regress, to mere abusiveness, to pointless yammering or to outrageous paradox. The answerer has won if he succeeds in keeping his wicket up until the close of play. The answerer is allowed to object to a question on the score that it is two or more questions in one or that it is metaphorical or ambiguous. The duel is fought out before an audience (cf. *Sophist* 230 C); and apparently it is sometimes for the audience to judge whether the questioner or the answerer has won. Certain debating tricks and manoeuvres are recognized as fouls (*Topics* 171 b 20; 172 b 20; cf. *Euthydemus* 287 C, 295 B, 296 A; *Theaetetus* 167 E). The exercise has to have a time-limit, or else the answerer can never win. The 'time's up' seems to be referred to in the *Topics* 161 a 10 and 183 a 25.

In the Greek world in general elenctic duelling is normally called 'eristic', but this word has acquired pejorative connotations for Plato and Aristotle. They use this word and its variants for commercialized forms of the exercise practised by certain sophists who stoop to all sorts of tricks in order to make sure of winning. Plato's *Euthydemus* depicts such sophists in action. Aristotle uses the word 'dialectic' for the contest as practised with intellectual seriousness and without conscious trickery. We shall see that Plato does so too. The word 'eristic' continues to be used, often with no pejorative connotations, after Plato's and Aristotle's time, and we should often employ it too. The word 'dialectic' now carries too many daunting and uplifting associations for us to rely on it. It also obscures the inter-personal because match-playing aspect of the exercise, which the word 'eristic' preserves.

Why do people engage in eristic matches? Aristotle gives several reasons:

(*a*) There is the pedagogic or tutorial motive. A student's wits are sharpened if he is made to practise argumentation by trying to defend his own theses against criticisms and by trying to think up and organize criticisms of other people's theses. So the teacher may either himself engage his pupil in eristic bouts or else pit one pupil against another, subject to his own tutorial criticisms of their arguments. This is dialectic conducted with a *gymnastic* purpose. Obviously students may for extra practice conduct their own debating matches without tutorial supervision.

(*b*) Sometimes people are intellectually complacent or reckless. They need for the good of their souls and wits to be punctured. When they discover that they can be driven without trickery into acknowledging things patently inconsistent with other things which they had felt perfectly sure of, they become warier and intellectually humbler. This is what Aristotle calls the *peirastic* or probing purpose. It is a part or species of the pedagogic or tutorial dialectic.

(*c*) The exercise is an absorbing game—difficult, exciting and competitive. It has much in common with chess and fencing; or with draughts, as Adeimantus says in the *Republic* VI 487 and as Cleinias says in the *Laws* VII, 820. It is fun to win, and fun even to try to counter one's opponent's stratagems. Aristotle calls this the *agonistic* or match-winning purpose of the exercise. He says, what we could have guessed anyhow, that even those who debate for intellectual gymnastic cannot be stopped from trying to win (*Topics* 164 b 8–14). The students are after all young men; and their coach, Aristotle, is not very old.

(*d*) Sometimes sophists put on public tournaments in which, presumably, they take on challengers from the audience, or else challenge one another. Their object is to win at all costs and so to build up such a reputation for invincibility that they will make money from the fees of the pupils who will flock for coaching in such duelling and, conjecturally, from the gate-money paid by the audiences who come to hear the champion performing. This is the prize-fighting or eristic purpose, in the abusive sense that this word has for Plato and Aristotle. We may wonder whether they did not magnify the dimensions of the practice for diplomatic reasons.

(*e*) Finally, serious thinkers engage in duels with each other from an interest in conceptual issues themselves. Though Euthydemus and Dionysodorus use as a mere booby-trap the question 'Does not he who says that something is the case say something that is the case?', that is, 'are not all significant statements true?', a Plato or an Aristotle will debate this very same question in order to bring out into the light of day the relations between *significance* and *truth*. We may call this the *philosophical* purpose of the dialectical exercise. As we shall see, this purpose is in the end going to involve an historically crucial inversion of the duelling process. The Socratic Method culminates, when successful, in the answerer being caught in an argumentative *impasse*. But the philosopher's operations culminate, when successful, in his finding the way out of an *impasse*. What had been the destination has become the starting-point. But it took Plato something like a dozen years to convert his skill in constructing ambushes for others into skill in extracting himself and us from them. The latter can be a solitary and silent undertaking, where the former must be sociable and conducted *viva voce*. The word 'philosophy' correspondingly changes in significance between Plato's early and his latest dialogues.

In whichever of these five spirits the exercise is conducted, its rules are the same. Certain sophistries are disallowed in an Academic *milieu* (see *Topics* 164 b 8, 171 b).

We cannot from internal evidence fix the date when Aristotle composed the *Topics*. But in 354–353, some seven years before Plato's death, Isocrates in his *Antidosis* 258–69 makes it clear that the teaching of eristic is, with geometry and astronomy, now a part of the curriculum of the Academy. In the *Panathenaicus* 26–9 and in his *Letter to Alexander* of 342 he is likely to be sniping at Aristotle in person as a teacher of eristic. Plato, in what must be a late composition, the *Parmenides*, Part II, represents the venerated old Parmenides as demonstrating to the young Socrates the Zenonian gymnastic which he must practise if he is to become a philosopher. He then produces the most unrelieved and formalized model of a two-way question-answer exercise that has come down to us. The model conforms well with the rules and prescriptions collected in Aristotle's *Topics* for a serious exercise in dialectic, though Plato himself does not here use the word 'dialectic'. There can be no doubt, then, that what Isocrates calls 'eristic' and Aristotle calls 'dialectic' is, despite the drastic veto in the *Republic* VII, being taught to young men in the Academy by about the middle 350's; that Plato approves of this teaching; and that it is Aristotle who teaches the practice and the theory of it, in close connexion with his teaching of rhetoric. It is not by coincidence that in a dialogue composed well on in the 350's Plato unearths a coeval of Socrates called 'Aristotle' to be Parmenides' answerer.

Xenocrates too must have been closely associated with the teaching of this *gymnastic*. Of his numerous writings the titles of which are recorded by Diogenes Laertius IV 13 at least five have to do with dialectic, including one, in twenty books, *Of Theses*, another, in fourteen books, τῆς περὶ τὸ διαλέγεσθαι πραγματείας. At least two of the writings of Heracleides Ponticus must also be of this *genre*. That the exercise continues to be an important ingredient of college education throughout the succeeding centuries is shown by, among other things, the book-titles of the later Academics, Peripatetics and Stoics.

We are, however, confronted by this major historical enigma about Plato himself. We have good evidence from Isocrates' *Helen*, as well as that provided by Plato's own early dialogues, that Plato himself had during the 370's taught elenctic debating to young men. The Socratic Method had up to a certain moment been the sole or the main thing that Plato taught. Yet this teaching ceases outright when Plato founds his Academy. Its students must learn the *fortes* of Theaetetus and Eudoxus. They may on no account learn Plato's *forte*. It is left to Aristotle in the 350's to introduce the teaching of eristic, with that of rhetoric, into the Academy. Plato had not taught Aristotle dialectic. Why not?

3. THE EARLIER HISTORY OF DIALECTIC

The eristic Moot was not the invention of Aristotle. Its history goes well back into the fifth century. According to Diogenes Laertius' *Plato* 24 Favorinus says that Plato coined for eristic the noun 'dialectic', and therewith 'dialectician' and 'dialectical', from 'διαλέγεσθαι'; this last was the general verb for 'discuss', 'debate' and, specifically, 'debate by the method of question and answer'. The verb, though not the noun, occurs in Plato's very early dialogue, the *Laches*, and much earlier still in the *Dissoi Logoi*.

There are two other recurrent titles for eristic disputation. It is sometimes called '*antilogike*', and its practitioners are abusively described as 'antilogical' when emphasis is being laid on their readiness to argue impartially *pro* or *contra* any given thesis. Old Parmenides insists on this two-way argumentation in the *Parmenides* 136; so does

Aristotle in his *Topics* 101 a 35 and 163 b 10. It is sometimes called '*agonistike*' to emphasize the fact that its practitioners are primarily out to win their matches. This match-winning spirit is regularly called 'φιλονικία' by both Plato and Aristotle. We could call it 'eristic gamesmanship'.

Diogenes Laertius credits a number of people with the invention of the eristic Moot.

(i) *Zeno*

Diogenes Laertius quotes Aristotle as saying that Zeno was the inventor of dialectic; and Sextus Empiricus tells us that Aristotle said this in his *Sophist* (see Aristotle, *Selected Fragments*). Plato virtually says the same thing in the *Parmenides* where he makes old Parmenides tell the juvenile Socrates that if he is to become a philosopher he must put himself through a certain sort of training, namely in the pattern of reasoning of which Zeno has just produced an example. This method, however, requires a certain expansion. The argumentation should be two-way argumentation, deriving consequences both from a given proposition and from its negative. The student must learn to argue both *pro* and *contra* any given thesis. Parmenides then demonstrates the method in full question-answer style, with his answerer duly responding with 'yes' and 'no'. Commentators sometimes grumble at the unconversational role given to Parmenides' young interlocutor. But it is one of the first rules of the eristic exercise that the answerer has, with certain exceptions, to confine himself to assent and dissent.

Zeno's own argumentation had not, apparently, taken

the form of a questioner driving an answerer into elenchus after elenchus. It had been a chain of *reductiones ad absurdum*; and this is probably what Aristotle has in mind. An elenchus is, so to speak, a two-person incarnation of a *reductio ad absurdum*. But it was not Zeno who invented this incarnation. He pitted arguments against arguments. It was someone else who first pitted questioners against answerers. If Zeno was the grandfather, he was not the father of dialectic.

(ii) *Euclides*

According to Diogenes Laertius, Euclides of Megara studied the writings of Parmenides; his followers were called 'Megarians', 'Eristics' and, later, 'Dialecticians', because they put their arguments in the form of question and answer. Euclides, we are told, rebutted demonstrations by attacking, not their premisses (λήμματα), but their 'ἐπιφορά', that is, the inference from those premisses to their alleged conclusions. Eubulides, a follower of Euclides, is reported to have produced many dialectical arguments in interrogative form, including the famous and important crux, 'The Liar'.

Suidas says that Bryson, together with Euclides, introduced the eristic dialectic.

We know very little about the Megarians, but we know that they had very sharp noses for logical cruces. They consequently get short shrift from commentators on Plato. So does Zeno, of whose earth-shaking discovery of the *reductio ad absurdum* the Megarians may well have been the transmitters.

(iii) *Protagoras*

Diogenes Laertius says that Protagoras was the first to say that there are two opposite *logoi* about every subject; and was the first to argue in this way, by means of questions, συνηρώτα. He was also the first to institute λόγων ἀγῶνας, eristic matches or duels; he introduced the Socratic Method; and he was the father of the whole tribe of eristical disputants. Protagoras wrote an *Art of Eristic*, and this may be hinted at in Plato's *Sophist* 232. Protagoras did apparently introduce the exercise into Athens; and he was the first to give coaching in its techniques and to do so for a fee. As a teacher of rhetoric, wishing to train his pupils for forensic advocacy, he might well have been the inventor of the questioner-answerer Moot.

At the beginning of his *Against the Sophists*, which can be dated *c.* 390, Isocrates scolds some unnamed teachers who devote themselves to disputation. They profess to search for the truth; they promise to teach the young what to do and how to prosper; they inculcate virtue and self-control; they claim to be able to foretell the future; they charge fees which have to be deposited with a person of trust before the course of instruction begins. Protagoras did write a famous lecture-treatise called *Truth*, and Plato tells us in the *Theaetetus* 178 D–179 A that he claimed to foresee the future. All the rest of Isocrates' charges fit Protagoras. So Isocrates almost certainly here associates Protagoras with eristic and the teaching of it. In his *Helen* 2 he explicitly associates Protagoras with eristic.

Plato associates Protagoras with eristic in his *Protagoras*, *Theaetetus* and *Sophist*. In the *Theaetetus* 167D–168 Socrates, acting as spokesman for Protagoras, makes Protagoras say that his critics may either set up a doctrine in opposition to his own, or 'if you prefer the method of questions, ask questions; for an intelligent person ought not to reject this method, on the contrary he should choose it before all others'. He goes on to distinguish the mere match-winning eristic from the serious, truth-hunting eristic and urges his critics to pursue the latter, since familiarization with the match-winning eristic nauseates the young with philosophy (cf. *Republic* 537–9 and *Phaedo* 89–91). In Plato's *Protagoras* 329B Protagoras is described as being able to deliver a long and excellent speech, but also as able when questioned to reply briefly; and after asking a question to await and accept the answer (cf. *Sophist* 225B). When Socrates at a later stage asks Protagoras to confine himself to brief replies, Protagoras huffily says, 'I have undertaken in my time many disputation-matches, ἀγῶνα λόγων, and if I were to do what you demand and argue in just that way that my opponent, ὁ ἀντιλέγων, demanded, I should not be held superior to anyone...'. The expressions ἀγών λόγων and ὁ ἀντιλέγων were standard parts of the parlance of the eristic exercise. The dialogue largely consists of regulation question-answer moves, which duly result in Protagoras being driven to contradict his original thesis, but result also in Socrates' own position being turned upside-down. At one point, when Protagoras has lost his temper (337A–B), Prodicus exhorts Protagoras and Socrates 'to debate, not to wrangle' (cf. *Theaetetus* 167E–168A and *Republic* v 454A). Hippias urges the appointment of an umpire, ἐπιστάτης, 338A. The proposal is rejected as unworthy of serious thinkers, but it is interesting as suggesting, what would *a priori* seem necessary, that at least in the students' Moots and in the exhibition-bouts staged by sophists the contests may have been umpired. In the *Sophist* 225 Plato may be alluding to Protagoras, *inter alios*. At 232 Protagoras is mentioned as the author of *Arts* of wrestling and of a lot of other things; and, since what is in question is the possibility of anyone writing an *Art* which could teach people how to debate on any subject whatsoever, it may be that Protagoras' *Art of Eristic* is being alluded to. Though Plato thus associates Protagoras with the eristic exercise, he nowhere hints that he invented it or even introduced it into Athens. But Protagoras was not an Athenian, and he was disapproved of by the best people. He is seldom mentioned without some reference to his fee-taking. Protagoras probably died, aged seventy, a dozen years before Socrates. So the eristic exercise must have been a familiar thing well before the last decade of the fifth century.

(iv) *The 'Dissoi Logoi'*

At the end of vol. II of Diels–Kranz, *Fragmente der Vorsokratiker*, there is a little piece, entitled *Dissoi Logoi* from a phrase occurring both in its first sentence and elsewhere. '*Dissoi Logoi*' means 'Arguments Both Ways' or 'Arguments *pro* and *contra*'. The *Dissoi Logoi* is in large part a sequence of theses, generally shocking ones, about which are marshalled first an array of arguments *pro* and then an array of arguments *contra*. Among the arguments *contra* the thesis that *Virtue is not teachable* there is one shrewd argument which, together with an illustrative example, Plato puts into the mouth of Protagoras in his *Protagoras* 327–8. This, with some corroborative evidence, strongly suggests that the backbone of the *Dissoi Logoi* derives from Protagoras himself, though some stretches, including a mention of the result of the Peloponnesian War, must be additions by a later hand. The whole piece is highly pemmicanized, somewhat jumbled, and fragmentary. It is written in amateurish Doric, with plenty of Ionicisms.

These arrays of *pro* and *contra* arguments seem to be designed for memorization by students as ammunition for their questionings and answerings in eristic Moots. The piece as a whole may therefore have been or belonged to a cram-book of eristic. Aristotle alludes scathingly to such primitive *Arts of Eristic* at the end of his *De Sophisticis Elenchis* 183 b 35–184 a 10. His description of them fits the *Dissoi Logoi* well. It teaches arguments: not how to argue. At the least the *Dissoi Logoi* shows us not only that, but also in some degree how students were being trained for participation in eristic Moots before the end of the fifth century B.C. They committed to memory batches of recommended and sometimes numbered points *pro* and *contra* some standard theses. It is worth noticing that the author of the piece, speaking of himself as 'I', sides with the arguments *contra* the shocking theses. Like the Socrates of Plato's Socratic dialogues he wants the arguments *pro* even the shocking theses to be fairly pitted and weighed against those *contra*, but he does not want the cynical or nihilist theses to win. He marshals the Worse and the Better Reasons, but his heart is with the Better Reasons.

(v) *The Hippocratic Writings*

The Nature of Man (*Hippocrates*, Loeb ed., vol. IV, p. 5) is thought to date from between 440 and 400 B.C. Its author begins by criticizing some people, not physicians, who discourse on What Man is Made Of. They are eristic debaters, ἀντιλέγοντες.

> Given the same debaters and the same audience, the same man never wins in the discussion three times in succession, but now one is victor, now another, now he who happens to have the most glib tongue in the face of the crowd. Yet it is right that a man who claims correct knowledge about the facts should maintain his own argument victorious always, if his knowledge be knowledge of reality and if he set it forth correctly. But in my opinion such men by their lack of understanding over-throw themselves in the words of their very discourse...
> (trans. W. H. S. Jones).

This passage shows or suggests several interesting points. Eristic Moots were familiar things before and perhaps well before the end of the fifth century B.C. They were conducted before audiences and the audience might decide who had won. A given thesis would come up again and again for discussion, and the same debater might attack or alternatively defend the same thesis on several successive occasions. So he could re-employ, discard or reshape arguments that he or others had used in previous Moots. Thus we can infer that as theses were in some measure stock topics, the arguments for and against them would enjoy an evolution by the progressive mending of proven weaknesses. The deliberate study of the profits and losses of particular eristic tactics was possible and expedient. Two or three generations later Aristotle was to provide a theoretical basis for such study. In his *Topics* 105 b 12 and 163 b 17 Aristotle gives concrete tutorial advice to students how to prepare for debates upon the themes that regularly crop up.

Against this background the recurrence of the problem *Is Virtue Teachable?* in Plato's *Laches, Protagoras, Euthydemus, Meno* and [*Alcibiades*] becomes explicable. It had been canvassed in the *Dissoi Logoi*, and Isocrates gives his own negative answer to it at the end of his *Against the Sophists*. There were compositions on this theme by Crito, Simon, Antisthenes and Xenocrates. It was a stock Moot theme, and consequently the arguments to it were in development. The frequent phrase λόγον διεξιέναι might therefore mean 'deploy a consolidated or consolidating sequence of argument-moves'. Chess players call their analogous sequences 'combinations'.

If Plato composed his early dialogues with *antilogike* going on under his nose and even under his tutelage, then their argumentative content is likely to reflect stretches of actual argumentations from recent Moots. Perhaps these dialogues were, in part, dramatized Hansards of combinations deployed there.

(vi) *Euthydemus and Dionysodorus*

Early in Plato's *Euthydemus* Socrates says that the two sophists had learned their brand of eristical all-in-wrestling only a year or two ago, that is before about 402 B.C. They give public exhibitions of their art and also, for a fee, tuition in it. They are exponents of the match-winning eristic from which Protagoras dissociated himself. The sophist Dionysodorus may have been a pupil of Protagoras.

At 275C the lad Cleinias is described as having already had a good deal of practice in debating and the answering of questions. This suggests that the uncorrupted eristic exercise had become popular with the young men by the last decade of the fifth century. What was new to them was eristic gamesmanship, though they could swiftly pick up the tricks of it. In the course of the dialogue Socrates exhibits a couple of pieces of serious and edifying eristic. He does not even altogether despise the sophists' eristic tricks. He thinks that he and others ought to find out how to cope with them. Aristotle in his *Topics* does deal fairly carefully with a number of the sophistical elenchi that fill the *Euthydemus*.

(vii) *Socrates*

Nearly all the specimens that we possess of eristic contests are the elenctic question-answer tussles with which in his early dialogues Plato credits Socrates. We have to distinguish, as commentators have not always distinguished, between mere philosophical discussions on the one hand, and on the other hand the rule-governed concatenations of questions, answerable by 'yes' or 'no', which are intended to drive the answerer into self-contradiction. The latter is what should be meant by 'the Socratic Method'. Socrates

himself is made to say in the *Apology* 27 B 'if I may put my
arguments in my accustomed manner' before notionally
driving his prosecutor into an elenchus by a duly con-
catenated sequence of questions. With much or little conversational relief eristic moves are the dramatic action of
the *Laches*, *Lysis*, [*Alcibiades*], *Euthyphro*, *Charmides*, *Hippias
Major* and *Minor*, *Protagoras*, *Ion*, *Euthydemus*, *Gorgias*,
Meno and *Republic* I. But this pattern of argument which
had dominated the Socratic dialogues prior to Book II of
the *Republic* was thereafter abandoned almost altogether
from the Socrates-led dialogues. Which Platonic Socrates
are we to believe in, if either: the one who does or the one
who does not employ the Socratic Method?

A propos this question there is a curious feature of the
Theaetetus. At the beginning and the end of the dialogue
Socrates declares almost apologetically that his sole intellectual power is the 'maieutic' one. He can extract
ideas from his pregnant answerer and test them, if necessary, to destruction. Apparently this destruction nearly
always is necessary. But Socrates can produce no offspring
of his own. In Aristotle's parlance he is capable only of
peirastic cross-questioning, or of what the Eleatic Stranger
describes as the *cathartic* elenchus in the *Sophist* 230–1.
Socrates admits that he is reputed to drive other men into
aporiai, *Theaetetus* 149 A (cf. *Meno* 80 A); but he now claims
that his function is that of both exacerbating and relieving
their travails, 151 A. Here Plato seems to be sitting on the
fence. He is representing Socratic dialectic as being at one
and the same time elenctic and solution-hunting, as thesis-
demolishing and thesis-establishing. Plato's conscious in-

version of the direction of dialectic has begun but is not yet complete. The actual argumentation of the dialogue does not anyhow conform at all well with this 'maieutic' picture. Socrates gives birth to babies of his own. Nor does the modest Theaetetus display 'conceit of knowledge' requiring for his soul's good Socratic puncturing.

Did the real Socrates, as distinct from the Platonic Socrates of the pre-*Republic* dialogues, practise the eristic method? We do not believe Plato when he represents old Parmenides as giving a demonstration of Zenonian argumentation in question-answer style; so perhaps we should not believe Plato when he represents Socrates as forcing elenchi by cunning concatenations of questions. Here we are without any relevant testimony from Isocrates or even from Diogenes Laertius; and we are without the evidence of treatise titles. The fact that the two presumably loyal Socratics, Plato and Antisthenes, both taught eristic and propagated it, one in dialogues, and the other, possibly, in cram-books as well as dialogues, is some evidence for their common master having taught them the use of it.

When Aristotle in his *Metaphysics* 1078b credits Socrates with the invention of Induction he credits him with one of the dialectical procedures that he describes in his own *Topics*. Socratic Induction could have been used independently of eristic cross-questioning, but its incessant employment in Plato's early dialogues, and Aristotle's treatment of it as a part of dialectic, suggest that it did in fact first live as a specifically dialectical procedure.

Subject to the debated proviso that Xenophon's ideas of the Socratic Method may all derive from Plato's dialogues, his *Memorabilia* supports the view that the real Socrates did practise the Socratic Method. Xenophon employs the semi-technical terminology of the eristic exercise in his *Memorabilia* (III. viii. 1; IV. iv. 9; IV. v. 12–vi. 1; IV. vi. 13–15; and IV. viii. 11). We need not suppose that Xenophon understood this parlance or that he would have recognized an elenchus if he had met one. Even more significantly, although he consistently represents Socrates as asking one question after another, yet with a few exceptions the questions are rhetorical questions, Socrates' positive views expressed in interrogative form. Their sequence does not depend on whether the answerer says 'yes' or 'no'. His interlocutor is not an adversary and the questions do not drive him into checkmate, but merely lead him to a wiser view. It looks as if the unphilosophical Xenophon is garbling something that he has heard and misunderstood about Socrates' conduct of discussions; and this is some independent evidence that Socrates had used the Socratic Method, though independent only if Xenophon was not merely garbling the early Platonic representations of Socrates at work.

In the slender fragments from the dialogues of Aeschines given in Ch. XI of G. C. Field's *Plato and His Contemporaries* Socrates is represented as plying his interlocutors with chains of questions. Unlike Xenophon, Aeschines is known to have been a close associate of Socrates.

In his *Clouds* Aristophanes certainly accuses Socrates of pitting the Worse against the Better Reason, that is, of teaching the young men to argue as forcibly against a respectable thesis as in its favour. But this does not prove

that the argumentation was of the question-answer pattern. Anyhow Aristophanes might be pinning on to
Socrates things that belonged to Protagoras, as he certainly pins on to Socrates 'physical' theories about air
which belonged to Diogenes of Apollonia. Aristotle in his
Rhetoric II xxiv II accuses Protagoras of giving an equal
run to the Worse and the Better Reason. Eudoxus does so
too (see Diels–Kranz, vol. II, p. 260). Yet they must, like
Plato, have known the *Clouds*. Aristophanes does employ
a few of the semi-technical dictions of the eristic exercise;
and both the Worse Reason and Pheidippides do assail their
interlocutors with tail-twisting interrogations. So by 423
or else by the time when he revised the *Clouds*, Aristophanes may be crediting the real Socrates with something
like the Socratic Method.

In sum, we are warranted in taking it that the Socratic
Method was the method of the real and not only of the
Platonic Socrates. We have good reason to think that he
did not invent it or introduce it into Athens; but probably
he did improve its armoury and tactics. Above all he
seems to have stiffened dialectical arguments by requiring
definitions of their hinge-terms (see Aristotle's *Metaphysics* 987 b and 1078 b). There are no attempts at definition in the *Dissoi Logoi*. However, save for their pupils,
Protagoras seems more important in the history of dialectic than was the real Socrates.

(viii) *Antisthenes*

We know very little about Antisthenes. He is thought
to have died aged ninety in about 366. He probably

studied rhetoric under Gorgias and he had pupils of his own, some of whom he took with him to sit at the feet of Socrates, that is before 399. His school is likely to have been in the first instance a school of rhetoric, since a good many of his writings appear from their titles to deal with standard rhetorical themes. But he also wrote dialogues. What is of interest to us, however, is that his titles include περὶ τοῦ διαλέγεσθαι ἀντιλογικός, Σάθων ἢ περὶ τοῦ ἀντιλέγειν, περὶ ὀνομάτων χρήσεως ἐριστικός, περὶ ἐρωτήσεως καὶ ἀποκρίσεως, and δόξαι ἢ ἐριστικός.

Whether these were dialogues or *Arts of Eristic* or mere memorizable digests of *pro* and *contra* arguments, they show that the teaching of eristic, presumably as an ancillary to the teaching of rhetoric, had become an established thing with some kind of a literature of its own well before Aristotle came to the Academy. Aristotle himself at the end of his *De Sophisticis Elenchis* speaks witheringly of the quality of the training manuals of eristic that his fee-taking predecessors had composed. We have no reason to suppose that he here has Antisthenes in mind. The reference to fee-taking suggests that it is Protagoras whom he has chiefly in mind. But Aristotle's statement corroborates the impression given by the titles of Antisthenes' writings that there had for quite a long time been a market for technical coaching in eristic, reinforced by some kind of handbooks. Even if the training manuals that preceded Aristotle's *Topics* were, like the *Dissoi Logoi*, merely cram-books of particular arguments *pro* and *contra* particular theses written down and numbered off to be memorized by the students and quite devoid of any theory, still the

fact of their existence shows us the pre-Aristotelian be-
ginnings of an interest, however vocational, in the Art of
elenctic argumentation. It had become a proficiency to be
acquired and a subject to be studied. It had a careers-value.
But it was also interesting. Plato's dialectical dialogues
must have stimulated and been intended to stimulate this
interest, which was ultimately, though only after an important reversal of direction, to develop into what we
know as 'philosophy'. Doubtless the dialectical dialogues
of Plato and others displaced the boring cram-books of
pro and *contra* arguments, of which the *Dissoi Logoi* is our
solitary surviving specimen.

(ix) *Plato*

Diogenes Laertius in his *Plato* 48, confusing, as others
have done, the production of dialogues with the production of dialectical arguments, says,

in my opinion Plato, who brought this form of writing to per-
fection, ought to be adjudged the prize for its invention as well
as for its embellishment. A dialogue is a discourse consisting
of question and answer on some philosophical or political subject, with due regard to the characters of the persons introduced and the choice of diction. Dialectic is the art of discourse,
τέχνη λόγων, by which we either refute or establish some proposition, by means of question and answer on the part of the
interlocutors.

Later, 79, he says that Plato 'was the first to frame a science
for rightly asking and answering questions, having used it
himself to excess'. In his *Arcesilaus* he says, obviously
erroneously, that Arcesilaus was the first to argue on both
sides of a question and the first to meddle with the system

handed down by Plato and by means of question and answer to make it more clearly resemble eristic. So it looks as if a tradition grew up according to which dialectic was a Platonic invention. Favorinus says that the word 'dialectic' was invented by Plato. The eristic or dialectical exercise was certainly not invented by him, or even by his own master, Socrates. When in his *Metaphysics* 1 987b Aristotle says that Plato's forerunners did not participate in dialectic, he cannot mean merely that they had not got the word 'dialectic'. Aristotle is surely here referring only to the forerunners whom he had just been describing, namely the Pythagoreans, not to Plato's forerunners in general.

Evidence is adduced in Chapter VI that Plato did not confine himself to producing dramatic representations of the Socratic Method in action. Until some crisis occurred late in the 370's, he himself trained young men in the practice of the Socratic Method. His dialectical dialogues may embody dramatized minutes of his tutorial Moots. If so, then we can well imagine that the rigorousness and the range of the disputations conducted in these Moots greatly exceeded those of the eristic matches that had been or were then being held anywhere else, unless in Megara.

4. PLATO'S DIALECTIC VIS-À-VIS ERISTIC

We have seen that what Aristotle means by 'dialectic' is just what other people meant by 'eristic', save that Aristotle is in the main concerned with those question-answer matches which are conducted in a pedagogically or philosophically serious spirit. But what about Plato? His accounts of dialectic in his *Republic* VII, *Philebus* and

Sophist give such lofty places in knowledge to the results of dialectical thinking that he seems here to be talking about something entirely different from what the *Topics* is the Art of, or from what his own *Hippias Minor*, say, is a dramatized specimen of. We get the impression that in the Academy at the same moment the word 'dialectic' is being used in two entirely different ways, in one of which dialectic has everything, in the other nothing to do with the Moots that are held, so to speak, on Wednesday evenings between a young Coriscus and a young Theophrastus, with the not very old Aristotle or Xenocrates acting as coach, umpire and timekeeper. There is good evidence that for Plato as for Aristotle the concrete or, so to speak, Wednesday evening activity of prosecuting dialectic is the eristic match conducted in an academic spirit; that where Plato differs from Aristotle—and also from himself—is in his accounts of the heuristic profits of the exercise; and that even here some of Plato's accounts of these profits are not more disparate from those given by Aristotle than we should expect from our knowledge of Aristotle's logical and methodological interests, as well as from our knowledge of the growth and systematization of the special sciences in the Academy during the 360's and the 350's.

In the *Cratylus* 390 C Socrates says, 'And the man who knows how to ask and answer questions you call a dialectician?' In the *Meno* 75 C–D he says,

if my questioner were a professor of the eristic and contentious sort I should say to him: I have made my statement; if it is wrong, it is your business to examine and refute it. But if, like you and me on this occasion, we were friends and chose to have

127

a discussion together, I should have to reply in some milder tone more suited to dialectic. The more dialectical way, I suppose, is not merely to answer what is true, but also to make use of those points which the questioned person acknowledges that he knows.

Here we get the contrast credited to Protagoras and constantly made by Plato and Aristotle between the match-winning and the truth-hunting spirits in which the question-answer exercise may be conducted, with the adjective 'dialectical' used just as Aristotle uses it.

In the *Republic* Book VII 534 dialectic is set up in a sovereign position over the so-called sciences. But in 537-9 we are to our surprise told of the immense evil of insubordination that at present accompanies dialectic. For a young man of twenty or so,

when met by the question What is beauty? and, having given the answer which he used to hear from the legislator, is confuted by the dialectic process, ἐξελέγχῃ ὁ λόγος; and when frequent and various defeats have forced him to believe that there is as much deformity as beauty in what he calls beauty and that justice, goodness and all the things which he is used to honour most are in the like predicament

he will become cynical and lawless. So only selected thirty-year-olders are to be introduced to dialectic.

Whenever boys taste dialectic for the first time, they pervert it into an amusement and always employ it for purposes of contradiction, imitating in their own persons the artifices of those who study refutation, delighting, like puppies, in pulling and tearing to pieces with logic anyone who comes near them.

The senior men, however, will imitate those who are resolved to discuss and examine truth, rather than those who play at contradiction for amusement. Here too Plato is distinguishing dialectic from match-winning eristic by the different spirits in which the same question-answer disputation-exercise is conducted.

In the *Phaedo* 75 C–D (and cf. 78 D) we hear of '... absolute beauty and the absolute good and the just and the holy and, in short, with all those things which we stamp with the seal of "absolute" both in our questions when we are questioners and in our answers when we are answerers'. Plato does not here use the word 'dialectic'; but he is likely to be referring to some regulation question-answer disputations and saying that the Theory of Forms is common to both sides in these disputations. So apparently these disputations were philosophically serious and conformed to the pattern described in the *Topics*. In the *Republic*, Book V 454 A, Socrates distinguishes the Art of *antilogike* from dialectic, those who wrangle from those who debate against one another. The former are content with making empty verbal points. But both are pursuing τοῦ λεχθέντος τὴν ἐναντίωσιν, the controverting of the thesis. The concrete procedure of dialectic is for Plato just what it is for Aristotle. It is the serious employment of the method of driving an answerer into elenchi by strategically arranged sequences of questions (see also *Philebus* 17 A and *Theaetetus* 161 E).

5. THE MINOR VALUES OF DIALECTIC

Plato and Aristotle are in agreement about the subordinate values of elenctic cross-questioning.

(*a*) What Aristotle calls 'peirastic' (e.g. *Topics* 169 b 26,

Met. 1004 b 26) is the dialectical method as employed to prick the bubble of an individual's intellectual conceit. He thinks he knows things, but is driven to concede propositions which he recognizes to be inconsistent with what he thought he knew. Plato does not use the noun '*peirastike*', but he and Aristotle both use the phrase πεῖραν λαμβάνειν (*Topics* 171 b 4; Plato, *Gorgias* 448 A; *Protagoras* 348 A; *Euthydemus* 275 B; cf. *Theaetetus* 157 C). In his *Sophist* 229–30, especially 230 B–D, Plato gives a full account of how his last variety of sophist, who merits a better title than 'sophist', purges by cross-questioning the false conceit of knowledge. At the beginning of the *Theaetetus* (149–151 D, and compare 210 C) Socrates explains at length how his powers are only 'maieutic', emphasizing that his kind of midwifery involves the extinction of spurious offspring. Seemingly they usually are spurious.

(*b*) The *gymnastic* value of dialectic, mentioned by Aristotle (e.g. *Topics* 159 a 25, 161 a 25, 164 a 12), is what Parmenides gives as the reason why the young Socrates should practise the two-way Zenonian method. This training exercise is indispensable for the young man who wishes to become a philosopher (*Parmenides* 135–6). It is an important fact that Socrates must be about twenty years old, just the age at which in Book VII of the *Republic* Plato had declared it dangerous for people to get even a taste of dialectic. It is also an important fact that here Parmenides is made to distinguish philosophy from Zenonian argumentation. This is now an indispensable training exercise for those who later on are to be philosophers. This distinction was not realized by Plato in the 370's. In the

350's the distinction comes to be common ground to Plato and Aristotle. Elenctic debating is now a means to an ulterior theoretical end.

In the *Phaedrus* Plato acknowledges, what he had denied in the *Gorgias*, that there is a teachable Art of Rhetoric, but he requires that the student of it must also learn psychology and, more conjecturally, dialectic (265–6, 269 E–272 B, 273 D–274 A, 277 B–C). Presumably such a student would be of the normal age of a student of rhetoric, that is a young man. Even Isocrates, whose educational ideals were far from Platonic, admits the gymnastic value of astronomy, geometry and eristic in his *Antidosis* 261–9 and *Panathenaicus* 26–8. These pursuits should, however, be dropped when student-days are over.

(*c*) Both Plato and Aristotle rank *agonistic* eristic low. Aristotle's strictures, however, are less wholehearted than Plato's. Plato does now and then let Socrates score by fairly raw argumentative tricks. But Aristotle gives a lot of tips in sheer eristic gamesmanship. He is after all a much younger man than Plato, and Plato seems to have needed conspicuously to purge himself from some scandal that had been caused by his propagation of elenctic disputation. (On eristic gamesmanship see *De Sophisticis Elenchis passim*; also *Topics*, e.g. 112 a 10–15, 134 a 3, 142 a 32, 148 a 21, 155 b 25–157 a 5, 158 a 25–30, 159 a 16–25.)

(*d*) Plato and Aristotle are at one in their emphatic contempt for sophistical eristic, that is eristic prize-fighting. Doubtless Athenian citizens did find rather unobvious the distinction between elenctic prize-fights and tutorial disputations.

6. THE PHILOSOPHICAL VALUE OF DIALECTIC

First for a verbal point. When Aristotle uses the word 'philosophy', save when he speaks of First Philosophy, he normally has in mind what we mean by 'science'. Arithmetic, geometry, astronomy and medicine are for Aristotle branches of philosophy. In this sense of 'philosophy' dialectic is not the whole nor even a part of philosophy, that is, of science, though it is in important ways ancillary to scientific knowledge. Plato on the other hand tends to equate the dialectician with the philosopher; though he does sometimes, in late dialogues, talk in Aristotle's idiom and treat, for example, geometry as a branch of philosophy (*Theaetetus* 143 D and *Philebus* 56 D–E, 57 C–D). At the very end of his *Euthydemus* Plato seems ready to class the two sophists as philosophers, though not of the best sort. This partial terminological divergence of Aristotle from Plato by itself reduces a good deal the apparent gap between their views about the major value of dialectic. That the word 'philosophy' was still very fluid in meaning is shown by Isocrates' use of it for, roughly, rhetorical cultivation. In his *Antidosis* 270–80 he grumbles at Academic misappropriations of the word. In the pseudo-Platonic dialogue, *The Lovers*, Socrates criticizes the idea that a philosopher is just a generally well-informed man.

Next, the terminal Plato and Aristotle agree that the dialectician's concern is with what is 'common' to, that is, shared by and neutral between the various special branches of knowledge. He is concerned with those concepts which are ubiquitous or trans-departmental; or with those truths

which are in some way presupposed by all alike of the pro-
prietary truths of the special sciences. The concepts of
*existence, non-existence, identity, difference, similarity, dis-
similarity, unity* and *plurality* are such 'common' or
ubiquitous concepts (see *Theaetetus* 185–6; *Sophist* 254–9;
Parmenides 136; cf. Aristotle, *Metaphysics* 995 b 19–26,
998 b, 1004 a, 1004 b–1005 a 18). Aristotle's emphasis is
a little less on the ubiquitous *concepts* than on the trans-
departmental *truths*. Even here, however, he may have
Plato with him in one of his moods; for in the *Republic* VII
532–3, arguably, the 'hypotheses' of the special sciences
and, presumably, the unpostulated first principle or principles are truths and not concepts. (For the trans-departmental truths with which the dialectician is concerned see
Aristotle: *Topics* 101 a 34–b 4, 170 a 20–b 11, 171 b 35–
172 b 8; *Metaphysics* 1005 a 19 *et seq.*; *Rhetoric* I i 14, ii 21,
iv 6.) Nor is there a total disparity between Aristotle's view
of the role of dialectic *vis-à-vis* the special sciences and the
view that Plato had held in *Republic* VII. True, for Aristotle
the special sciences rest on their own special axioms, and
these departmental axioms are not the mere postulates
which Plato, in the *Republic*, held them to be. So for
Aristotle there is no question of dialectic being a hunt for
trans-departmental axioms from which the departmental
principles of the special sciences will be deducible. Plato,
for a time, did hold this view, though he gives us no specimens of his super-axioms; nor do any of his dialectical dialogues portray such a hunt in progress. So far Aristotle does
differ from Plato and is right where Plato had been wrong.
From completely topic-neutral premisses the truths of the

special sciences *could* not follow. Plato had venially mis-located a precedence that dialectic really does possess over the special branches of knowledge. The historical impor-tance of Plato's theory in the *Republic* is that it is his second essay at stating the constructive or heuristic task of dialectic in contrast with the purely gymnastic and cathartic tasks of the Socratic Method. His first essay had been his Theory of Forms. Then dialectic had been an inquiry into some special entities. Now it is a search for some special truths.

It is the business of dialectic according to Aristotle to be in some way analytical or critical of the departmental axioms of the special sciences; though he does not clearly explain how or why these axioms require or benefit from such criticism. Some trans-departmental principles, which do not function as axioms, are presupposed by the special axioms of all the sciences. The Principle of Non-contradic-tion is one such principle. The establishment of such under-lying and neutral principles is still dialectical in pattern (see *Metaphysics* 1004 b 15–27, 1005 a 19 *et seq.*, 1006 a 16–28, 1012 a 17–28; *Topics* 101 a 34–b 4, 155 b 10–16, 163 b 9–11). In *Metaphysics* 1005 b 7 Aristotle requires the philosopher to study, *inter alia*, the principles of syllogistic reasoning, though 'syllogistic' here has not the highly determinate sense that it gets in the *Prior Analytics*, but only the very broad sense that it has throughout the *Topics*. As we might put it, there are trans-departmental formal or logical principles presupposed by the departmental truths of the special sciences; and these logical principles need to be ex-tracted, and can be extracted only by dialectic.

So Plato and Aristotle both credit dialectic with the task

of discovering some very important trans-departmental principles which hinge on the ubiquitous, non-specialist or 'common' concepts. They differ about the status of these principles. Plato and Aristotle are talking about the same exercise, but Aristotle is controverting an important error in what, in the *Republic* only, Plato had said about its philosophical proceeds. Even so, when Aristotle comes to speak of First Philosophy as the Science of Being *qua* Being, he is a bit nearer to Plato's position in the *Republic*, e.g. in *Metaphysics* 1005 b 9–34.

However, now Plato himself, in his *Phaedrus* 265–6, *Politicus* 286 and, more debatably, *Philebus* 16–18, seems to give a role to dialectic quite different from that given in the *Republic*. We hear no more of the discovery of non-hypothetical first principles functioning as super-axioms for all the special sciences; nor is any reason given for the disappearance of this view. Perhaps daily intercourse with mathematicians, astronomers, and other researchers had taught him that no such super-axioms were to be looked for, since their absolute generality or formality would prevent special or material consequences from being derivable from them. Nor had the lack of them prevented new geometrical, astronomical or physiological truths from being discovered. Plato's own *Timaeus* does not try to be Euclidean in structure. Plato now in the *Phaedrus*, the *Politicus* and, debatably, the *Philebus* seems closely to connect the task of dialectic with the tasks of Definition and especially Division, that is the task of articulating higher or more generic kinds into their lower, more specific kinds (cf. *Republic* 454 A). He is tempted to treat this articulation as being necessarily dichotomous, though he prudently resists this temptation some of the time. In the *Sophist* and *Politicus* we are presented with detailed kind-ladders on the bottom rungs of which are the concepts of *sophist* and *statesman*.

The pedagogic value of trying to build such ladders of kinds was doubtless considerable. The practice of systematic definition presupposes such exercises in division. But it is immediately clear that eristic cross-questioning cannot be the way of constructing such ladders of kinds. The answerer could not, except in some very special cases, be driven into elenchus by rejection of a suggested division. Aristotle saw this in his *Posterior Analytics* 91 b. Nor for that matter does Plato make his Eleatic Stranger try to establish his divisions by argumentation. A chain of *summa genera, genera, species, subspecies* and *varieties* is not itself a chain of premisses and conclusions. But what is more, it cannot in general be deductively established or established by *reductio ad absurdum*. The work of a Linnaeus cannot be done *a priori*. How could Plato who knew exactly what question-answer arguments were really like bring himself to say, if he did say, that the philosophically valuable results of such arguments are kind-ladders? In the jewelled examples of the Socratic Method that fill, for example, the *Protagoras, Gorgias* and *Republic* I not a single kind-ladder is established. Quite often Socrates has, *en route*, to draw attention to differences between different species of a genus, just as very often he has by means of his induction to draw attention to their generic affinity. But until we get to the *Sophist* we have nothing reminding us of the contribution of Linnaeus to botany; nor should we have been grateful or philosophically enlightened if we had. No such divisions result from the dialectical operations in the *Parmenides*, Part II.

Before trying to assess the claims made by Plato for division and definition in his *Phaedrus* 265–6 let us consider what place is actually occupied by division and definition in the curriculum of the Academy. In his *Topics*, especially Book VI, Aristotle describes carefully various failings to which debaters' definitions are liable. But he does not here introduce his students to the Rules of Definition. They know them already. Similarly in his *Rhetoric*, though he frequently employs division and constantly produces definitions, mostly very good ones, of virtues, passions, temperaments, etc., he does not have to explain what he is doing.

The so-called *Platonic Definitions* contains nearly two hundred definitions or would-be definitions. For some of the terms to be defined half a dozen or a dozen different definitions are collected. Quite a lot, though far from all of the definitions are or try to be of the genus-differentia pattern; and quite a lot of them embody semi-logical or semi-philosophical parlance of obviously Aristotelian provenance. Two or three of the definitions have been culled from Plato; eight or nine may have been culled from Aristotle. But most of the terms defined are terms of so little scientific or philosophical sophistication that any adolescent would be familiar with them; and a large number of the definitions offered are amateurish and juvenile. Over a dozen of the definitions are or closely resemble definitions which are justly demolished in the *Topics*.

It seems plausible to suppose that the *Platonic Definitions* is a class-album of definitions, partly culled from Plato, Aristotle and maybe Xenocrates and others, but mostly subscribed as beginners' essays by Aristotle's own pupils. To put it anachronistically, definition was a Pass Moderations subject for freshmen in the Academy. These beginners were not yet supposed to know any science or dialectic. That they were not yet even being taught rhetoric is suggested by the fact that not one of the scores of definitions in Aristotle's *Rhetoric* has been garnered into the album, though two or three dozen of the terms defined, often very badly, in the album are terms defined, usually very well, in the *Rhetoric*.

At the end of Diogenes Laertius' *Plato*, we have ten pages of divisions, erroneously said to have been collected by Aristotle out of the works of Plato. Many, though not all of these divisions are again amateurish and even puerile attempts at the division of frequently unsophisticated and unimportant generic concepts. We could take them too to be extracted from a class-album of divisions, that is a collection of, mostly, juvenile essays in division assembled for tutorial criticism.

Diogenes Laertius credits Xenocrates with eight books of divisions; Aristotle with seventeen; Theophrastus with two; and Speusippus perhaps with one. Speusippus is given one book of definitions; Aristotle seven; Theophrastus three or perhaps five.

It looks, therefore, as if, whatever Plato promised or

dreamed for division and definition, in mundane curricular fact they were taught to young, even very young, students in the Academy before they were qualified to study the Arts of rhetoric and dialectic. We can well imagine that the *Sophist*'s half-dozen kind-ladders terminating in the notion of *sophist*, though philosophically and scientifically quite unrewarding, were intended to serve as exemplary models for the propaedeutic course on which the eighteen-year-olders were embarked. As the ladders presented are apparently alternatives to or rivals of one another, these could stimulate some educative comparisons and criticisms.

Similarly with the *Politicus*. Here the Stranger's voice and manner are markedly, even irksomely, those of the schoolmaster. The political concepts to which he applies his division-procedures are concepts familiar to any bright lad. Save for some discussion of the notion of the Mean the dialogue imposes no philosophical labours upon its recipients. It was not written to interest those more senior students who were equipped to cope with the philosophical core of the *Sophist* or with either part of the *Parmenides*. Dialectic is alluded to only twice, at 285 D and 287 A, and then only in the Stranger's explanation of the preparatory role of the intellectual exercises that he is giving. So Plato may have composed the *Politicus* for the special benefit of the philosophically innocent novices who were at that moment getting their freshmens' training in the ABC of thinking.

The *Sophist* consists queerly of a stretch of highly abstract and sophisticated philosophical reasoning sand-

wiched between some division-operations which presuppose no philosophical sophistication whatsoever. In
the philosophical stretch dialectic, here equated with
philosophy, is described at 253 C–D as the science which
discovers how the 'Greatest Kinds' are 'joined' with and
'disjoined' from one another. Among a lot of other metaphors the term 'division' occurs once or twice. This makes
it tempting, though not compulsory, to infer that Plato
thought that the task of constructing kind-ladders was not
only a propaedeutic to the philosopher's or dialectician's
task; it was a part of it or else the whole of it. But then we
have to recognize that the Stranger's exploration of the
mutual dependences and independences of the Greatest
Kinds does not yield one kind-ladder, however short. For
the Greatest Kinds are not related to one another as genus
to species, or as species to co-species. Aristotle seems to be
saying this in *Metaphysics* III 998 b. Even to render 'γένη'
by 'kinds', and *a fortiori* by 'classes', is to prejudice the interpretation of the Stranger's operations. *Existence,
identity* and *otherness* are not sorts or sets of things, embrac-
ing subsorts or subsets of things. The Stranger produces
here neither dichotomous nor trichotomous divisions; he
produces no divisions at all.

In the *Parmenides*, Part II, between which and this stretch
of the *Sophist* there are probable echo-relations, scores of
implications, real or apparent, are traced between propositions anchored in, *inter alia*, the Stranger's Greatest
Kinds. Again no kind-ladders are generated. So at least
Plato did not work as if he thought that these dialectical operations were of a piece with his own exercises

DIALECTIC

in division. We should have lamented it if he had so worked.

There is, however, one argument, besides the natural interpretation of the *Phaedrus* 265–6, for the view that Plato did assimilate division to dialectic, namely that Aristotle does scold some unnamed persons for failing to see that a division is not a demonstration, and is not even the product of demonstration. There need be nothing illogical in refusing to accept a recommended division (*Posterior Analytics* 91 B and cf. *De Partibus Animalium* from 642 b). So maybe Plato did for a time fail to see that dividing is not reasoning and is therefore not dialectic.

None the less the inferred propaedeutic place of division and definition in the curriculum of Plato's own Academy, together with Plato's own non-production of kind-ladders in his *Parmenides*, Part II, and in the philosophical core of his *Sophist* itself, show that Plato knows quite well that to be good at division does not yet amount to being good at dialectic, and so require us to suppose that in the *Phaedrus* he means but omits to say explicitly that division is only a preparation for dialectic. Plato's commentators often kow-tow to the notion of division and to the imputed equation of dialectic with division. They adduce from the whole history of philosophy no specimens of philosophically illuminating divisions, and *a fortiori* no specimens of divisions philosophically established. Nor do they volunteer any specimens elaborated by themselves.

If all this is so, then after Book VII of the *Republic* Plato gives us only one statement of what kind of contribution dialectic makes to human knowledge, namely the statement in the *Sophist* 253 that dialectic reveals the mutual dependences and independences of the Greatest Kinds. As these Kinds seem partly to coincide with what Aristotle calls the 'first kinds' (*Metaphysics* III 998 b), and with what he elsewhere calls the 'common' terms or notions, Plato's present account of the role of dialectic seems to have some close affinities with that of Aristotle (e.g. *Rhetoric* I ii 20–2, *Metaphysics* III 995 b 21).

It is difficult to extract a hard-edged doctrine out of the metaphors in which Plato talks of those relations between the Greatest Kinds which it is the task of dialectic to disclose. But as in the *Parmenides*, Part II, Parmenides is all the time drawing consequences, legitimately or illegitimately, from propositions that hinge on the formal or 'common' concepts, including those listed as 'Greatest Kinds' in the *Sophist*, it is arguable that in the *Sophist* itself Plato is gropingly beginning to explore what we, but not yet he, can identify with the implications, incompatibilities, and compatibilities that hold between propositions in virtue of the 'common' concepts that they embody. If so, then here in the *Sophist* and with fuller awareness in the *Parmenides*, Part II, he is ascribing to the dialectician inquiries which Aristotle ascribes to the dialectician, namely what we can now call 'logical' inquiries. Plato is, perhaps, adumbrating the route on which in his *Topics*-lectures Aristotle is already toddling, and in his *Analytics* will before long be marching.

In his *Topics* Aristotle is, as yet, only toddling, for though his purpose is to construct an Art which shall enable eristic questioners and answerers to force and rebut

DIALECTIC

elenchi, he is still quite unclear about the difference between (1) an argument generating an untenable conclusion
because the *inference* is *fallacious*, and (2) an argument
generating an untenable conclusion because the answerer
has not noticed that at least one of the *questions* put to him
was equivocal, or many questions in one, or unrestrictedly
general, or metaphorical, etc. There is one and there is only
one fallacy about which Aristotle is perfectly clear in the
De Sophisticis Elenchis, namely the Fallacy of the Consequent. An answerer may erroneously think that having
conceded that *if p then q*, and having also conceded *q*, he
must concede *p*. But in the main Aristotle here tries to
diagnose the treacherousness of arguments in terms only of
trickinesses internal to their premisses. Nowhere in the
Topics, not even in the reputed Handbook of Fallacies, the
De Sophisticis Elenchis, does Aristotle mention such formal
fallacies as *Undistributed Middle*. His *Art of Dialectic* is not
yet a work of formal logic. The *Topics* could have been
taught without the Academic equivalent of a blackboard.
The *Prior Analytics* could not.

Aristotle makes it a defining property of a dialectical
argument that the thesis which the answerer undertakes to
uphold is an 'endoxon' and not a paradox. It should be a
truism, or something attested by the experts, or something
obvious to the man in the street. Now it really would be a
sensible piece of practical advice to a participant who wants
to win an eristic duel to tell him to defend only those theses
of which he and the members of the audience feel quite
sure. It is much easier to think of points supporting what
one believes than to think of objections to it or to think of

points supporting what one disbelieves. But Aristotle is wrong in making this a defining property of the exercise. For he himself allows, what Parmenides insists on, that the would-be philosopher should practise constructing and rebutting arguments both *pro* and *contra* each thesis and its negative. But if a thesis is a truism, its negative will be a paradox; so the defender of this negative will be arguing, even if with his tongue in his cheek, for something which he does not believe and yet will still be operating dialectically (see *Topics* 101a34, 163b1–15). We may suspect that Aristotle overstresses the importance of the unparadoxicalness of theses for another reason. His grasp of the notion of fallaciousness of reasoning is still so unsure that he is inclined to assume that a paradoxical conclusion must derive directly, that is validly, from something overtly or else covertly paradoxical in a premiss. The answerer must have conceded something inadvertently, so that the truism that he meant to start from has been replaced by a paradox that he never meant to start from.

7. CONCLUSION

The correct answer to the question What is the philosophical value of elenctic argumentation? is much the same both for the terminal Plato and for Aristotle. Both of them know that the exercise of driving answerers into *impasses* is a preparation, and only a preparation, for the task of finding the ways out of *impasses*. Both know that the 'common' or topic-neutral concepts are the hinges on which turn both confutations and philosophical discoveries. Aristotle knows that *aporiai* are the driving force of philosophical, as distinct from scientific thinking. In the *Theaetetus* (187D, 190E–191A, cf. 149A–151A) and in the *Sophist* (236E, 238A and D, 241B, cf. 264C) Socrates and the Stranger open their philosophical inquiries with explicit formulations of the *aporiai* that demand resolution. But neither Aristotle nor Plato is able satisfactorily to state what sort of knowledge or insight comes from the unravelling, λύσις, of an *aporia*. Aristotle says, with his enviable pungency, 'the resolution of a perplexity is discovery' (ἡ γὰρ λύσις τῆς ἀπορίας εὕρεσις ἐστίν, *Nic. Eth.* 1146b6; cf. *Metaphysics* 995a24–b5); and in his practice he often first marshals *aporiai* and then moves to their resolutions. But even Aristotle never explains clearly why the person who has never been in an *aporia* is to be pitied rather than envied. It is, however, not for us to complain. We too know in our bones how philosophical perplexities differ in kind from scientific problems; but our statements of the differences continue to be inadequate. Wittgenstein's *fly-bottle* is the *aporia* of the Academy. But what has the fly missed, that has never got into the bottle and therefore never looked for or found the way out of it?

CHAPTER V

THE CRISIS

I. THE CHARGES AGAINST SOCRATES

Several of the Platonic dialogues are centrally or peripherally concerned with the trial, defence, condemnation and execution of Socrates in 399. The *Euthyphro* begins with a meeting between Socrates and Euthyphro, while Socrates is waiting at the King Archon's Court in which he is to be charged with irreligion and the corruption of the young men. The *Theaetetus* ends oddly with an unheralded and perfunctory reference to Socrates going to this Court. In the *Phaedo* we get the description of Socrates' end, after his farewell discussion of the soul's immortality. The *Apology* gives us the sequence of Socrates' three speeches to his judges. In the *Crito*, a sort of sequel to the *Apology*, Socrates rejects Crito's entreaty that he should save his life by escaping from prison and from Athens. In the *Gorgias* (486, 508 C–D, 509 B–C, 521–2, 527 A) and the *Meno* (94 E–95 A, 99 E), there are apparent allusions, dramatically in the future tense, to the trial and condemnation of Socrates. The *Politicus* 299 B–C seems again to allude to the condemnation of Socrates.

From the opening of the *Euthyphro*, from Diogenes Laertius' *Life of Socrates*, from Xenophon's *Apology* and *Memorabilia*, from the *Seventh Letter*, from the end of the *Theaetetus* and from Plato's *Apology* certain facts can be established with certainty. Socrates was tried by the

Court of the King Archon; the charge against him was the dual charge of (*a*) irreligion and (*b*) the corruption of the young men by inculcating irreligion in them. For the second part of this charge we are without the support of the *Seventh Letter*. Diogenes Laertius does not specify the kind of corruption. Xenophon says that the corruption in question was corruption by the inculcation not of religious scepticism but of moral cynicism.

The Court of the King Archon was competent to try only for murder and irreligion. Both were capital offences. The Athenians had little mind for juridical niceties, so possibly enemies of Socrates blurred the distinction between the inculcation of religious scepticism and the inculcation of moral cynicism. But by the letter of the law only the former could have been a capital offence. In Plato's *Apology* 26 B Socrates does briefly rebut the charge of inculcating religious scepticism in the young men. In the *Euthyphro* 6 A Socrates suggests that he is being prosecuted for being sceptical of the popular theological fables. In Aristophanes' *Clouds*, 904 and 1080, two such stories to the discredit of Zeus are cited by the Unjust Reason. The former is cited in the *Republic* 377 E and the *Euthyphro* 6 A. The latter may be echoed in the *Republic* 390 C. Such scepticism of theological fables is expressed in the *Republic* II, from 377, and in Isocrates' *Busiris* 38–43. Though it seems a likely ground for a charge of irreligion, the *Apology* is silent about it. Indeed the *Apology* leaves it completely unclear what Socrates was supposed to be sceptical of or what new-fangled religious doctrines he was supposed to have espoused. He makes no apology for his private divine voice; indeed he overtly refers to it, as if no one could take theological exception to this. In Aristophanes' *Clouds* Socrates is pilloried for his rejection of the popular theological fables. In the *Phaedrus* 229-30 Socrates is, perhaps defensively, made to speak unsceptically of such fables.

2. THE CHARGES AGAINST 'SOCRATES'

If we now examine the trial-prophecies made by Anytus in the *Meno* 94 E–95 A and by Socrates in the *Gorgias* 522 B we find this extraordinary fact. What Anytus warns Socrates against has nothing whatsoever to do with irreligion; it is saying defamatory things about people in public life. In the *Gorgias* Socrates predicts that he will put up only a lame defence against the charges of corrupting the young men by driving them into logical quandaries, and of saying defamatory things against their seniors. Defamation, κακηγορία, was indeed a legal offence, but it was not a capital offence and not an offence which could officially have been tried by the Court of the King Archon. Tying young men up in logical knots by the Socratic Method was not, *pace* Xenophon, a legal offence at all; and the young men themselves loved the exercise.

Plato and everyone else knew quite well that Socrates had not been tried in the Court of the King Archon for the defamation of public men or for driving young men into logical quandaries. Why then does Plato in the *Meno* and *Gorgias* misdescribe, dramatically in the future tense, the charges against Socrates? Plato cannot here be trying to be historical about the year 399. He is instead, it will be argued, alluding to an actual trial for defamation which took place not in 399, but in the not very early 370's; not in the King Archon's Court, but in another court; and it was the trial not of Socrates but of 'Socrates'.

If we examine the *Apology* itself, we find other queer facts. Socrates begins his defence by describing the wide-spread prejudice that exists against him because of his plaguing, not of the young men, but of the politicians, orators, poets and craftsmen by eristic questioning in public places. Out of the twenty-four Stephanus pages of the *Apology* two pages, 26–27, are devoted to Socrates' very esoteric and question-begging defence against unspecific charges of being irreligious and inculcating irreligion in the young men, with nothing said about his rejection of the popular theological fables. Save for a few lines in 35 D we hear almost nothing more of the charge of irreligion. Nearly the whole of the remainder of the *Apology* is Socrates' Defence of the Socratic Method; and now the mischief allegedly done to the young men is that they have acquired the taste and the ability to drive their elders and betters by means of this Socratic Method into logical quandaries (23 C, 33 C, 37 D, 39 D). Socrates' three accusers, Meletus, Lycon and Anytus, are described in 23 E–24 A as the champions of the politicians, orators, poets and artisans against their eristic gadfly. We hear hardly a breath more of their being the champions of religion. In the *Crito* there is not a hint of the charges made against Socrates, or of the court in which they were made, save that in 53 C it is suggested that if Socrates were to escape from Athens, he would wish to continue to exercise the young men, in

Thessaly perhaps, in the eristic exercise. In the *Apology* itself, 41 C, Plato makes Socrates look forward to an after-life of cross-examining the people whom he will meet in Heaven. He says, 'At any rate, the folk there do not kill people for it', as if it was for his practice of the Socratic Method that Athens condemned him to death.

The eristic exercise, or the Socratic Method, was not even illegal. It had been taught by Protagoras and was certainly taught in Antisthenes' school. Isocrates reprobates it in his *Against the Sophists* and at the beginning of his *Helen*, but never hints that it is or ever has been a criminal offence. Twenty years later in his *Antidosis* 260–9 Isocrates more tolerantly recommends the young men to train their grow-ing intellects in the exercise, without a suggestion that it is or ever has been illegal. In the *Gorgias* 484 C, 485 Callicles approves of the training of young men in 'philosophy', provided that they give it up in time to work for worldly success. The *Antidosis* shows that the Academy itself was giving systematic instruction in dialectic by about the middle 350's, and giving it to the young men. Aristotle's *Topics* and Plato's *Parmenides*, Part II, show what sort of in-struction this was and who gave it. There is no suggestion in the *Antidosis*, *Topics*, *Parmenides* or anywhere else that any law had to be repealed to make this instruction possible. In the *Republic* VII 537–9 dialectic is indeed for-bidden to the young men, but it is permitted to, or even required of the thirty-year-olders whose minds and cha-racters have been duly trained. How then can Plato repre-sent Socrates' defence as having been, for by far its greater part, a defence of the Socratic Method before the Court of the King Archon, when this method was not a legal offence and, if it had been a legal offence, could not have been a capital offence coming within the jurisdiction of that court?

The *Apology* is discrepant with the *Meno* and the *Gorgias* in that the *Apology* is silent about the charge of defamation which is the sole charge prophesied in the *Meno* and one of the two charges prophesied in the *Gorgias*. Conversely the *Meno* and *Gorgias* are silent about the charge of irreligion and the inculcation of irreligion. The *Meno* is silent about the Socratic Method, and the *Gorgias* mentions it, very unconvincingly, only as corrupting the young men by driving them into logical quandaries. Neither dialogue says a word about the young men driving their elders and betters into quandaries, any more than the *Apology* says a word about the young men being themselves driven into quandaries.

In his *Apology* Xenophon says nothing about the charge of defamation *or* about the mischief of young men or their elderly victims being driven into logical quandaries *or* about Socrates being prosecuted for, or even on account of his practice of the Socratic Method. The *Seventh Letter*, Diogenes Laertius and Plato's *Euthyphro* and *Politicus* are totally silent about all these alleged charges.

One conclusion from all this is inescapable. Plato was not writing even a romantic history of the trial of the real Socrates in the *Gorgias*, the *Meno* or even the *Apology*, save in the last case for the two Stephanus pages in which Socrates rebuts the charges of being irreligious and inculcating irreligion, plus the page, 32, where Socrates describes his defiance of unjust orders from the government. The bulk of Socrates' defence is no more historical than Thucydides' speeches are historical. The *Apology* is for the most part a defence of the Socratic Method against an attack which was not made in 399, but was made well on in the 370's. The martyr's name was not 'Socrates' but 'Plato'. The startling disappearance of the Socratic Method from Plato's dialogues comes after the composition and publication of the *Euthydemus*, *Gorgias* and *Meno*, which are eristic dialogues *par excellence*. The *Apology* is Plato's protest against the suppression of Plato's practice of the Socratic Method. In the *Crito* Plato is explaining why, despite its suppression, it would be wrong for Plato to desert Athens in order to continue teaching the Socratic Method in Thessaly, Thebes or Megara. Perhaps Simmias, famous for being one of the philosopher-revolutionaries who freed Thebes from Sparta in 379, had, with Cebes, invited Plato to take refuge in Thebes (see *Crito* 45 B); and perhaps the honorific prominence given to the two Thebans in the *Phaedo* and their mention in the *Crito* were Plato's tribute of personal gratitude to them for this or for some other support. (For Simmias see Plutarch's *De Genio Socratis* in *Moralia* VII, and the *Phaedrus* 242.)

The total hypothesis is this. By a certain moment quite well on in the 370's Plato had composed and recited to his normal audiences the *Euthydemus*, *Gorgias* and *Meno*—the *Gorgias minus* its terminal monologue by Socrates and the *Meno minus* its Anytus episode. Conceivably because offence was given by these dialogues *inter alia*, but anyhow very soon after their public delivery, some legal action occurred in which some of Plato's adherents and Plato himself were prosecuted for the defamation of some senior persons of social and political importance. Somehow Plato's teaching of eristic to his pupils was implicated, so that the success of the prosecution somehow involved the suppression of this teaching and therewith, by indirect causation, the cessation of his eristic dialogues. Plato's first reaction was to add to the books of the *Gorgias* and *Meno* Socrates' long monologue at the end of the *Gorgias* and his short colloquy with Anytus near the end of the *Meno*. Here we get the dramatic prophecies of the charge of defamation, together with the unplausible and obviously invented subcharge of the corruption of the young men by driving them into logical quandaries. Eristic may well have been objected to, but not conceivably on this ludicrous ground and therefore possibly not on any alternative specific ground either. Dialectically proficient young men can be troublesome hecklers, particularly if their politics are reactionary or revolutionary.

A little later Plato wrote his Defence of the Socratic Method. We might rename it the *Apologia Platonis*. Here Plato is out not to report the actual defence made by the defendants or made on their behalf against the charge of defamation, nor even to produce *post eventum* an imaginary defence which might or should have been made on their behalf. He is defending his own philosophical mission, not its penalized acolytes. Not a word is said now about influential persons being slandered. But a lot is said about influential persons being offended by the eristic gadfly and his disciples, without it being explained how there could have been a legal remedy for the offence, unless it was defamation.

It was now or very soon afterwards that Plato joined forces with Theaetetus, who had had a mathematical school at Heraclea on the Black Sea, and Eudoxus, who had had a mathematical and astronomical school at Cyzicus. The Academy was formed as a merger between Plato's suppressed school of eristic and the other two immigrant schools.

The founding of the Academy, the curriculum of which is described and justified in Book VII of the *Republic*, was a salvage operation. It was not Plato's realization of a dream; it was his building of a raft after the shipwreck of his own teaching-vocation. In this new curriculum dialectic is sternly vetoed for the younger men, who have first to study the subjects taught by Theaetetus and Eudoxus. Only later, when mature men, will they study what Plato is now debarred from teaching to adolescents.

The Academy had certainly started before 369, since Theaetetus, reputedly a foundation-member of the Academy, perished on military service in the summer of that year. But it was not founded more than a handful, perhaps not more than a half-handful of years before Aristotle joined it in 367. It had not been founded when Isocrates wrote his *Helen* towards or at the end of the 370's.

3. EVIDENCE

It is now time to assemble positive evidence for parts of this seemingly unhistorical hypothesis. For there is no story in Diogenes Laertius' *Life of Plato* of Plato's being in-

volved in any legal proceedings between the trial of
Socrates in 399 and that of the general Chabrias in about
365. Nor does the *Seventh Letter* say a word about any such
event. Yet the cumulative evidence for it seems to out-
weigh the fairly strong argument against it from the total
silence of history about it. It is only fairly strong, since
history tells us very little about Plato's life, and much of
that little derives from the [Platonic] *Letters*, the unauthen-
ticity of which is proved in Chapter III. It is worth mentioning that the *Seventh Letter* is silent both about the existence
of the Academy and about Plato's activity as a composer of
dialogues. Not all of this *Letter*'s silences can be credited
with negative probativeness, even by those who believe
that Plato wrote it.

(*a*) In Book VII of the *Republic* 537–9 Socrates explains
why the twenty-year-olders are forbidden to study the
coping-stone of knowledge, dialectic. Having learned to
enjoy worrying, puppy-like, any thesis, however lofty,
they fall into total cynicism, *and thereby both they and the
whole cause of philosophy have been prejudiced in the eyes of the
world.* This is a very vehement assertion and a surprising
one from Plato who in his eristic dialogues has again and
again, and very recently, represented Socrates as devotedly
exercising adolescents in questioner-answerer disputations. In the *Euthydemus* the young Cleinias is shown that
he needs to be well enough trained in genuine eristic to be
able to combat the trick-eristic of the two sophists. Something has radically changed Plato's mind, or at least
radically changed his practice and his public professions.
What had been the best higher education for young men

has become something from which they are to be wholly screened until they are in their thirties. The exercise itself and its young participants have come under a black cloud, and quite suddenly.

(b) Isocrates' *Helen* is dated by some scholars about 370, rather earlier by others. In its first few pages, without any apparent relevance to the theme of the oration, some un-named contemporary teachers of young men are castigated both for teaching them foolish philosophical doctrines and for teaching them eristic. Several of the foolish philo-sophical doctrines mentioned in the opening paragraph and in Section 9 are easily identified with points argued for in Plato's *Protagoras*, *Euthydemus*, *Meno* and *Gorgias*; and this idea that it is Plato who is the prime target of Isocrates' attack is borne out by the theory, argued in Chapter VII, 2, that Plato's *Phaedrus* contains a riposte to Isocrates' *Helen* as a whole. The *Helen*, it is there argued, is as a whole an attack in pretty lame allegory on Plato's *Gorgias*; and the apparent irrelevance of the opening pages of the *Helen* to its proper theme is apparent only. At the end of its first paragraph Isocrates says that eristic disputations are not only useless but are sure to 'make trouble', πράγματα παρέχειν, for their participants. Isocrates uses this phrase or kindred phrases several times in his *Antidosis* (8, 148, 163, 241, 287), where each time, save one, it patently has the special sense 'get into legal hot water' or 'hale before the court' or just 'prosecute' (see also his *Against Callimachus* 7). So Isocrates is apparently alluding to some specific legal proceedings in which some members of Plato's circle have been involved. In spite of his disapproval of eristic disputation and of the teaching of eristic to young men, Isocrates nowhere suggests that it is or ought to be made a legal offence. Their teachers 'deserve censure' (7).

If it is Plato who is being castigated for the bad education which, from mercenary motives, he gives to the young men, then the *Helen* must be prior to the foundation of the Academy, since Isocrates says nothing that pertains to the mathematical and astronomical curriculum of Plato's Academy, and *a fortiori* nothing about its ban on dialectic for the young men. The somewhat similar oration, the *Busiris* 23, does seem to refer, under cover, to the curriculum of the Academy, and if so it must have been composed later than the *Helen* and at least twenty years later than the date commonly ascribed to it. It may also allude to what is now Book VII of the *Republic*, which is likely, though not in its present form or setting, to have been delivered when the Academy was launched. In the *Busiris* the elements of the curriculum are arithmetic, geometry and astronomy. No mention is made of eristic.

(c) In his long monologue at the end of the *Gorgias* 508 C, 509 D, Socrates surprises us by twice saying prophetically that he will flounder incompetently in his defence of *himself, his associates and his relations,* οἰκείων. But in 399 Socrates was the sole defendant; he had no co-defendants for whom he had to try to state the defence. The prosecution prophesied in the *Gorgias* was not that of a solitary defendant for irreligion; it was the prosecution of a plurality of defendants for defamation. Apparently at least one of these defendants was a relative of 'Socrates'. Who?

Why is Socrates made to prophesy that he will flounder hopelessly in court? Xenophon reports no floundering; and Plato's *Apology* will live for ever as a powerful speech. A very creditable minority of the judges voted for the acquittal of Socrates. There are other places where Plato makes Socrates declare that the true philosopher is bound to flounder in court against the ready-witted, mean-minded prosecutor, though their roles will be happily reversed when they come to discuss more cosmic matters. One place is the long and philosophically quite pointless digression in the *Theaetetus* from 172 C. Here Socrates says nothing about himself in particular. In the *Republic* 517A we get a similar but briefer statement of the forensic incompetence of the true philosopher, who again is not identified with Socrates. In the *Gorgias* 526B–527A the politician Callicles is warned that he, but not the philosopher, will gape and feel dizzy before Rhadamanthus and Minos, as Socrates is going to do before his Athenian judges. We may conjecture that Plato had had to speak on behalf of his fellow-defendants and himself in their trial for defamation and that his performance had been embarrassingly inadequate. His pitiful showing left an abiding sore place in his memory. His dream in the *Gorgias* and *Theaetetus* of an eventual turning of the tables upon the 'lawyers' was a compensation-dream. It is noteworthy that in the *Theaetetus* the philosopher is described as an unworldly innocent who does not even know his way to the *agora* or the courts. In the *Apology* Socrates had not been so represented. He was a frequenter of the *agora*. In the *Theaetetus* Plato was thinking about someone else than

Socrates as his unworldly, forensically ineffective philosopher.

(d) The impression that the early dialogues give us of Socrates' personality is that of the gay, avuncular, combative, shrewd and predominantly scrupulous champion of eristic ring-craft; a mixture of Dr Johnson, D'Artagnan and Marshall Hall. The last twenty pages of the *Gorgias*, the *Apology*, the *Crito* and the *Phaedo* introduce us to a very different man. Socrates is now a prophet, a reformer, a saint and a martyr. The hemlock reminds us of the crucifix. Plato is writing here with a passion which was not there before. Some quarter of a century has elapsed since Socrates' execution, and during this period Athens has repented of her crime. Socrates' name no longer needs to be retrieved from disgrace. Plato himself has written, surely to the great satisfaction of his Athenian audiences, a number of cheerful, down-to-earth stories of the champion's victories and, in the *Euthydemus*, of his technical defeat in the disputation-ring. Whence come the new tones of Plato's voice? No mere twenty-five-year-old piety could explain the new moral passion or the new political venom of Socrates' monologue in the *Gorgias*; his relish in the myth in the *Gorgias* for the eternal tortures in Tartarus that await the men of power; his apostolic vindication of his mission in the *Apology*; the deep and almost merry seriousness of his Farewell to This Life in the *Phaedo*. The earlier eristic dialogues are the products of Plato's talents, but these immediately succeeding dialogues come out of his heart as well. What has happened to Plato's heart? The fact that history records nothing shows only that there is a big gap in history; and this should not surprise us, since nearly all that history tells us about Plato's life derives from those so-called Platonic *Letters* which were forged by a pro-Dionist in order to misrepresent Plato's connexions with Dion and Dionysius. There must have been a crisis in Plato's life in the later 370's, which is reflected at once by the disappearance of the elenchus from his dialogues; by the foundation of the Academy with its dialectic-barred curriculum for the young men; by the passion with which Plato writes in the *Gorgias* monologue and in the *Apology*, *Crito* and *Phaedo*; and even, perhaps, by Socrates' very uncharacteristic lament at the divine veto on suicide in the opening conversation of the *Phaedo*.

(*e*) The *Antidosis*, composed in the later 350's, is Isocrates' *Apologia Isocratis* against an avowedly notional prosecution. Isocrates tells us that he has invented the fiction of a prosecution of himself in order to provide a setting in which he may deliver a vindication of his life and especially of his pedagogic mission. Now it is not just once or twice, but again and again that Isocrates here plagiarizes Plato's *Apology*. This Isocrates might certainly have done if he had taken Plato's *Apology* to be the faithful reconstruction of what the real Socrates had actually said in 399, or at least the *post eventum* construction of what Socrates could or should have said, that scholars have commonly taken it to be. Isocrates must have known from his own memories of 399 which of the two it was, if it was either. But another view is possible. Perhaps the uninventive Isocrates borrowed the whole idea of composing an *Apologia pro Vita Mea* from Plato's *Apology*; that is, perhaps he and everyone else took the *Apology* to be, in the main, Plato's dramatized vindication of Plato's life and Plato's pedagogic mission. Isocrates followed a *genre* of which Plato was the inventor, with the big difference that Isocrates' teaching-mission was only notionally in jeopardy, where Plato's had been all too actually done to death.

Isocrates was thirty-seven and resident in Athens when Socrates was tried and executed. Yet his fictional self-defence in his *Antidosis* seems to draw nothing directly from the self-defence of the real Socrates in 399. Isocrates modelled his personal *Apology* only on what Plato had written and apparently not also on his own memories of what the real Socrates had said. The *Antidosis* is not even an inferential source-book for what had happened in 399. This strongly suggests that Plato's *Apology* is not one either, else Isocrates would now and then have diverged from Plato's report by enlarging upon it or differing from it.

(*f*) We should not forget that there is a serious anachronism in our natural assumption that the literary art of which Boswell was the great genius was an art in which Plato could and therefore should have been a conscientious practitioner. We too easily assume that it is Plato's duty to Socrates and to us to introduce us to his teacher in person. We need to remember that Isocrates tells us in his *Evagoras*, which must be dated at least a year or two later than 374, that he is the first person to try to give in prose a biography-cum-encomium of a man. The craft of describing type-characters has yet to be inaugurated in Aristotle's *Art of Rhetoric* and *Ethics* and perfected in Theophrastus' *Characters*. Plutarch's *Lives* are half a millennium off, and in them biography is still ancillary to encomium.

It is not merely that Plato's hearers and readers might have been unshocked to find his *Apology* diverging slightly or grossly from the canons of faithful biography. The very idea of faithful biography was not yet theirs. Plato could neither respect nor betray the ideals of Boswell. He had never heard of them. Our question 'Is Plato's story—or Xenophon's story—of the trial of Socrates myth or history?' was not a natural question to ask in the middle of the fourth century B.C.; nor our question 'Is it *the* story or just *a* story?' It was the perquisite and the duty of the dramatists to tell stories about persons. In his *Memorabilia* III and his *Oeconomicus* Xenophon puts into the mouth of Socrates views about the Duties of a Cavalry Officer and about Farm Management which no one could suppose not to be the views of Xenophon himself. Yet Xenophon, unlike Plato, was an historian.

(*g*) The trial-prophecies in the *Meno* and *Gorgias* are our sole direct evidence for the theory that there was a trial specifically for defamation in which Plato was involved. As this trial somehow resulted in the suppression of Plato's teaching of eristic and the indirectly consequential disappearance of the elenchus from his dialogues, the *Meno* and the *Gorgias*, which are eristic dialogues *par excellence*, must have been composed and publicly delivered before this trial, and the passages containing these prophecies must have been added to the books of these dialogues after the trial. Is there any internal evidence to corroborate this hypothesis that the passages containing the prophecies are subsequent additions?

In the *Meno* it is Anytus, one of Socrates' prosecutors in 399, who warns Socrates of the danger of saying defamatory things against persons in public life. Socrates prophesies, 'As for Anytus, I shall be conversing with him again', that is, in court. Now there is one unparalleled thing about this short colloquy between Socrates and his new interlocutor, Anytus. The *Meno* is the only one out of all Plato's dialogues in which an answerer is introduced into the discussion who had not been on the stage when the curtain rose. The sole partial parallel is the irruption of the tipsy Alcibiades into the Dinner Party; but the *Symposium* is not a discussion-dialogue and Alcibiades is not an answerer. The actual introduction of Anytus in the *Meno* 89 E is artificial enough to arouse by itself suspicions of interpolation. Socrates' last remark to Meno, before he notices that Anytus has taken his seat by them, joins smoothly on to his first remark, in 95 A, after his valedictory comment on Anytus. The whole Anytus episode looks as if it had been intercalated *en bloc* without any stitching or patching.

In the *Gorgias* Socrates' prophecies of the poor showing that he will make in court occur in the long monologue at the end of the dialogue. This long monologue contains several odd features. First, after Socrates had in earlier stages of the discussion been so severe on others for introducing long speeches into what ought to be staccato questioner-answerer exchanges, it seems inconsistent for Socrates to conclude the discussion with a long monologue. He admits the inconsistency, which is forced on him by the sulking of Callicles. Next, from the beginning of Socrates' long monologue two things have changed. The subject under discussion is no longer merely the original subject of the dialogue, namely the worthlessness of popular rhetoric and rhetoric-teaching. Socrates is now arguing for the disastrousness of popular democracy and popularity-hunting politicians. Popular rhetoric is now only incidentally mentioned. Callicles is an ambitious democratic politician; he is not just a political orator, and certainly not an epideictic orator. He is not a mere Isocratean. It is his political vocation which is wrong, not only his misemployment of rhetorical skills. Moreover Socrates is now a very different person from the dialectical puncturer of Gorgias and Polus. Then he had been championing philosophy against rhetoric, as well as, after a while, confuting the moral thesis that it is worse to suffer than to do wrong. But now he is contrasting what the Demos wants with what it needs, its pastry with its surgeon's knife. Athenian society is under the lash. Socrates reminds us of Jeremiah. He jars our ears by claiming 'I am the only statesman of my time.' Here too we get the *prima facie* puzzling references to the 'genuine rhetoric', that is, the medicinal and therefore unpopular oratory, of which, apparently, Socrates is the solitary practitioner and for which the politicians will destroy him.

Isocrates in his *Helen* as well as in his *Nicocles* 1 and 9 seems, rightly, to take the *Gorgias* to be an attack on his school of rhetoric and what it stood for; but in Socrates' terminal monologue the target is no longer the school of

Isocrates; it is Periclean and post-Periclean democracy. In the *Gorgias* 521 E–522 B Plato is surely hinting that the suppression of his teaching to the young men has resulted from some action taken by the democratic politicians, not by mere orators.

Next, though the Athenian theatre-going public had been tolerant enough to enjoy its gay but stinging whippings from Aristophanes, it is hard to believe that it could have sat quietly through the end of the *Gorgias*. So perhaps this part was composed not for its ears, but for sympathetic readers only.

Finally, the *Gorgias* is 26 or 27 Stephanus pages too long, longer, that is, than what seems to be the standard or regulation length of about 53 pages for middle-sized dialogues (see pp. 39–40).

We do have therefore some internal corroboration for the independently based hypothesis that the passages in the *Meno* and *Gorgias* which contain the prophecies of a trial for defamation were added after this trial to the books of the dialogues which had been composed and orally delivered shortly before it.

(*h*) There are one or two biographical incongruities which could be explained by the theory that 'Socrates' in the terminal *Gorgias* and the *Apology* represents Plato himself. In the *Gorgias* (486 C, 508 C–D, 511 A and 521 C–E) apparent prophecies of Socrates' trial and punishment are made by both Callicles and Socrates. Side by side with the death penalty there is mentioned forfeiture of property (cf. *Crito* 46 C). In 521 C Socrates says that the man who unjustly despoils him of his property will get no good out of his ill-gotten gains. But the real Socrates had no money. He could not pay even a very small fine out of his own resources. Plato on the other hand had been quite wealthy. Did his inferred prosecution result in Plato losing his fortune? The *Thirteenth Letter*, a forgery but one concocted at its ostensible date early in 365, represents Plato as the salaried agent and virtually the pensioner of Dionysius II. He will require from Dionysius the money to provide a dowry for a female relative and funeral expenses for his mother. We need not suppose that there is a word of truth in this. But if the readers of the *Letter* had known or believed that Plato was still a rich man, they would on this ground alone have recognized the *Letter* for a forgery. If the *Letter* was written to deceive, its writer and its intended readers must have known or believed that Plato was in 365 no longer at all well off, and been at least prepared to believe that Plato was dependent on Dionysius' munificence. (Compare also *Letters* VII 333D, II 312C, III 318E, and see Diogenes Laertius' *Life of Plato* 3 and 9.) Plato's will is not that of a man with much ready money or treasure, or a big retinue of slaves; but the two pieces of land which he bequeathed may, for all we can tell, have been worth a good deal (Diogenes Laertius, *Plato* 41).

If the *Helen* was aimed against Plato, then Isocrates seems to say, 6 and 8, that Plato taught pupils for money. But as it is the teaching of eristic that Isocrates has primarily in mind, Plato's alleged teaching for pay would be prior to the trial, since this trial resulted in the suppression of Plato's eristic teaching. So either Isocrates was lying, or Plato was already before the trial an unwealthy man, or Isocrates was here scolding other teachers of eristic, such as Antisthenes. As Socrates in the *Apology* denies that he taught for money, we may safely infer that, whatever Isocrates says, Plato had hitherto charged no fees for the tuition that he gave.

If Plato did become impoverished and in this sort of way, the bitterness inspiring *Republic* VIII 564–5 and IX 573–5 might have something personal in it. Certainly his reduction to comparative poverty would have thwarted for good his political ambitions; and this might have been part of the intention behind the inferred judicial confiscation of his property.

Next, in the *Apology* (31 C–32 A, 32 E and 36 B–C) Socrates explains why he had kept out of politics. But the real Socrates, unlike Plato, had not the means, the interests, the connexions or presumably the ambitions of a might-have-been politician. In the *Gorgias* 473 E–474 A Socrates confesses to Polus his quite recently displayed incompetence, in his position of prytany-president, even to take the votes, and says 'I am not a public man.' But Plato had political aspirations. The *Seventh Letter* 324–6, no matter who wrote it, is unlikely glaringly to misrepresent Plato on this matter; and Plato surely wrote *Republic* VI 496 in an autobiographical spirit. The reasons for abstention from politics given by Socrates in the *Apology* tally well with those credited to Plato in the *Seventh Letter*, 325 D and 331 C–D, the *Fifth Letter* 322 and with those credited to the true philosopher in the *Republic* 496. In the *Gorgias* (484 C, 485 D–E, 486 C–D) Socrates is invited by Callicles to give up philosophy and come into politics. Plato seems to forget that at this dramatic date Socrates was already well over sixty. Socrates refers to this advice, 487D, 500C, and gives reasons why it is wrong (e.g. 510D–511A, 512E–513D, 515A–B, 527D). These reasons tally in part with those of the *Seventh Letter* and the *Apology*. One or two of the idioms for 'going into politics' which occur in the *Gorgias* and *Apology* occur also in the *Seventh Letter*. They are standard idioms, but they slightly reinforce the idea that the authors of the *Seventh Letter* and the *Fifth Letter* identified the Socrates of the terminal *Gorgias* and of the *Apology* with Plato.

In his *Helen* 9–10 Isocrates reprobates someone for claiming political science, περὶ τῶν πολιτικῶν ἐπιστήμην, and is doubtless referring to Socrates' astonishing claim to this science in the *Gorgias* 521D and/or *Euthydemus* 291 and/or *Protagoras* 319, 321, 322. Isocrates is equally incensed by the claim to possess the true theory of government and by the refusal to participate in the practice of it. Isocrates is talking not about Socrates, but about one or more contemporary political doctrinaires, and almost certainly about Plato, as he may be doing in the penultimate sentence of his *Letter to Dionysius*. It is therefore a plausible hypothesis that accusations of political doctrinaireness had been made not against Socrates but against Plato, including that by Isocrates in his *Helen*; and that it is for that reason that a defence of his non-participation in active politics is put into Socrates' mouth in the terminal *Gorgias* and the *Apology*, despite the historical incongruity of making the real Socrates, what Plato passionately, though surely mistakenly, felt himself to be, the statesman *manqué*. Plato meant his public to identify his 'Socrates' with himself.

(*i*) It is argued in Chapter VII that the *Phaedo* was composed just before Plato's departure for Sicily in 367, and that therefore Socrates' Farewell to Athens, his friends and his philosophical mission is also Plato's Farewell, for over a year and perhaps for ever, to Athens and the Academy. Socrates' journey to the Next World is sometimes described in maritime similes; and as Socrates laughed at his friends' fears about his hosts-to-be, so Plato is encouraging his friends and himself to think that the tyrant's court in Syracuse will be a civilized court. Maybe the queer passage in *Phaedo* 78 A hints at the Academy's practical problem 'Who is to be Head of the Academy if Plato does not return?' It is pretty certain that Socrates' incongruous announcement at 108 E of the shape and structure of the Earth is Plato's announcement of something that he had just learned in Sicily, twenty-two years after Socrates' death. This suggested identification by Plato of his dramatic Socrates with himself would both give some needed support to, and draw some needed support from the theory that in his *Apology* Plato is identifying the Socratic Voice of the Socratic Method with the Platonic Voice of the Socratic Method; the trial of 399 with a trial in, say, 372–371; the execution of Socrates with the pedagogic gagging and property-spoliation of Plato.

(*j*) In the *Apology* 37 D Socrates perplexes us by saying that if he escaped from Athens to continue his dialectical vocation elsewhere, the young men *whom he refused to admit would get their elders to drive him out from those asylums too*. Had 'Socrates' offended some politically influential persons not by teaching but by refusing to teach dialectic to their sons or nephews? In the *Republic* VI 495 Plato makes Socrates speak rancorously of the dishonour brought on philosophy by the incursion of aspirants to the title of 'philosopher' who were contaminated by their humble origins and by their associations with trades and crafts. Plato forgets that Socrates himself was so contaminated. In the *Apology* 23 C Socrates says that the young men who listen to his cross-questionings and imitate them are those who have the greatest leisure and are the sons of the wealthiest men, a dictum which does not tally with the practice of the real Socrates, whose disciples included poor men like Aeschines, Antisthenes, Aristippus, Phaedo, Simon and Apollodorus, as well as rich young men like Plato, Alcibiades and Critias. Indeed Socrates says as much in the *Apology* 33 B. Xenophon, in his *Memorabilia* I, quite elaborately exculpates Socrates from the allegation of having trained up the young Alcibiades and Critias in their anti-popular politics; and the same intention might be read into Alcibiades' contribution in the *Symposium*; into the *Alcibiades* I and II, if Plato wrote them; and into the *Republic* VI 494–5. Was it Plato who needed this exculpation? Perhaps the democratic politicians had some grounds for objecting that not Socrates', but Plato's circle was exclusive to the anti-democratic *jeunesse dorée*.

In the *Politicus* 299 B–C there is a probable allusion to the condemnation of Socrates, or else of 'Socrates'. Here the corruption of the young men is explicitly equated with their indoctrination with ideas and intentions subversive of the democratic régime. Nothing is said about dialectic being an instrument of this indoctrination, and it is not easy to see how an eristic duel terminating in an elenchus or a draw could be supposed to have an ideological effect. But certainly young men who have been trained in the techniques of disputation can be thorns in the flesh of politicians to whom they are hostile; and we can be sure that Plato's disciples tended to be hostile to the Callicles of their day (see *Apology* 39D). It might well be that though the prosecution in, say, 372–371 was a prosecution for defamation, much of its animus was animus against what was seriously thought to be a nursery of anti-democratic politicians.

(*k*) In Xenophon's *Memorabilia* I ii 31–8 two members of the Thirty, Critias and Charicles, explain to Socrates the terms of their new law which forbids him to interrogate young men under thirty. Did the Thirty really make such a law against questioner-answerer disputation and make it *ad hominem*? Socrates was not prosecuted in 399 for breaking any such law, though this proves little since the acts of the Thirty were generally rescinded after their fall. But Plato's Socrates does not allude to such a law in any dialogue, not even in the *Apology* where his resistance to the Thirty is mentioned. Nor does the *Seventh Letter* say anything about the matter. In the *Gorgias* Callicles inveighs against long continuation of the dialectical exercise, but not on the score that the exercise is or has ever been against the law. It is worth while considering the possibility that Xenophon is antedating an actual but much later *ad hominem* prohibition of the teaching of eristic to the under-thirties. For this alleged ban on eristic for young men is combined with the permission of it for the over-thirties, and this reminds us forcibly of the *Republic* VII 539 and therefore of the actual curriculum of the Academy. In this stretch of his *Memorabilia*, 32 and 37, Xenophon does seem to echo, imprecisely, the *Gorgias* 491 A and 516 A. So he might be drawing on Plato's Socrates and if so he might be alluding with prudent indirectness to an *ad hominem* ban imposed by democratic politicians upon the teaching of dialectic not by Socrates but by Plato.

What sort of a ban could this have been? Xenophon's idea of *ad hominem* legislation and even the idea of an *ad hominem psephisma* seem politically unlikely; and Plato himself in his most vitriolic attacks on democratic politicians does not charge them with such *privilegium*.

It is more likely that the court which convicted him of defamation made a court order, if such powers then existed, forbidding Plato to teach eristic to the under-thirties. Or, more likely still, that this court, in fixing the penalties, first confiscated Plato's fortune and then gave him the choice between going into banishment and giving his undertaking never to teach eristic or perhaps anything else to the under-thirties; and that Plato chose the latter option. Or, most likely of all, that Plato proposed that his punishment should be expropriation *plus* the suppression of his teaching to young men; and that the court accepted this alternative to the prosecution's proposal of banishment. The *Crito* might then be his vindication of his tame-seeming choice to 'die', that is to stay in Athens pedagogically muzzled, rather than to live exiled but unmuzzled in Thebes or Megara. Some of Socrates' reasons for not going abroad do strike us as special pleading. The stern call of duty is given some rather trumpery reinforcements. It may be significant that in the *Apology* 37D Socrates prophesies, if he were to go abroad, one banishment after another and not one death sentence after another. Other slender straws which could be thought to point in this direction are to be found in the *Gorgias* 508 D, the *Apology* 29 C and 37 C–E, the *Crito* 52 C and 53 B–E and the *Phaedo* 98 E–99 A. A few references to loss of civil rights, ἀτιμία, suggest the possibility that Plato suffered this penalty as well, for example *Apology* 30 D; *Gorgias* 486 C, 508 C, 527 A; *Phaedo* 82 C; *Republic* 492 D. That an insuperable fine could have this effect is shown by Demosthenes' *Against Aristogeiton* and *Against Theocrinas*.

In his *Antidosis* Isocrates parades a Socratic heroism in the face of a threatening death penalty, although the notional charge against him, whatever it was supposed to be, could not have been a capital charge. He inflates the notional danger in order not to leave out the heroics. Maybe Plato in an authentic crisis proclaimed over-heroically, 'Give me dialectic or give me death', when the alternative was not death and when what he actually chose was just this alternative.

(*l*) On this hypothesis Plato would never have taught dialectic, or even possibly anything else, to the young men in the Academy. What Aristotle would have learned, except by hearsay, of Plato's philosophy would have been what was contained in Plato's published dialogues. Now this seems to coincide with the facts, as Harold Cherniss has brilliantly shown in Chapter III of his *The Riddle of the*

Early Academy, though without rendering these facts un-perplexing. Save for the unpublished *Lecture on the Good* the Platonic dialogues that we possess seem to be the sources of nearly every philosophical argument or doc-trine that Aristotle ascribes to Plato. Aristotle transmits to us not one echo of Plato's expository, tutorial or even elenctic voice. On the present hypothesis he never heard it. It was this muzzling of Plato that saved or debarred Aristotle and his fellow-students from being the echoes that the personal disciples of a genius are almost bound to be.

The first we hear of dialectic being taught to the young men in the Academy is what Isocrates says in 354–353 in the *Antidosis* 258–69; what we find, without certainty of date, in Plato's *Parmenides*, Part II, where the interlocutor is a coeval of Socrates with the name of 'Aristotle'; and what is exhibited in Aristotle's *Topics*, and alluded to in his *Art of Rhetoric*. Aristotle was not muzzled by the court verdict of, say, 372–371; it was he who, surely with the backing and the envy of Plato, introduced into the Academy the teaching of dialectic to the young men, side by side with that of rhetoric. At the end of his *De Sophisticis Elenchis* he says that he had himself to begin the methodology, τέχνη, of dialectical argumentation. He acknowledges no debts to Plato's teaching of dialectic. On this hypothesis he owed none, save for the examples of it that are the sub-stance of the pre-372 Platonic dialogues, and these Aris-totle does draw on. These final pages of the *De Sophisticis Elenchis* virtually prove that Plato had not been teaching philosophy, that is dialectic, to the young men since

174

Aristotle joined the Academy in 367, and so force upon us the crucial question 'Why not?', to which this current chapter proffers an answer.

(*m*) All of us have the picture of Socrates, followed by his troop of upper-class young men, strolling round the bankers' tables and the market place of Athens. Every now and then he waylays some citizen, a politician, maybe, or an orator or a rhapsode, and subjects him for an hour or two to ordeal by the Socratic Method.

The *Apology* 17C, 22 and 23E–24A is our solitary source for this popular picture and for its corollary that the politicians, orators, poets and artisans so deeply resented being thus personally probed and punctured in public that they got Meletus, Anytus and Lycon to prosecute Socrates, somehow on a capital charge, for so quizzing them on their walks abroad. Did anything like this really happen?

First, as noted before, Socrates was prosecuted in the Court of the King Archon for irreligion and inculcating irreligion. The dialectical badgering of citizens in public places was no more a legal offence than was gossiping; but if it had been one, it could not have been tried in the Court of the King Archon. If Meletus, Anytus and Lycon prosecuted Socrates in the Court of the King Archon, it was not, whatever the *Apology* suggests, for subjecting grumpy citizens to eristic canvassing in the *agora*. Or if they got Socrates convicted for plaguing citizens in the *agora*, then it was not by this court that Socrates was tried, despite what the *Euthyphro* and *Theaetetus* say, and what the death sentence proves.

Next, a Greek *agora* is a noisy and bustling place, as unsuitable a *venue* for a sustained questioner-answerer duel as Covent Garden or Fleet Street. Not only would Socrates' retinue of young men be unable to hear what was being said, but a reluctant citizen would find it easy to dodge or shake off his would-be interrogator. Perhaps a co-operative acquaintance might try, despite the shindy, to indulge the old inquisitor for a while; but then he would not be so resentful as to enlist the law—what law?—to protect himself from such treatment or to revenge himself for it. In fact, not in a single other Platonic dialogue, not even in the *Gorgias*, is Socrates represented or described as ever conducting his questioner-answerer examinations in such unsuitable surroundings. They take place in someone's private house, or in the young men's gymnasium, or in the school-room where Hippias has just been lecturing. In about a dozen dialogues the company is described as seated or reclining, which is what *a priori* we should expect. Xenophon's stories are economical in dramatic background, but what there is does not support the picture proffered by the *Apology*. Nor does Aristophanes' *Clouds*.

Next, the eristic duel, as Adeimantus says in the *Republic* VI 487 B–C (and cf. *Laws* 820), has several things in common with draughts. Among others it is a voluntary undertaking on both sides. A person cannot be lassoed into playing or coerced into adhering to the rules. Hippias, Protagoras and Callicles do indeed sulk when confuted, as a chessplayer may sulk when checkmated. But there is no question of Hippias, Protagoras or Callicles being dragooned into the role of answerer, or therefore of resenting Socrates taking the part of questioner. Interlocutors are not conscripts. Nor would mere complaisance on their part be enough. The participants in the duel must take some interest in the matter under discussion and in the development of the argument. Socrates' answerers in the Platonic dialogues generally are or become eager. Even Hippias is not actuated only by *amour propre*. But if so, then Socrates was not prosecuted for injuring people's *amour propre* by extracting contradictions out of their answers to his questions, since these answers were voluntary.

Finally, there is a further reason for being sceptical of our habitual picture. In the *Apology* Socrates is made to provide too many inadequate reasons for inflicting his elenctic interviews upon his reluctant victims. At one moment he cross-questions a public man in order, not very piously, to satisfy himself, but not his victim, that the Delphic Oracle was wrong. At the next he does so in order, not very piously, to satisfy himself, but not his victim, that after all the Delphic Oracle was right. The young men listen to and imitate Socrates' kerb-side pesterings not for either or both of these discordant reasons but because they get malicious fun from witnessing the deflatings of the conceited. Or Socrates has, like a gadfly, to sting Athens into wakefulness, with almost nothing to show what she is to be awakened to, save to the existence of the gadfly. Just in four or five sentences or phrases Socrates avers that his task is that of exhorting Athens to virtue, but he does not explain the connexion between this edifying task and the practice of puncturing the conceit of artisans, poets and others by pavement-questionings upon their specialties. An elenchus is not a sermon; and in Plato's own eristic dialogues Socrates is not always or even usually trying to impart a moral lesson. Indeed, the *Gorgias* is our first dialogue in which Socrates is represented as a moral teacher. The *Thrasymachus* would have been another.

The factitiousness of these discordant reasons for Socrates forcing his pavement interviews upon resentful interlocutors has a simple explanation. Such interviews did not occur. They are Plato's invention. The twice-mentioned resentment of the politicians, orators, poets and artisans did genuinely exist, but it was resentment for something quite different from what in the *Apology* Plato's Socrates is made to allege.

For what, then, did the exacerbated politicians, orators, poets and artisans not only seek, but get a legal remedy? The *Apology* 22 A–C provides a possible clue. Socrates went on from examining the politicians to examining the poets, and he found that they were the mere vehicles of knowledge which they did not themselves possess. They were inspired to say good things without themselves being the thinkers of these good things. Now this doctrine is the whole burthen of Plato's dialogue, the *Ion*, and it is echoed in his *Meno* 99 C–D. This suggests the hypothesis that what the politicians, orators, poets and artisans had resented was not things supposedly said on the pavement by the real Socrates before 399, but things that Socrates had been represented as saying in some of Plato's dialogues that were composed and publicly recited in the 370's. The prosecution was a prosecution of Plato for publishing to general audiences Socratic dialogues and maybe other discourses containing arguments or sentiments damaging to politicians, orators, poets and artisans. If so, then in his *Apology* Plato was, so to speak, dramatizing the offensiveness of some of his own recent compositions into an invented vexatiousness of the real Socrates' notional inquisitions in the market place a generation earlier.

Following up this idea we can see at once that the *finale* of the *Euthydemus* and the bulk of the *Gorgias* could have been taken as frontal attacks upon both practising orators and teachers of rhetoric. We know that they were so taken by Isocrates, who in the *Helen* and the *Nicocles* reacts with understandable acerbity to the treatment accorded by Plato's *Gorgias* to Isocrates' profession. The acerbity is still there twenty years later in the *Antidosis* 258–85. The democratic politicians might well have taken offence on their own behalf and on behalf of the Demos at the short shrift given to Callicles and to his darling in the *Gorgias*.

The inspiration theory of the *Ion* by itself could not have been more than a slight vexation to the poets. They could not have protested 'slander' or 'defamation' merely for this, especially as Ion is a rhapsode and not a poet. They might very well, however, have resented the *Gorgias* 502 B–D.

But in Plato's early dialogues we can identify no special cause of offence to the artisans unless just as forming a large part of the Demos; yet they are twice listed with the other three classes of people on whose behalf Meletus, Anytus and Lycon prosecuted Socrates. There is no Platonic dialogue in which a craftsman or a tradesman is an interlocutor. Xenophon's *Memorabilia* is less exclusive.

Remembering Aristotle's statement in his *Politics* II

1264 b 39 that Socrates (*sic*) filled up the *Republic* with ἔξωθεν λόγοις, extraneous discourses, we are warranted in looking to see whether our *Republic* contains, besides Book I, any other stretches which might have been independently composed and delivered, but not allowed to go out in book-form until incorporated much later in our *Republic*. Books VIII and IX of our *Republic* are an obvious candidate. The opening of Book VIII is very awkwardly safety-pinned on to Books IV and V, with no reference to Books VI and VII intervening. Nothing in the building of the Ideal State had prepared us for the disheartening news that despite its promised inherent stability it was after all doomed to degenerate through oligarchy and democracy to tyranny (see Book VI, 497 D). Nor in Book VIII do we hear a word about the sons of the rulers and guardians benefiting from the higher education described in Book VII. The crucial transformation of the governing class from being property-less to being propertied is only very hurriedly described in 547 B and 548 A–B. The collapse of the communal family is not even mentioned. When Plato originally composed what is now Book VIII of the *Republic* he was not thinking of an inevitable decline of his Callipolis. He was diagnosing the actual downfalls of ordinary Greek aristocracies, and warning their opponents of the inevitable culmination of their opposition in the horrors of tyranny. It is as factual political diagnosis that Aristotle criticizes Books VIII and IX in his *Politics* V 10.

Book IX's opprobrious treatment of the tyrant must antedate Plato's honorific invitation to Syracuse and his friendly and perhaps munificent treatment by its young tyrant, to whom he pays his high tribute in the *Laws* 710–11. If the original version of Books VIII and IX was composed before Plato's invitation to Sicily in 369 or 368, it could have been composed near to the *Gorgias*. The colour and temperature of the political sentiments of the two compositions, especially as they concern the Democratic State and the Democratic Man, are very similar. If so, it would be surprising if democratic politicians and their constituents had not cried κακηγορία.

Another stretch of our *Republic*, in Book VI 487–96, on The Worthlessness of Actual Philosophers, seems to have a certain self-containedness; and its concluding justification for the abstention of the true philosopher from active politics rings very much like those given in the *Gorgias* and *Apology*, and in the *Seventh* and *Fifth Letters*. If this stretch had been delivered to the public, the artisans and tradesmen could hardly not have protested at their denigration at 495 B–496 A. We, two thousand years later, cannot read without vicarious shame the blistering words of the pupil of Socrates about the would-be philosophers who come from humble homes and have associations with trades and crafts. It should have provoked a prosecution for defamation; so perhaps it did.

Finally, the first half of Book X of our *Republic* on the damage done by the poets makes no pretence at pertinence to the argument which it protractedly interrupts. This stretch, *minus* its rather perfunctory attachment to the Theory of Forms, had surely existed in some shape or other either as a separate discourse or more likely as the *finale* of the attack on the poets and dramatists which begins in Book II of our *Republic* and which also seems to break the thread of the argument. There is no mention of this topic in Socrates' résumé at the beginning of the *Timaeus*; or in Aristotle's résumé in *Politics* II; or in the summary at the beginning of *Republic* VIII. If this attack on Homer and poetry had existed at the required time, the poets and rhapsodes would have had very good cause, not by itself provided by the *Ion*, for thinking that their profession was being damagingly slighted. For Plato demands the extrusion from the State of tragedians, comedy-writers and poets, including Homer.

It may be objected that if Plato had in, say, 372-371 been penalized for certain dialogues or other published discourses, he could not then have incorporated these same discourses in our *Republic* a few years later without expecting to suffer even more stringent penalties. In Chapter II, 4 it is argued on mostly independent grounds that the two mammoth dialogues, our *Republic* and our *Laws*, were not meant to be issued or delivered to the general public. They were meant for dissemination solely within some reliably private clubs or coteries, the members of which were politically on Plato's side. Before Plato's death neither the Athenian public nor the Academy heard or read our *Republic*. It was known only inside certain closed circles of right-minded Athenians.

4. PLATO'S CO-DEFENDANTS

If the prosecution for defamation was a prosecution of Plato for dialogues and perhaps other discourses that he had composed and delivered, why should some of his 'associates and relatives' have been joined with him in the prosecution, as the *Helen* 1 and the *Gorgias* 508 C and 509 D indicate? It is difficult to think of a satisfactory answer. The members of Plato's circle were doubtless in political ill-odour; we can picture the populace grumbling: 'Every one of them an Alcibiades or a Critias and all of them full of money.' Though the charge against them was, on some pretext or other, the charge of defamation, their real offences were those of all aristocrats and plutocrats. But some plausible pretext must have existed as well.

One possibility which should be considered, partly for independent reasons, is that during the 370's Plato was teaching his upper-class young men not only the craft of elenctic disputation but also, in some shape or other, political 'science'; and that it was the tenor of this latter teaching that provided part of the gravamen of the charges that the democratic politicians made against Plato and his associates.

In his *Helen* 9–10 Isocrates grumbles at some people who 'try to persuade us that they possess the science, *episteme*, of political matters, though they take no part in practical politics'; at the end of his *Letter to Dionysius* he sneers at some people 'whose statecraft has been but guesswork, though they have acquired great renown'; and in his *To Nicocles* 51 he refers to teachers of philosophy 'who dispute about the proper training-exercises of the mind, of whom some claim that their students will get this training through eristic disputations, others that they will get it through political discourses...'.

Isocrates' *Helen* seems to be a sustained retort to Plato's

Gorgias; and it is in the *Gorgias* 521 D that Socrates makes his astonishing claim to a near monopoly of the genuine art and even the practice of statesmanship. In the same passage Socrates surprisingly seems to refer to some occasional public speeches that he delivers, which, being medicinal, are unpalatable to the people. What public speeches?

If it is Plato at whom Isocrates is girding, then the questions arise, What shape did Plato's political teaching take? How had he acquired great renown for his politics? Did Plato, like Isocrates, deliver his political ideas in public speeches? For Plato's early dialogues are not only almost entirely unpolitical, but they are designed to terminate in the refutations of answerers' theses. Out of them no positive doctrines and, *a fortiori*, no positive political doctrines can be extracted. On the other hand, Plato's *Menexenus*, stripped of its conversational setting, is an orthodox funeral oration; the speeches that are put into Socrates' mouth in the *Apology* and *Phaedrus* are the reverse of amateurish; the myths at the end of the *Gorgias* and *Republic* are flights of homiletic eloquence; and the *Symposium* is a sequence of speeches. The *Critias*, *Timaeus*, the original *Laws*, and, inferentially, the original *Ideal State* were addresses, not conversations. Plato did know how to compose addresses. Well, then, did Plato during the 370's teach politics by teaching his young men to compose political orations? And did he deliver to Athens political orations of his own? In a word, did he do just what Isocrates did?—with the differences (*a*) that he also taught dialectic; (*b*) that in his orations he did not avoid saying highly unpopular things; (c) that he did not charge tuition-fees; (d) that his speeches were even remoter than those of Isocrates from immediate practical politics; and (e) that his orations were uniformly unsuccessful.

In the *Politicus* 299 the Eleatic Stranger speaks ironically of the need for a law to prevent anyone from corrupting the young men by teaching them unorthodox political seamanship and medicine, with the extreme penalties for infraction. He purports to cite the phrase 'stargazer... loquacious sophist', μετεωρολόγον, ἀδολέσχην τινὰ σοφιστήν. The same phrase, or near variants of it, occurs also in the *Phaedrus* 269 E, the *Parmenides* 135 D and *Republic* 488 E, 489 C, as being a vulgar sneer at the true philosopher. Its origin seems to be Isocrates' phrase in his *Against the Sophists* 8 at the expense of teachers of eristic or dialectic, ἀδολεσχία καὶ μικρολογία, repeated in his *Antidosis* 262. The sneer obviously rankled with Plato. The youth-corrupting teacher in the *Politicus* 299, who can hardly not be Plato, had taught political heresies to students and been severely penalized for it.

In the *Laws* 634 D–635 A the Athenian Stranger proposes to prohibit by law any investigations by young men into the merits or demerits of their own State. This time there is no irony. Plato here recommends the exclusion of young men from political discussions, though he differentially compliments their seniors by requiring that such discussions shall be prosecuted without inhibition by the elderly men and in particular by the members of the Nocturnal Council (951–2, 962–5). It is argued in Chapter II that the *Laws* was intended for consumption only by middle-aged and elderly men. Its congenial ban on political studies for their juniors would have had no point unless such studies had existed and caused troubles.

If Plato did combine the teaching of the composition of orations with the teaching of elenctic disputation, he would have been doing what Protagoras had done before him, what Antisthenes did, and what, in and after the 350's, Aristotle did. According to Favorinus and Idomeneus, even Socrates had taught rhetoric. Did he teach Plato rhetoric? If not, who did? That training in the Art of Discourse should include training both in the Art of Oratory and in the Art of Argumentation was a familiar idea before Plato and after Plato. Aristotle's *Art of Rhetoric* and *Topics* are closely interlocking training treatises. In the *Euthydemus* we are introduced to the two sophists as men who had until recently been teachers of, among other things, forensic oratory but have recently concentrated on eristic disputation. Gorgias and Isocrates, in omitting to teach the Art of Argumentation, were departing from a familiar pattern. Isocrates' frequent objurgations against this teaching may have been partly defensive. Perhaps some of his own pupils complained, 'Why must we go without any training in argumentation?'

This suggestion that in the 370's Plato was teaching his young men both dialectic and politics, the latter *via* instruction in the composition of political orations, seems at first sight totally irreconcilable with the central theme of Plato's own *Gorgias*. This dialogue is, and is taken by Isocrates to be, an attack on rhetoric. How could Plato be at the same moment a teacher of oratory, a producer of orations and the vehement critic of the art or knack of rhetoric?

If we look at the *Gorgias* more carefully, we find Socrates not only attacking popular oratory, but also contrasting with it an oratory of a quite other and this time valuable sort, namely medicinal and therefore unpopular oratory. The latter should exist, though it virtually does not yet exist. 'Socrates' is its solitary practitioner. It is this medicinal oratory that is 'genuine rhetoric', ἡ ἀληθινὴ ῥητορική (517A). Socrates says at 521D–E that his own speeches are of this latter sort, so when he is brought up for trial he 'will be like a doctor tried by a bench of children on a charge brought by a cook'. This genuine, medicinal oratory is mentioned in several places in the *Gorgias* (namely 480C–D, 502E–503A, 504D–E, 508B–C, 517A, 521A, 521D–522B, 527C–D; cf. *Politicus* 304A). The orator of the right kind teaches the people what is really for its good, however unwelcome this tuition may be; the orators of the wrong kind persuade the people of what it is already inclined to, however deleterious or wrong its predilections are.

Plato, then, in his *Gorgias* is explicitly championing one sort of oratory; and as his Socrates prophesies that he will be prosecuted and condemned for practising just this medicinal oratory, with no mention made of irreligion, we can use the *Gorgias* as a source of direct evidence that Plato himself did deliver orations on social and political matters, that these did bring him great unpopularity, and that his prosecution was partly motivated by the resentment of the Demos and its leaders against the author of

these unpalatable orations. The *Gorgias* does not provide
evidence that Plato taught his young men to compose
political orations, or, therefore, to compose unpopular
orations. The tenuous evidence for this is to be found in
passages already cited from Isocrates and from Plato's own
Politicus and *Laws*.

In the *Apology* (29D–30A, 31A–B, 36C, 39D) Socrates
talks of the exhortations and reproaches that he delivers to
his fellow-Athenians. Yet in the eristic dialogues outside
the terminal *Gorgias* there is almost nothing that could
qualify as civic exhortation or civic reproach. If here, as in
many other places, 'Socrates' is Plato, then Plato might be
referring not to his eristic dialogues but to other public
discourses in which he had told Athens what was good for
her. The fact that, apart from the Funeral Oration in the
Menexenus, not one of the inferred orations survives, in its
original shape, would be easy to explain. The orations,
being antipopular, were unpopular; being unpopular, they
were unsuccessful; and, being unsuccessful, they were not
issued as books. But in the *Republic* the attack on Homer
and the account of the Decline of the State might well be
conversationalized revisions of earlier unpopular speeches;
and the *Republic* might embody other such ingredients
as well. If the extraneous discourses, ἔξωθεν λόγοι, with
which according to Aristotle 'Socrates' filled out the
Republic, included not only such dialogue-fragments as
the *Thrasymachus* but also recastings of rejected addresses,
this could explain the precipitous decline from the conversational vitality of the *Euthydemus*, *Meno*, *Gorgias*,
Phaedo and *Republic* Book I to the conversational debility of

most of the last nine books of the *Republic*. Where Callicles, Simmias and Thrasymachus are persons, Adeimantus and Glaucon are nearly all the time cardboard dummies. Few readers can recollect which of the two is Socrates' interlocutor at the end of Book VIII, say. Conversational parts were not designed for these two speakers. Rather the speakers were intercalated in order to give the show of conversation to what had originally been composed as monologue. In the *Laws* we see in an uncompleted condition the same process of conversion from monologue to dialogue. Where the conversion has been made, the interlocutors again fail to capture our interest or our memory. Adeimantus and Glaucon are nearly as featureless as Megillus and Cleinias, and for the same reason. The composer of mimes has here been ousted by the composer of allocutions. There can be no cut and thrust in an allocution, even when this has been remodelled into the outward shape of a dialogue. It is no accident that the *Republic* is apt to be the favourite Platonic dialogue of those who prefer homilies to arguments. It was for them that the bulk of our *Republic* had originally been composed.

Well then, if some of Plato's past or present students had delivered similar anti-popular orations, this might account for their being joined with Plato in the inferred prosecution for defamation.

It is an objection to this guess, however, that Isocrates, in his *Helen* 1, connects the legal trouble into which Plato's associates got specifically with their training in eristic and not with their conjectural training in oratory, which he does not mention. It is another objection to this guess that

Plato, in the *Republic* 539 C, connects the scandal, whatever it was, solely with the premature participation by the young men in eristic. The *Apology* 23 C–D and 41 C points in the same direction.

The one remaining hypothesis seems to be that some members of Plato's circle had also published impolitic eristic dialogues. The two Thebans, Simmias and Cebes, are credited by Diogenes Laertius with dialogues, of which we know only the titles. *Letter* XIII shows that Cebes was as late as 366–365 on friendly terms with Plato.

Diogenes Laertius also credits with dialogues an Athenian Socratic named 'Glaucon'; and scholars have conjectured that this Glaucon is identical with the brother of Plato, who, with their brother, Adeimantus, occupies the role of Socrates' answerer in the *Republic*. Plato's two brothers are represented in the *Republic* (487 B, 505 A, 507 A and 532 D) as belonging to Socrates' circle. Two Athenian Socratics of the name of 'Glaucon' seem too many. Since Glaucon, the dialogue-writer, entitled one of his compositions *Aristophanes*, this was presumably composed after Aristophanes' death in or after the 380's. So this Glaucon would have been composing dialogues roughly when Plato was doing so. Unlike Adeimantus, his brother Glaucon is not mentioned in the *Apology* 34 as attending Socrates' trial. Perhaps he was present in another capacity at the trial of 'Socrates', that is of Plato. Plato's brother, Glaucon, is described by Xenophon, in his *Memorabilia* III, as having rhetorical and political ambitions. From his family we can guess what was the complexion of his politics, and perhaps infer it from the *Republic* 548 E–549 A.

In the *Republic* 548 E he is credited with φιλονικία, the love of victory which is regularly identified by Plato and Aristotle with polemical zest in eristic disputations. As in the *Gorgias* Socrates speaks of having to defend himself, his friends and his relatives, the idea suggests itself that Plato and his brother Glaucon, with others, were prosecuted for publishing eristic dialogues disparaging influential persons or groups. Glaucon's role as minor hero in the *Republic* might then, like the roles of Simmias and Cebes in the *Phaedo*, be honorifically intended by Plato. This hypothesis is riddled with many irremediable 'perhapses', but it possesses just enough plausibility to make it worth proffering.

5. EPILOGUE

We are bound to find distasteful the idea here presented that Plato in his *Gorgias*, *Apology*, *Crito* and *Phaedo* is not trying to be a Boswell. For it entails first that the real Socrates is much further from our ken than we had imagined, since our chief picture of him has now to be discounted as, in large measure, a camouflaged self-justification of the painter; and second that though Plato himself comes much nearer into our ken, he is now neither the Great Disciple nor the Great Teacher. Moreover, if the mission that Plato is vindicating is Plato's mission and if the protest against the martyrdom is the protest of the martyr himself, we are nagged by the Anglo-Saxon feeling that the man who protests however justly on his own behalf is the man with a grievance. The passion with which these dialogues are written is not an impersonal or even a vicarious passion. Though the distance between the egotism of Isocrates' *Antidosis* and the serious call of Plato's *Apology* is very wide, still it is not infinitely wide, and we wish that it were. However, our reluctance that the facts should be so is no argument for them not being so. It may spur us to look for such arguments, but it cannot do duty for them.

For philosophers the transformation of Plato from something superhuman to something human is compensated by the transformation of Plato from the sage who was born at his destination to the philosopher who had to search for his destination. We lose a Nestor, but we gain an Ulysses.

CHAPTER VI

THE DISAPPEARANCE OF THE ERISTIC DIALOGUE

I. THE ABANDONMENT OF THE ELENCHUS

By the end of the 370's Plato had written and recited to Athenian audiences about a dozen dialogues in which Socrates debates with his interlocutors according to the Socratic Method. He plies his interlocutors with chains of questions, their successive replies to which entrap them in self-contradictions. The theses which they had begun by championing are by their own admission demolished by answers voluntarily given by themselves to interrogations strategically deployed by Socrates. In the *Euthydemus* it is the two sophists who are the questioners; Socrates is for once a hapless answerer. Dialogues of this structure can be called 'eristic dialogues'. Plato's eristic dialogues are: the *Laches, Lysis, Charmides, Euthyphro, Hippias Major, Hippias Minor, Ion,* [*Alcibiades* I and II], *Protagoras, Euthydemus, Gorgias* and *Meno*. Book I of our *Republic* is also of this structure, and seems to be the torso of what, if finished, would have been the *Thrasymachus*, an eristic dialogue of the same *genre* as the *Protagoras* and *Gorgias*.

At this point, when at the acme of his powers, suddenly and apparently in the middle of composing his *Thrasymachus* Plato stops producing eristic dialogues. The dialogues which he now writes mostly contain argumentation, but the argumentation does not often, until the *Parmenides*, terminate in elenchi. The checkmate has nearly vanished. Socrates' interlocutors are now only occasionally more than nodders, and the dramatic form of Plato's dialogues becomes more and more of a pretence. They have no dénouements. They are conversations, not combats. A major revolution has occurred, and we ought to wonder what has overcome what.

It is argued in Chapter v that this abandonment of the eristic dialogue synchronizes with Plato's enforced abandonment of the eristic exercise itself. He may no longer conduct eristic Moots for the young men. His dialectical occupation has gone. But why does the suppression of his actual participation in elenctic debates involve the suppression of his dramatic representations of such debates? Even if Plato may no longer be the teacher and practitioner of the Socratic Method, why can he no longer be the Boswell or the Landor of the exploits in it of his Socrates?

We cannot suppose that the ban on Plato's conduct of eristic Moots carried with it a ban on producing Socratic dialogues of one pattern, combined with leave to produce Socratic dialogues of other patterns. In what terms could Plato have been told that he might represent Socrates as arguing against someone else's theory that the Soul is a Harmony or that Knowledge is Sense-Perception, but not as forcing his interlocutors to eat their words? Or that Socrates might ask himself questions, but not ask his interlocutors questions, unless untactical ones like rhetorical or pedagogic questions? Anyhow Plato in his non-eristic dialogues has no qualms in pretending that the Socratic

Method is still being employed. In the *Republic* VI 487 B–C Adeimantus complains that the Socratic draughts-playing defeats but does not convince its victims, although in fact Socrates has not played eristic draughts since Book I. In the *Theaetetus* Socrates repeatedly professes that his role is merely that of the midwife of ideas, and even then the demolisher of most of these unpromising babies. Yet the dialogue incorporates only a little questioner-answerer confutation, and Socrates produces and develops positive views of his own. Conversely, the *Parmenides*, Part II, is an unmitigated questioner-answerer debate; there is a short elenctic passage in the *Phaedo*; and there is a slight revival of questioner-answerer debating in the *Cratylus*.

We cannot suppose that Plato's audiences, which surely consisted largely of discussion-hungry lads, suddenly lost their taste for eristic dialogues merely because their author had got into judicial hot water. Rather we must suppose that there was a close internal connexion between Plato's activity as the conductor of eristic Moots and his activity as the playwright of eristic dialogues. Because he was debarred from continuing the former activity he was disabled from continuing the latter activity. But what sort of internal connexion could there have been between the two activities? If an ex-soldier can continue to write war-novels, or if Boswell can, after Johnson's death, compose his *Life of Samuel Johnson*, Ll.D. from notes, letters and memories, why is Plato disabled from depicting the Socratic Method in action by his own enforced exclusion from it?

2. THE ORGANIZATION OF THE ERISTIC MOOT

A set disputation begins with the adoption by the answerer of the thesis that he will defend and the questioner will try to demolish. The match terminates in victory for the questioner if his sequences of questions elicit from the answerer admissions inconsistent with that thesis. The answerer is victorious if he has made no such admissions by the moment when time is up. It is not necessary that the answerer believes his thesis or the questioner disbelieves it. What is at stake is only whether the case against the thesis is unrebutted or rebutted. Disputants are expected to practise themselves both in attacking and in defending the same thesis on different occasions. They are not adherents, but advocates. Indeed it is efficient advocacy that they are learning.

From what sources are these theses drawn? At least at a later date there exist written collections of theses. Diogenes Laertius credits Xenocrates, Aristotle and Theophrastus with dozens of books of theses. It is natural to suppose that the theses which prove in practice to make good Moot points are assembled into a common stock of re-employable debating themes. In Plato's *Euthydemus* the two sophists operate with their own battery of theses for which they have previously prepared themselves with effective confutation-gambits. One of their most paradoxical theses, which embodies a genuine philosophical *aporia*, may derive from Antisthenes or, as Socrates says, from some followers or even forerunners of Protagoras (286 c).

One regularly recurring thesis is the thesis that virtue can or, alternatively, cannot be taught. This thesis is at or near the heart of the debates in Plato's *Laches*, *Protagoras*, *Euthydemus* and *Meno*, as well as in the *Alcibiades I*, the *Theages* and the fragmentary *Cleitophon*, whoever wrote these dialogues. Diogenes Laertius ascribes books on this theme to Simon, Crito, Antisthenes and Xenocrates. At the end of his *Against the Sophists*, written in about 390, Isocrates forcibly rejects the thesis that virtue can be taught. Earlier even than this the *Dissoi Logoi* 6 presents arguments *pro* and *contra* this thesis, and, since Plato in his *Protagoras* 328 puts one of its arguments *pro* the thesis, as well as one of its illustrative examples, into the mouth of Protagoras, it may be that Plato knew that Protagoras was the original author of this *pro* argument and perhaps of the thesis itself.

In the *Crito* 46–9 Socrates seems to be reminding Crito of theses which had often been argued before and had been either established or else refuted on those previous occasions. It looks therefore as if eristic Moots, whether conducted by Plato or by anyone else, sometimes drew their theses from a presumably accumulating general fund or stock. Plato did not, or did not always, invent the disputation-themes for his young men to debate; he adopted them and sometimes used them again and again, when they proved to make for good hunting. The questions debated did not have to be Platonic questions, even supposing that during this period any such questions yet existed. We have no evidence that they did yet exist. For nearly every dialogue-theme that Plato uses, we can find other dialogue writers who compose dialogues with the same theme.

The Hippocratic writings unexpectedly give us another piece of evidence, in the passage already referred to on p. 117. It is convenient to cite it again.

Given the same debaters and the same audience, the same man never wins in the discussion three times in succession, but now one is victor, now another, now he who happens to have the most glib tongue in the face of the crowd. Yet it is right that a man who claims correct knowledge about the facts should maintain his own argument victorious always, if his knowledge be knowledge of reality and if he set it forth correctly. But in my opinion such men by their lack of understanding overthrow themselves in the words of their very discussions...

This passage shows us that organized eristic matches were familiar things before and perhaps well before the death of Socrates; that the matches were held before audiences, and it was the audiences that decided who had won (for audiences see Plato's *Sophist* 230 C, *Gorgias* 474 A, 487 B and Aristotle's *Topics* 1169 b 31, 1174 a 37); and that the same disputant might, before the same audience, attack or else defend the same thesis on several successive occasions. Now when the thesis thus remained constant, the disputants could and therefore presumably would develop their arguments to it by discarding or mending arguments which were rebutted last time and by repeating with or without improvements arguments which had worked well hitherto. Like the chess-players' 'combinations', tried argument-sequences can be learned by heart and studied for their strengths and weaknesses, and the successful ones can, *en bloc*, become parts of the common repertoire of all who may ever debate the same thesis. Naturally for this evolution, consolidation and dissemination of effective argument-sequences to be possible the courses of past debates on the same thesis must be remembered or recorded.

3. THE MINUTING OF DEBATES

We hear about the recording from Aristotle. In his *Topics* 1105 b 12 Aristotle advises the students of dialectic to make extracts from 'the written handbooks of argument', τῶν γεγραμμένων λόγων, and draw up 'sketch-lists', διαγρα-φάς, of them upon each several kind of subject, putting them down under separate headings, for example 'On Good' or 'On Life...'. Later, at 1163 b 17, he advises them

to know by heart arguments upon those questions which are of most frequent recurrence... You should try, moreover, to master the heads under which other arguments tend to fall. For just as in geometry it is useful to be practised in the elements and in arithmetic to have the multiplication table up to ten at one's fingers' ends... likewise also in arguments it is a great advantage to be well up in regard to first principles, ἀρχαί, and to have a thorough knowledge of premises, προτάσεις, at the tip of one's tongue... So these habits too will make a man readier in reasoning, because he has his premises classified before his mind's eye, each under its number... Records of discussions should be made in a universal form, even though one has argued only some particular case, for this will enable one to turn a single rule into several. (*Topics*, trans. G. R. G. Mure.)

At the very end of his *De Sophisticis Elenchis* Aristotle, describing how he had no precursors in the construction of the theory or the methodology of questioner-answerer disputation, says that the money-making teachers of eristic had given their pupils to learn by heart particular arguments *pro* and *contra* particular theses, which is like presenting someone with some shoes when what he wants is to acquire the science of the care of the feet. They taught arguments: not how to argue. The *Dissoi Logoi* seems to exemplify the sort of Manual of Eristic against which Aristotle inveighs, if it is not the manual which he has specially in mind.

In the *Metaphysics* XI 1063 b 13 Aristotle speaks of the *aporiai* that have been 'handed down', παραδεδομέναι, which suggests that in his own practice, when he assembles a battery of *aporiai* on a particular theme, he includes, besides specimens excogitated by himself, specimens recorded in the Academy and elsewhere. Their unevenness of quality supports this suggestion. In Book III Aristotle ascribes a few specified *aporiai* to contemporaries of his own.

It is clear from all this that minutes of dialectical matches were written down and that these records were studied, abstracted from and memorized by students of dialectic. The teaching of eristic was subserved by Moot-Hansards, and the learning by heart of arguments and argument-sequences was facilitated by numbering off the points recorded in these minutes. Such numbering off can be found once or twice in the *Dissoi Logoi*, and Aristotle recommends it.

4. DIALOGUES AND THE MINUTES OF DEBATES

So now the question raises its head: How were the dialectical dialogues of Plato and of the other composers of Socratic dialogues related to the actual occurrences of eristic Moots? Did Plato just invent out of his head the interrogation chains of his Socrates and the defence-manœuvres of his Protagoras, Polus or Thrasymachus? Or had he encountered them in operation or himself deployed or redeployed them in recent disputations? In particular, had the outlines of them and even their individual steps been recorded, perhaps by Plato himself, as the minutes of those disputations?

In the *Protagoras* we find a few argument-moves repeated from the *Laches*; and an important and quite powerful argument is put into Protagoras' mouth which, highly compressed, had already been employed in the *Dissoi Logoi* 6. It occurs with an improvement in *Alcibiades I* 111. The *Meno* inherits from the *Protagoras* the Socratic argument for the unteachability of virtue, namely that the most distinguished Athenian statesmen did not in fact manage to impart their qualities to their own sons. The argument is used also in *Alcibiades I* 118. But perhaps most significant of all, in the *Protagoras* 352–60 we find a sustained and careful argument-sequence for the Hedonistic Calculus. Yet not even in adjacent dialogues does Plato seem to accept the conclusion of this argument or to be much interested in the *pros* and *cons* of hedonism. In the *Gorgias* and *Phaedo* Socrates is an anti-hedonist. So Plato seems to be ready to produce in a dialogue and to credit to his Socrates an argument which did not come, so to speak, out of his own philosophical heart, if at this stage he yet had such a heart. So perhaps he had encountered the argument, or perhaps he had in the course of a series of recent Moots himself experimentally constructed it. He chronicles it because it had proved in recent practice to have some potency. At this stage Plato and his young men are interested in match-winning and match-losing arguments; they are not yet primarily interested in tenets. The objective of an eristic match is the demolition of a thesis, not the solution of a problem. For them a good argument is a knock-down one.

We need therefore to consider seriously the possibility that, to start with, the composition of a Socratic dialogue, whether by Plato or by Aeschines, say, was much less the invention of an imaginary questioner-answerer duel than the dramatization of an actual duel; or, more likely, the dramatization of 'rounds' culled out of a progression of actual debates on a particular thesis. A Socratic dialogue may have been, to start with, a dramatized documentary, compiled out of a run of fresh Moot-memoranda, supplemented by the memories of the composer and of his fellow-participants. In the *Lysis* the dramatic stretches are so uncunningly tacked on to the interrogation-stretches that in reading the latter we might well be reading the raw verbatim records of actual Moot-rounds. Sometimes we find Socrates switching from the culmination of one 'combination' to the inception of a new one with such abruptness that we get the impression that these argument-combinations had existed before the dramatic story had been composed that was to incorporate them (e.g. *Gorgias* 491 D, 495 C, 497 D, 499 C; *Protagoras* 332 A, 351 B).

Plato's *Euthydemus* is obviously a collection of sophists' actual stratagems and teasers. One of these is declared by Socrates to have originated with the Protagoreans or their forerunners. Two or three more seem to have been extracted out of the *Dissoi Logoi*. In this dialogue Plato has not invented all of the trick-arguments that he assembles. Here his invention certainly has been, in part, that of the dramatizer of debate-gambits that he had not invented.

Doubtless this dialogue was composed with the double didactic purpose of explaining to Athens the unobvious distinction between prize-fighting eristic and tutorial dialectic; and of interesting the young students and would-be students of dialectic in the tasks of detecting and re-butting fallacies that were already extant and already giving trouble. What Aristotle tries to do scientifically in his *De Sophisticis Elenchis* Plato tries to do dramatically in his *Euthydemus*. If so, then it becomes reasonable to suppose that Plato's other eristic dialogues were designed at least partly for the same recipients and with the kindred purposes of giving to the young men unforgettable, because dramatized specimens of questioner-answerer disputation, and of showing to the play-loving Athenians pedagogically serious eristic in cut-and-thrust action.

For these purposes, while the dramatization would need to be original, the representation of the argument-sequences deployed would not need to be original; it could just be faithful. The arguments would need to have proved to be unrebuttable or rebuttable by having in live disputations been unrebutted or rebutted. Actual success and actual failure before live Moot-audiences were the prime tests of strength and weakness. Naturally Plato would have carefully sifted, polished, compressed, expanded and arranged these already extant argument-combinations to suit his dramatic ends.

5. WHY THE ERISTIC DIALOGUE VANISHED

A necessarily speculative answer to our original problem is, then, this. The reason why the suppression of Plato's practice of the Socratic Method involved the abandonment of the eristic dialogue was that Plato now had no more Moot-records or memories to dramatize. His home source of elenctic arguments dried up when his personal participation in dialectical debates stopped. Hitherto he himself had, in the course of live tutorial disputations, been the constructor of some argument-sequences and the re-employer, improver, target, critic, umpire and chronicler of others. In composing his eristic dialogues he had drawn on minutes and memories of the argument-combinations that had progressively developed and crystallized through sequences of such disputations. But he had not yet learned, since he had not yet had to learn, to excogitate arguments to be notionally pitted against merely imagined counter-arguments; any more than most chess-players have learned notionally to counter the imagined moves of merely imagined opponents; or any more than most boxers have learned to think up feints and parries in the course of their shadow-boxing. At this stage arguments are team-products. They are not the handiwork or property of individuals.

The *Crito* and the *Phaedo* seem both to belong to the years immediately following upon Plato's exile from eristic debating. Both embody acknowledged réchauffés of arguments that had been used before, in the *Gorgias*, the *Meno*, and the *Alcibiades I*, as if Plato's fund of argument-sequences is not being replenished.

6. FROM ERISTIC TO PHILOSOPHY

Commentators have sometimes expressed disappointment that these early dialogues terminate in the mere demolitions of theses defended by Socrates' interlocutors. On the hypothesis here put forward a Socratic dialogue is and is meant to be the dramatized Hansard of an elenctic debate; nothing but a demolition, that is, an elenchus, provides such a composition with its needed dramatic dénouement. Unless the questioner drives his answerer into surrendering his position, the duel ends undramatically in a mere draw. Plato wrote these dialogues not from an interest in what we would classify as philosophical problems, but from an interest, only partly pedagogic, in serious eristic debating and in the mimes that he composed out of these debates. He was not trying without success to resolve philosophical *aporiai*. He was trying with great success to depict eristic tournaments ending in acknowledged checkmates. It is the checkmate that proves the cogency of the arguments. Plato's eristic dialogues are instructional models of eristic manœuvres that had in recent fact proved efficacious. Plato is interested in elenchi both as a dramatist and as a match-player and coach. His interest in the resolution of *aporiai*, that is, in philosophical problems, is still only embryonic. In his pupils and his public audiences it is not yet even embryonic.

We with wisdom after the event can see, as the late Plato and Aristotle saw, that though the sorts of arguments which are effective in confuting answerers are the sorts of arguments which are effective in resolving philosophical cruces, there are radical differences between the directions of the deployments of these arguments, according as they are directed towards the knocking-out of an adversary or as they are directed towards the resolution of an *aporia*. To have learned to tie someone else up in conceptual knots is to have learned part of what is needed in order to untie conceptual knots. But victories are one thing; discoveries are another, as is said in the *Philebus* 14 B. Theses are argued *against*, but solutions of problems are argued *for*. An elenctic debate terminates in an *aporia*. Philosophy starts from *aporiai*.

While composing the latest of his eristic dialogues Plato was beginning, for example in the *Gorgias*, to be aware of the differences between arguing against an answerer and arguing against an *impasse*; between trying to rebut an opponent and arguing something out with oneself; between winning a battle of wits and solving a problem. In the *Hippias Major* Socrates fictionally personifies his own intellectual conscience. It is this which must be convinced of the goodness of an argument; and not the easily satisfied sophist or man in the street. The notion of a valid argument is just beginning to separate itself off from the notion of an unrebutted argument. But the answerer's surrender is still the solid criterion of the inescapability of an elenchus. What other criterion could there, in the beginning of things, have been? How could even that criterion have become a definite and unsubjective one but for the existence of the rule-governed exercise of questioner-answerer duelling under the eyes of a vigilant, practised and sporting jury? Anachronistically we have all assumed that

Plato just knew from the start the differences between good and bad *pro* and *contra* arguments. We have not wondered how he or anyone else learned to look for these differences or to satisfy other people that they were there. It was the debating-match with its rules and its controls that gave the lessons. These Socratic dialogues reflect the daily exercises which gave to Plato and his associates the training and hence the knowledge. After Zeno it was Plato who introduced systematized argument, that is, dialectic, into philosophy. We have uninquisitively failed to ask what trained his dialectical powers.

In his *Topics* 1163 b 3 Aristotle surprises us by advising his students of dialectic that if they cannot find anyone else to argue with they should argue with themselves. Our very surprise that Aristotle should trouble to recommend this, to us, familiar solitary exercise shows how much we have been enabled to take for granted by Plato and Aristotle, who had had to find out this secret. It was just his dramatization of chronicled debates that put Plato, and then mankind in the way of *pro* and *contra* thinking in the absence of adversaries. It always is playing, including romancing, that first loosens the grip of the usual. Plato's initial dependence on the presence of flesh and blood opponents was partly overcome by his playwright's art of putting rearrangements of recorded arguments into the mouths of merely imagined adversaries. It enabled him first to rethink recorded arguments and later to think out new arguments enjoying match-free lives of their own. Plato the composer of dialectical mimes eventually gave to Plato the nascent philosopher detachment from the reverberating actualities of last week's Moot. But while he was still composing his eristic dialogues he had not yet taught himself the art of solitary debating. He could not yet 'hear' the answer unless he could hear an answerer. He was not yet sure of the conclusiveness of a rebuttal, unless the jury was sure of it.

In the *Gorgias* 513C–D Callicles concedes that Socrates has argued correctly, yet he does not believe what he says. Socrates replies, '...if we come to examine these same questions more than once, and better, you will believe'. The two-party debate has to be gone through again and again. It is not even suggested that Callicles might reach conviction by private rumination over its steps and stages (cf. *Lysis* 211 A–B; *Meno* 85 C–D; *Philebus* 24 E; *Republic* VII 532 D).

At the end of the *Apology* Socrates says that the supreme happiness that he hopes for from the Next World is to be able 'to examine and investigate the people there, as I do here, to find out who among them is wise and who thinks he is when he is not... To debate with them, διαλέγεσθαι, associate with them and examine them would be immeasurable happiness.' To be Inquisitor in eristic matches through eternity! But when Plato composes the *Phaedo* 65–9 he no longer tethers inquiry to inquisitions (cf. *Symposium* 209–11).

What forced Plato to find out the secret of solitary debating was the suppression of his practice of conducting eristic Moots with the young men. It was his exile from this duelling that drove Plato, though only after years of frustration, into solitary *pro* and *contra* reasoning. Plato did not write the eristic dialogues because he was a philosopher; he became a philosopher because he could no longer participate in questioner-answerer Moots, or any longer be their dramatic chronicler. His judges broke Plato's heart, but they made him in the end a self-moving philosopher. No longer had the Other Voice to be the voice of another person. No longer was the objective the driving of another person into an *impasse*; it was now the extraction of oneself from an *impasse*.

The Boy-Love *motif* is very strong in the eristic dialogues. We find it in the *Lysis*, *Charmides*, *Protagoras*, [*Alcibiades*], *Euthydemus*, *Gorgias* and *Meno*. We hear hardly a whisper of it in the later dialogues with the two important exceptions of the *Symposium* and the *Phaedrus*. In Diotima's speech in the *Symposium* the darling of Eros is sublimated into an Otherworldly Beloved, in what sounds like a valedictory tone of voice. It is the sixty-year-old Plato's 'Farewell for Ever' to his darling twenty-year-olders. He must now think without them. He must now think alone. The much later *Phaedrus* is a new call to the twenty-year-olders, but this time not to dialectic-hungry young men, but to the rhetoric-hungry young men for whom at last the Academy is going to provide rhetoric-teaching of a philosophically fortified kind.

It seems plausible to infer from the prevalence of this *motif* in Plato's early dialogues that these dialogues were composed primarily for the ears of the young men; and that therefore their argumentative content was meant primarily for their benefit too. But of what benefit to young men could exhibitions of elenctic argumentation be unless as demonstrations of elenctic argumentation itself? What Aristotle's *Topics* teaches the theory of, the eristic dialogues teach, by examples, the practice of. Indeed the strictures which at the end of his *De Sophisticis Elenchis* Aristotle passes, with some genetic unfairness, on the early cram-books of eristic, as teaching arguments but not how to argue, could have been passed on Plato's eristic dialogues too, with the marginal exception of his *Euthydemus*. For while Plato vividly depicts Socrates and his interlocutors deploying now unrebuttable, now rebuttable arguments, he does not, save incipiently and unsystematically, extract out of them that which renders them potent or impotent. His dialogues supersede the *Dissoi Logoi*, but they do not anticipate the *Topics*.

None the less the students whom Aristotle taught in his *Topics* classes in and after the 350's had the same needs and zeals as the students whom Plato had taught in his Moots and by his dialogues in the 370's. The proficiencies that they were meant to acquire were the same. Though these did not include proficiency in what we know as philosophy, Aristotle is clear that dialectical argumentation is an indispensable preliminary training for philosophy (see Aristotle, *Metaphysics* IV 1004 b 18–27). In the end Plato is clear about this, too, in his *Parmenides* 135 C–136 E. In the 370's no such discipline as what we think of as philosophy was yet discernible from serious eristic match-play. It was first becoming clearly discernible in the 350's. Like Aristotle Plato can now treat elenctic debating as a training exercise preparatory to philosophy. Philosophy is no longer itself elenctic debating. At the end of the *Euthyde-*

mus the two sophists can still be graded as 'phil
But in the *Parmenides* a Zenonian training is c
paration for 'philosophy'.

7. ERISTIC AND THE THEORY OF FORMS

Plato's Theory of Forms appears on the scenes very quickly
after the suppression of his teaching of dialectic to young
men and the consequent cessation of his eristic dialogues at
the end of the 370's. The Forms are eloquently mentioned
in Socrates' speech in the *Symposium*, and the Theory of
Forms is expounded with relative fulness in the *Phaedo*.
Both these dialogues were composed in the year or two
before the spring of 367. More is said about the Forms in
the *Timaeus*, which was composed in Sicily in 367–366.
Books VI and VII of the *Republic*, in which the Theory of
Forms is also expounded and drawn on, would seem to
have been originally composed before the *Timaeus*, and
near to the foundation of the Academy in, say, 371–370.
When the seventeen-year-old Aristotle arrived in the
Academy in 367, the Theory of Forms was in its heyday.

It is legitimate, therefore, to speculate whether there
may not have been a causal connexion between Plato's
compulsory divorce from the practice of dialectic and his
excogitation of the Theory of Forms. Such a speculation
will have to do solely with Plato's intellectual motives and
not with any of the disparate reasons on which the Theory
is based.

Plato's traumatic separation from the practice of dialectical match-play with the young men might be expected to force him to explain to the censorious world, but

especially to himself, wherein consisted the paramount value which he placed upon this now forbidden or forsworn exercise. All the more so since not only did contemporary Athens believe that the exercise did the young men harm and not good, but Plato himself has publicly, if not wholeheartedly, to admit its demoralizing effects on the twenty-year-olders in the *Republic* VII 537–9 and therewith to exclude instruction in it from the curriculum of his own Academy.

In his *Apology* Socrates defends his vocation of practising and teaching dialectic. Yet the justifications that he there adduces for the exercise are too numerous, too factitious and too discrepant to satisfy us or, therefore, to satisfy Plato. The only impressive justification adduced is that by means of his elenctic questioning Socrates has tried to awaken Athens to her moral duties (*Apology* 29 DE, 31 B, 36 C, 39 D). Yet in fact out of the pre-*Republic* dialogues it is a single stretch of the *Gorgias* only which can be read as such a moral spur, though the *Thrasymachus* would have been another. In most of these eristic dialogues the theses debated, though often concerned with moral concepts, have no moral content and the confutations of these theses generate no messages of moral reform. How indeed could an elenchus convey or suggest any positive moral message unless, as in the *Thrasymachus*, the thesis confuted was itself a morally cynical one? Socrates does debate in the *Meno* what Virtue is and whether it can be taught, and he duly demolishes his interlocutor's answers. But Socrates has no satisfactory answers of his own to give, and there is no suggestion that his lack of answers to these questions carries with it a lack of virtue itself. Nor in the *Laches* does their inability to say what Courage is show that the old soldiers and Socrates himself are short of that quality or need to be awoken to the importance of it.

Plato knew in his bones that elenctic disputation had some important and positive heuristic value over and above the modest values of proving the Delphic Oracle wrong or right, of deflating the intellectually conceited, of rebutting cynical theses, of amusing the young men and of whetting their forensic wits. An argument-sequence too cogent for the answerer to circumvent does not lead only to the questioner's victory in the ring. The employer of it, the victim of it and the audience that follows it also learn something, and learn something over and above the mere techniques of winning such victories. Plato is already realizing this in his *Gorgias* and even in the *Hippias Major*. What then do they learn new things *about*? Well, they come to know new things, if seemingly only negative things, about Courage, say, or Beauty, or Knowledge *versus* Belief, or Teaching *versus* Persuading, or Friendship, or Justice. But what are these? Let us label them, non-committally, 'Notions', 'Ideas' or 'Concepts'. Is it worth while coming to know new things about these un-concrete matters? Reasons for maintaining that these Ideas are supreme realities, the apprehension of which constitutes Knowledge or Science *par excellence*, will be step-reasons for maintaining that the dialectical dissection of them has a supreme, theoretical title. The ontological nobility of its objects confers a heuristic nobility upon the dialectical study of them. The very investigation which democratic Athens has rejected is the coping-stone of the sciences that are to be studied by the *élite* in the Ideal State; and what makes it the coping-stone of the sciences is the ontological primacy of its objects and the cognitive primacy of the faculty by which we apprehend them (see, for example, *Republic* 511 A–C, 534 B–E). It is some corroboration of this speculation about Plato's intellectual motives that in the late dialogue, the *Parmenides* 135 C, old Parmenides, after formulating powerful objections to Socrates' Theory of Forms, concedes none the less that a total denial of the existence of Forms would utterly destroy— what?—the faculty of dialectical disputation (τὴν τοῦ διαλέγεσθαι δύναμιν. The phrase occurs also in the *Republic* 511 B, cf. 511 C, 532 D, 533 A). The existence of Forms is still envisaged as providing the desiderated vindication of the eristic Moot.

It might be a relevant fact that in the *Dissoi Logoi*, which must be a lot earlier than the earliest of Plato's dialogues, theses are argued *pro* and *contra* about the ostensible Opposites, *Good and Bad, Just and Unjust, True and False, Beautiful and Ugly, Sane and Mad, Wise and Foolish,* and, *en passant, Greater and Smaller, More and Fewer, Heavier and Lighter, Alive and Dead, Existent and Non-Existent.* Forms frequently discussed or mentioned by Plato are among the notions that had been the targets of dialectical debates for a long time before the Theory of Forms had been thought of. In the *Dissoi Logoi* some of the issues are put in this way: 'Some say that Good and Bad are different things, just as their names are different. Others say that with difference of name there goes no difference of thing.' 'Thing' is rendered once by πρᾶγμα and once, interestingly, by σῶμα. The demand that these verbal oppositions between, *inter alia*, value terms and disvalue terms signify real oppositions creates a pressure to equate the reality of the oppositions with the real thinghood of what the opposing terms signify. In Plato's picture of the adolescence of the Theory of Forms in the *Parmenides* 129–30 the young Socrates concentrates on Opposites and is nervous of admitting as Forms notions like *Man, Fire, Water, Hair* and *Mud*, which have no polar opposites. It was the dialectically charged Ideas that were the first to be endowed with Form-status.

CHAPTER VII

THE TIMETABLE

I. FOREWORD

This chapter offers a chronological *catalogue raisonné* of Plato's dialogues. No precise individual dating is suggested for any but the latest of Plato's early, eristic dialogues. Some of the middle and later dialogues have had to be somewhat arbitrarily located. The two parts of the *Parmenides* were apparently composed at considerably different dates, and it has seemed expedient to locate the dialogue as a whole with its Part II. The *Republic*, it is argued, is a relatively late conflation of pieces of which the original compositions and oral deliveries were earlier and sometimes much earlier than their conflation. It is catalogued where its conflation date seems to belong, though individual datings are also suggested for certain of its component pieces.

Conversely, the *Laws* is located where the composition date of the *Proto-Laws* belongs, and not where its revision belongs, since this revision was unfinished when Plato died.

It is also important to settle, if possible, the approximate times at which Aristotle and the Academy got access to the texts of certain dialogues, since there are reasons for thinking that Plato sometimes withheld his compositions from the copyists. While a dialogue remained uncopied or 'unwritten', members of the Academy would sometimes know it, if at all, only from having heard its solitary recital to the Athenian public.

2. THE ERISTIC DIALOGUES

The latest of Plato's eristic dialogues, namely the *Euthydemus*, *Gorgias*, *Meno* and the unfinished *Thrasymachus*, seem to have been composed pretty late in the 370's. For one thing, the *Euthydemus*, at its close, describes someone, who must be Isocrates, as a writer of political orations. Isocrates' first political oration, the *Panegyricus*, cannot be earlier than 380.

Isocrates' *Helen*, which scholars date near or at the end of the 370's, will be shown, in the section of this chapter on the *Phaedrus*, to have been a riposte to the *Gorgias*. The irritation shown by Isocrates suggests that the *Gorgias* had been published fairly recently. Similar irritation against the author of the *Gorgias* is evinced in Isocrates' *Nicocles* 1–4, which must have been composed at least a year or two after the death of Nicocles' father, Evagoras, in 374, and would seem, from its reference to Sparta (at 24), to be earlier than the battle of Leuctra in 371.

It is in Socrates' long monologue at the end of the *Gorgias* that there occur the prophecies of the trial of Socrates and others for defamation; and if the hypothesis of Chapter v is right, the *Gorgias* is one of the compositions for which Plato was prosecuted for defamation. This terminal monologue must have been added to the book of the *Gorgias* after the trial, while the public recitation of the *Gorgias*, without this monologue, was before the trial. But as no book of the unenlarged *Gorgias* was issued, the trial must have ensued swiftly after its oral delivery. Isocrates' *Helen* 1 seems to allude to this trial.

For reasons adduced in the next section of this chapter, the *Crito* is likely to precede the *Phaedo*, but not by a long interval. The *Phaedo* was being composed during 368. The *Crito*, and therefore the *Apology*, must be later than the original *Gorgias* and the unfinished *Thrasymachus*, and are unlikely to be very much later.

Together these various straws indicate that the *Gorgias* was composed and delivered before, but only, say, two to four years before, the end of the 370's. The series of Plato's eristic dialogues terminates some half a dozen years before Aristotle comes to the Academy in 367.

When did the series begin? How long before writing the *Gorgias* did Plato write the *Laches*, say, or the *Lysis*? This question, which has little importance, does not seem susceptible of a definite answer. No internal dating clues seem to be presented by any of these very early dialogues.

Several of these dialogues are so short that they would not anyhow have taken long to compose; but if, what is argued in Chapter VI, Socrates' interrogation chains in these dialogues derive in substance from the minutes of recent elenctic Moots, then Plato's task of dramatizing these already recorded argument-sequences would have been a relatively light one. On this hypothesis he did not have to invent the arguments, but only to select, arrange and conversationalize them.

Plato composed the *Symposium*, the *Phaedo*, the original *Ideal State* and the torso of the *Critias* after receiving his invitation to Sicily and before his departure from Athens, that is, between, at earliest, the summer of 369 and the beginning of April 367. Not much in these dialogues could have been compiled out of pre-existing materials. So Plato, working at anything like this rate of production, might have composed the dozen eristic dialogues in comparatively few years. His activity as dialogue writer might have begun after the 380's. There is no stringent reason for thinking that any Platonic dialogue had been presented to an Athenian audience more than about a decade before Aristotle joined the Academy.

Save for the *Gorgias* and *Meno* the eristic dialogues were presumably all released to the copyists directly after their public deliveries. But the *Gorgias* and *Meno* both embody additions made after the trial, to which they prophetically allude, though the original dialogues had been recited to their audiences before the trial. For the *Meno* this need have involved no great delay. Its Anytus-talk is short; the discussion of Reminiscence in the *Phaedo* presupposes that its audience is acquainted with the discussion of Reminiscence in the *Meno*; and the *Phaedo* was composed before the spring of 367. We have no analogous dating clue for the date of publication of the book of the *Gorgias*. Certainly Isocrates' *Helen* of, say, 371–370 is as a whole a riposte to the *Gorgias*, but it might be a riposte just to the *Gorgias* as this had been orally delivered in, say, 373.

The vengeful myth in the terminal *Gorgias* suggests that it was composed on the morrow of the trial and before the composition of the *Apology* and *Phaedo*. In the *Gorgias* Tartarus is a place where the powerful and wicked suffer

eternal tortures. In the *Phaedo* the Next World is, for the
most part, a place of temporary purgation for the moder-
ate sinners and of release to blessedness for the virtuous
philosophers. This clue, if it is one, would put the composition of the terminal *Gorgias* before the *Apology* too,
since its Next World is a blessed place. We might conjecture 371–370 for the date when the additions to the
Meno and *Gorgias* were composed and when the books of
these dialogues were published.

3. THE 'APOLOGY' AND THE 'CRITO'

The *Apology* and the *Crito* have always been taken by
scholars to be earlier than the *Phaedo*, and the stylometrists
are unanimously of this opinion too, though they are far
from united about the positioning of these two dialogues in
relation to the other pre-*Phaedo* dialogues.

There is, however, one important feature which the
Crito shares with the *Phaedo* and with virtually all the post-
Phaedo dialogues, but with none of the other pre-*Phaedo*
discussion dialogues. There is next to no questioner-
answerer eristic in the *Crito* or the *Phaedo*. What little
cross-examination goes on in the *Crito* is explicitly a resur-
rection of points established or demolished in previous
discussions. Some of them derive from the *Gorgias*, one,
possibly, from the *Alcibiades I*. Questioner-answerer
eristic is the dramatic action of the *Laches*, *Charmides*, *Lysis*,
Euthyphro, *Ion*, [*Alcibiades*], *Hippias*, *Protagoras*, *Euthydemus*, *Gorgias* and *Meno*. In the *Republic*, Book I, the
Socratic Method is fully deployed, but just this book had
independently been thought to be of a considerably earlier

composition date than the other books of the *Republic*. Then suddenly the Socratic Method almost disappears from Plato's dialogues. Until the *Parmenides*, no one from now on plays for more than a few moments the part of a Charmides, a Polus, a Protagoras or a Thrasymachus. The elenchus has vanished.

Whatever may be the explanation of this elimination of the elenchus from Plato's dialogues, the *Crito*, like the *Phaedo*, seems to be subsequent to that elimination. The *Crito* and with it the *Apology* must therefore be later than the *Gorgias* and *Meno*. The *Crito* is Plato's first non-eristic discussion dialogue.

The *Crito* is a prison scene, dramatically two days prior to the prison scene in the *Phaedo*. In both dialogues Socrates refers to Thebes and Megara as possible refuges (*Crito* 53 B and *Phaedo* 99 A). In the *Phaedo* Socrates' two interlocutors, Simmias and Cebes, are Thebans; both are mentioned in the *Crito* 45 B. Now in the *Crito* 53 B Socrates says that Thebes and Megara are both well-governed states. In his *Rhetoric* II xxiii 11 Aristotle mentions the good government of Thebes as having been the result of her statesmen being philosophers. Thebes had been emancipated from Spartan occupation only at the end of 379. Simmias, after exile in Athens, was one of the liberators. Athens can hardly have learned much of the nature or the strength of the ensuing drastic reconstruction of the Theban polity by Pelopidas and Epaminondas until some while after 379. So the *Crito* cannot be earlier than the not at all early 370's.

Two ancillary arguments would tend to show that

the *Apology* and *Crito* belong to the later years of the 370's. The *Euthydemus*, and therewith the *Gorgias*, *Meno* and *Thrasymachus* have to be dated at least a little while after Isocrates' first political oration in 380 or later, and this will squeeze their successors, the *Apology* and *Crito*, a bit further down than themselves from the earliest 370's. Secondly, on the hypothesis that Plato, like the dramatists, wrote dialogues in steady succession for audiences that expected dialogue recitations at cyclical gatherings, it would be natural to date the *Apology* and *Crito* not very long before the *Symposium* and *Phaedo*, and to date the *Gorgias* and *Meno* not very long before the *Apology* and *Crito*. For we have no other Platonic dialogues, save the unfinished *Thrasymachus*, qualified to fill the temporal vacancies, if such vacancies existed.

So it looks as if the *Apology* and *Crito* were composed somewhere in the period 372–369. As neither dialogue hints at the possibility of a new kind of pedagogic role in Athens for 'Socrates', both may precede the foundation of the Academy. If so, these dialogues would have to be dated in 372 or perhaps 371.

4. THE FOUNDATION OF THE ACADEMY

Theaetetus, who died in 369, is said to have been a foundation member of the Academy. He was the only person yet capable of teaching the solid geometry that is anachronistically approved of by Socrates in the *Republic* VII 528. He was its inventor. So the Academy, with its curriculum described in this book of the *Republic*, had been founded before 369. Theaetetus had had a school at Heraclea on the

Black Sea. On one account he left Heraclea for Athens in the mid-370's. It is not known why he came to Athens or whether he brought any of his pupils with him. Heracleides Ponticus, who was a geometrician, did come to the Academy from Heraclea, but it is not known how early this was. Amyclas, another geometrician, also came from Heraclea to the Academy, but again it is unknown when this was. Bryson too was from Heraclea, but he may not have joined the Academy.

Eudoxus might also have been a foundation member of the Academy, since the theoretical astronomy required in the *Republic* VII 529–30 was his specialty. In his *Plato and his Contemporaries*, p. 36, G. C. Field makes Eudoxus' return to Athens occur in the later 370's, since it would be difficult to compress into shorter time Eudoxus' previous career as student, researcher, traveller and head of a successful school. E. Frank puts his return to Athens as late as 370, but gives no evidence. Eudoxus seems to have brought several of his students with him to Athens. Helicon of Cyzicus had been a pupil of Eudoxus, and we know from the *Thirteenth Letter* that he was not only in Athens in 366–365 but had been there for at least a little time. Plato is made to speak of his consultations with other men from Cyzicus about Helicon, and it is natural to infer that these acquaintances of Helicon had also come from Eudoxus' school at Cyzicus. So Plato, Theaetetus and Eudoxus might have merged their schools into the Academy in about 370. There are some grounds for thinking that Eudoxus was deputy-Head of the Academy during Plato's absence in Sicily in 367–366.

There is, however, an alternative chronology for Eudoxus' life, which would make him only twenty-four years old in 367, that is, only seven years senior to Aristotle. On this showing he certainly could not have been a co-founder of the Academy in, say, 370 or even a teacher in the Academy while Aristotle was still a student there. It would be impossible to reconcile the *Thirteenth Letter* with this alternative chronology.

Isocrates' *Helen*, which castigates, presumably, Plato for teaching eristic to young men, must precede the inauguration of the Academy's curriculum, in which eristic is vetoed for the under-thirties. If we could rely on the approved dating of the *Helen* at the very close of the 370's, we could be sure that the Academy began at earliest in 371 or 370. In his *Panathenaicus* 26 Isocrates refers to the curriculum of the Academy as having been set up 'in our own day', ἐφ' ἡμῶν. This part of the oration was probably written in about 342 when Isocrates was some ninety-three years of age. Unfortunately his longevity makes his phrase 'in our own day' quite uninformative.

The founding of the Academy must have been later than Plato's composition of the *Euthydemus*, *Meno*, *Gorgias* and the unfinished *Thrasymachus*. For these are elenctic dialogues and therefore prior to the inferred prosecution of Plato, which, according to the conclusions of Chapters V and VI, stopped Plato both from teaching dialectic to young men and from composing elenctic dialogues. We have already seen strong reasons for dating these dialogues in the 370's, and weaker reasons for dating the latest of them quite late in that decade. We have also seen one not very strong reason for dating the *Apology* and the *Crito* before the Academy was founded.

This idea that the Academy was founded only three or four years before Aristotle joined it in 367 clashes violently with the view commonly accepted, namely that the Academy had been in existence for about twenty years before 367. There is one fairly strong argument *ex silentio* against this standard view. We know from Aristotle and others the names of quite a lot of the students who were Aristotle's contemporaries and juniors at the Academy. With the possible exception of Xenocrates we cannot name any of its students senior to Aristotle. We do not know that Xenocrates ever belonged to the Academy *in statu pupillari*. If the Academy had been going for twenty years when Aristotle joined it, it had produced no students of mathematics, astronomy or dialectic worthy of favourable or even of caustic comment. Nor can we name any predecessors of Theaetetus and Eudoxus as its teachers of mathematics and astronomy. Their names do not survive, because they did not exist.

The *Seventh Letter*, on which the standard biographies of Plato are confidingly based, is of no help in this matter. Its notional Plato makes no mention of his Academy. That Plato had pupils other than the idealistic Dion and the disappointing Dionysius is indicated only by the single phrase, at 341 C, 'hearers of mine'. In brief, we can be sure that the Academy had been founded by 369. A consilience of faint indications points to 370 as the year of its foundation. The *onus probandi* rests on those who wish to date this foundation earlier than 370.

5. THE 'PHAEDO' AND THE 'SYMPOSIUM'

The *Phaedo* and the *Symposium* seem to be stylistic neighbours; both are predominantly non-dialectical dialogues; the *Phaedo* reproduces, with an important addition, the *Meno*'s doctrine of Reminiscence; and the *Symposium*, which, at 178 E–179 A, contains an indubitable allusion to the defeat of Sparta at Leuctra in 371, reproduces some of the argumentation of the *Lysis*. Both dialogues belong to the period shortly after Plato had stopped composing dialectical dialogues, that is, after his *Meno*, *Gorgias* and unfinished *Thrasymachus*.

The *Thirteenth Letter*, forged or genuine, proves that the book of the *Phaedo* had been published by the winter-spring of 366–365, and implies that the dialogue had been composed, though not yet published in book-form, before Plato left Athens for Syracuse in April 367. Both dialogues seem, therefore, to have been composed after 371 and before April 367.

Both dialogues share with the *Parmenides*, Part I, the peculiarity that the dramatic deliverers of the stories are narrators other than Socrates, namely, Apollodorus, Phaedo and Cephalus. These three dialogues could be delivered to audiences without Plato being present to recite the words of his Socrates. It is a fair inference that these dialogues were designed to be so deliverable. Plato composed them knowing that he would be away from Athens at the times of their public deliveries. He composed the *Phaedo* and the *Symposium* after receiving from the Elder Dionysius in 369–368 his invitation to Syracuse and before sailing from Athens in early 367. So both were being written during 368, the year before the young Aristotle began his studies in the Academy. In its author's mind and in the minds of the hearers of the *Phaedo* Socrates' Farewell to This Life is also Plato's Farewell, perhaps for ever, to Athens and the Academy; Socrates' Journey to the Next World is also Plato's long and dangerous sea journey to Sicily (see *Phaedo* 67 B, 77 D, 84 B, 85 D); Socrates' hope that he will find in Heaven good despots and friends (63 B–C, 69 E) is also Plato's hope that the Sicilian Despot's Court will prove a civilized one; and maybe Socrates' counsel, at 78 A, how to find a charm-singer to succeed himself is also Plato's advice how to find a new Head of the Academy if he himself should fail to return to Athens.

Many of Plato's middle-sized dialogues seem to adhere to a regulation length, namely 52–54 Stephanus pages. As the *Phaedo* is five or six pages in excess of this regulation length, it is worth while to see if it has been enlarged beyond its original length. There is a stretch of just the required length between 108 C and 113 C which does bear several marks of being a subsequent interpolation. This stretch, which tells us that the earth is spherical and cavernous, is totally irrelevant to the subject-matter of the dialogue as a whole and is only factitiously relevant to the subject-matter of the passages immediately preceding and succeeding it. Moreover there is a glaring incongruity between Socrates' exposition of 'someone else's' geophysical theory in this stretch and his renunciation of physical theories ten pages earlier. The theme interrupted in the middle of 108 C seems to be smoothly resumed at the beginning of 113 D.

In his *Plato und die sogenannten Pythagoreer*, from p. 184, E. Frank finds in this geophysical stretch of the *Phaedo* the first announcement to the Greek world of Archytas' discovery of the spherical shape of the earth. That the earth is a sphere had not been known even to Democritus. As Frank assumes the standard dating scheme for Plato's dialogues, including the *Phaedo*, he has to let Plato learn this doctrine from Archytas on his first visit to Sicily at the beginning of the 380's.

We can take things differently. It was between his arrival in Sicily in April–May 367 and his return to Athens in the late summer of 366 that Plato gathered from Archytas, Archedemus and Philistion the scientific content of his *Timaeus*. This was the time when he also learned of the spherical earth. When he returned to Athens, he reserved his newly written *Timaeus* for his Academy, since its doctrines were too unorthodox or difficult or minute or vocational to suit the laity. Moreover these doctrines were the discoveries not of Plato but of his Sicilian and Italian friends. But the shape of the earth and its external and internal structure could and should be presented to the world, though, very explicitly, not as 'Socrates'' own discoveries. So very soon after his return to Athens Plato inserted these pages of geophysics into his text of the *Phaedo*, which, though it had been recited to an Athenian audience during his absence, had not yet been made available to the copyists. It is worth while noticing, what would otherwise be surprising, that the *Timaeus* says nothing about the spherical shape of the earth, save by implication at 63 A. For this news the synchronous *Phaedo* was the vehicle. There is, of course, a gross anachronism in making Socrates in 399 learn from 'someone' that the earth is spherical. 'Socrates' is, as often, Plato and '399' is, this time, 367–366, and 'someone' is Archytas.

In his *De Caelo* 294 Aristotle speaks as if the champions of the tambourine-shaped earth were continuing to contest the spherical theory later than the year 357, which is fixed for us in 292 a 5. He quarrels with Anaximenes, Anaxagoras and Democritus for requiring the earth to be flat-bottomed in order to be supported by a pad of air compressed beneath it. In the *Phaedo* 108 E Plato too rejects the theory that the earth needs this or any other bolster. In his *Meteorologica* 356 a Aristotle justly criticizes the *Phaedo*'s hydraulics; but, from 365 a, he accepts and develops its compressed air theory of earthquakes and volcanoes (*Phaedo* 112 B and 113 B). In the *Phaedo* 111 E Sicilian eruptions are explicitly mentioned. Perhaps Plato had recently visited the lower slopes of Mount Etna.

There is nothing to show whether the *Phaedo* was completed before the *Symposium* was begun, or *vice versa*. Nor does it matter. What is of importance is that we have solid grounds for fixing within a few months the date of the composition of both the *Symposium* and the *Phaedo*, and to within a very short period the date of the publication of the book of the *Phaedo*. Not only have we now a well-defined chronological ridge against which to locate both the pre-*Phaedo* and the post-*Phaedo* dialogues; but we can also tell how fast Plato could, when under pressure, compose dialogues. For he must have composed the *Symposium*, the *Phaedo*, the original *Ideal State* and the fragmentary *Critias* between receiving his invitation to Sicily and his departure from Athens, that is during a period of well under two years.

6. THE 'CRITIAS'

Scholars have speculated about the reasons for which Plato failed to finish the *Critias* or even, apparently, to begin the *Hermocrates*. We need also to speculate about his reason for beginning the *Critias*. What could make Plato want to write a piece of fictitious pre-history?

We should begin by looking at the stage-setting. At the beginning of the *Timaeus* Socrates gives a résumé of the main points on which he had discoursed on the previous day. As these points cover the political gist of our *Republic*, Books II–V, it has sometimes been supposed that Socrates' discourse was our *Republic*. This is an error.

(*a*) It is made clear that the gathering to which, dramatically, this discourse had been delivered by Socrates had consisted only of Timaeus, Critias, Hermocrates, and a fourth unnamed person. Not one of the persons dramatically present in our *Republic*, namely Thrasymachus, Glaucon, Adeimantus or Polemarchus, is present on this occasion; nor are Timaeus, Critias or Hermocrates mentioned as present in our *Republic* gathering.

(*b*) It is pretty clear that the discourse that Socrates had delivered 'yesterday' had, unlike our *Republic*, been an address or allocution, that is a monologue and not a dialogue; as the *Timaeus* and *Critias* are monologues. The *Hermocrates* obviously was to have been a monologue.

(*c*) While the political gist of the *Republic* II–V might have amounted to the length of, say, the *Protagoras* and so have been short enough to be delivered in one session of a couple of hours, our entire *Republic* could not have been delivered in one session or even in two or three sessions. Socrates could not have gone through it yesterday.

(*d*) In the *Timaeus* 17B, 20B–C and 26A–D Socrates, Hermocrates and Critias all refer to tasks which Socrates had yesterday given to his listeners, namely the tasks of repaying him with corresponding discourses of their own. No such tasks are set in our *Republic*.

(*e*) If Socrates had been giving however selective a résumé of our *Republic*, he could hardly have omitted to mention the notion of justice. But in his résumé he does in fact not say a word about justice. So presumably this backbone idea of our *Republic* did not feature seriously in the discourse of which Socrates gives his résumé. Nor does Socrates say a word about Homer or the theological fables, topics which bulk largely in Books II, III and X of our *Republic*.

The conclusion is patent. The discourse of Socrates which is summarized at the beginning of the *Timaeus* is not our *Republic*. It is an earlier version of one section of it, in a different literary form and with different *dramatis personae*, including one Sicilian and one Italian. This short Socratic discourse can be labelled *The Ideal State* or the *Proto-Republic*.

When Socrates describes the task or tasks that he set to

his listeners yesterday (*Timaeus* 19–20), the description fits perfectly the task actually undertaken by Critias. Critias duly sets out to describe how an antediluvian Athens, with just the political structure of Socrates' ideal polity of our *Republic* II–V, had led Hellas in victorious war against Atlantis. We have no useful clue to the task which was to have been taken on by Hermocrates. Timaeus' discourse, on the other hand, being on cosmogony, astronomy, chemistry, psychology, anatomy, physiology and pathology, does not conform in any way to Socrates' description of the tasks that he had set. No explanation is even offered for Timaeus' discourse, on *The Origin of the World and of Man*, coming between Socrates' discourse and its requested and promised sequel, the *Critias*.

Indeed in the *Timaeus* up to 27 A nothing is said to suggest that we are to be given a discourse *About Nature* at all, much less that we are to be given such a discourse after Critias has, to the tune of some eight pages, described the Egyptian source of his forthcoming war-history and actually begun the history itself.

What has happened? It seems reasonable to suppose that our *Timaeus*, from 17 to 26 E, was the original opening of the *Critias*. The original *Critias* had begun with our *Timaeus* 17–26 E and gone straight on at *Critias* 108 E. The present opening of our *Critias* 106–108 D is so insipid that we must fear that Plato's powers were flagging sadly when he wrote it. For some reason not only did Plato not finish his *Critias* but he borrowed its original opening to be the opening of his *Timaeus*, though this discourse had not been originally composed to go with the discourses of Socrates,

Critias and Hermocrates at all. Timaeus is not mentioned with Critias and Hermocrates at the end of 19 c.

Now for the subject-matter of the *Critias*. What would an ordinary Greek have read into Plato's description of Atlantis? 'A mighty host which, starting from a distant point in the Atlantic ocean, was insolently advancing to attack the whole of Europe and Asia to boot...of the lands here within the straits [of Gibraltar], they ruled over Libya as far as Egypt and over Europe as far as Tuscany...' (*Timaeus* 25). Poseidon, equated with Dagon, founded the island of Atlantis (*Critias* 113 c). 'The wealth they', the Kings of Atlantis, 'possessed was so immense that the like had never been seen before in any royal house nor will ever easily be seen again...' (114 D). Atlantis 'contained a very large stock of elephants' (114 E). Its shipyards were full of triremes. The sea-way and the largest harbour were filled with ships and merchants coming from all quarters... (117 D–E). Bulls were sacrificed to Poseidon (119). Already the ordinary Greek, and *a fortiori* a Sicilian Greek would have said 'Ah, there is Carthage.' The story of a war 9,000 years ago between Hellas and Atlantis had lessons in it for a Hellas whose western colonies in Sicily and Italy were her outposts against a currently menacing Carthage, which already occupied Sardinia and half of Sicily.

There are many more coincidences between Plato's Atlantis and the real Carthage. Most of the requisite information about Carthage is to be found in R. Bosworth Smith's *Carthage and the Carthaginians* (1879). Carthage did, like Atlantis, have a circular naval basin, the 'Cup', with a circular island in the middle linked to the shore by a causeway. Exit from the 'Cup' to the sea was through a narrow cutting into a larger mercantile basin, the exit from which into the sea was through a second narrow cutting. There was also a third basin or lagoon, the Lake of Tunis, in which countless ships could lie at anchor. This lagoon was not channelled to the other two basins. In Plato's Atlantis not only the naval basin but all three basins were circular. They formed a concentric series of salt-water moats. The cuttings from the inmost to the middle, and from the middle to the outside moat were just wide enough for one trireme. The width of Plato's middle moat is almost exactly that of Carthage's mercantile basin; and the width of water between the central island and the shore of the 'Cup' is 200–300 yards in both Atlantis and Carthage, though the central island in Atlantis is very much larger than that in Carthage. 'Cups', that is, artificial naval basins, existed at other Carthaginian ports as well.

Plato's arrangement is beautifully though unpractically geometrical. Conceivably it was merely a geometrically romanticized reconstruction by Plato of the correct information that the mercantile basin in Carthage was 'outside' the naval basin, and the lagoon was 'further out' than both.

Atlantis and Carthage both have many huge reservoirs, open and roofed, and bathing-pools, of which one is reserved for the blue-blooded. The main temple in Atlantis is externally plated partly in silver and partly in gold, and it contains a roof-high statue of their god, standing in a chariot. In Carthage there was a temple plated in gold and containing the colossal statue of 'Apollo' that was carried

off to Rome after the sack of Carthage. In both Atlantis
and Carthage the sacrifices in the temple are performed by
the rulers themselves, not by priests. Both places are
served by large and elaborate irrigation-canals. Both enjoy two crops in the year. According to Strabo, Carthage
has hot and cold springs, as does Atlantis. Both have
quarries of red, white and black (or green) stone. Both use
archers, slingers and javelin-throwers; both have huge
numbers of triremes and war-chariots. The war-chariots of
Atlantis are two-horse chariots; according to Plutarch's
Timoleon, those of Carthage at the Battle of the Crimessus
were four-horse chariots, but those described by Diodorus
Siculus (XVI 67 2) were two-horse chariots. Both Atlantis
and Carthage are protected from the land side by three
parallel walls of stone, about five miles out from the city
centre. Even the mosaic pavements which can still be un-
earthed on the site of Carthage may correspond to the
many-coloured patterns of stones which decorate some of
the dwellings of Atlantis.

In the *Critias* 114 B Plato gives the name 'Gadeira' to the
part of Atlantis nearest to the Pillars of Hercules. 'Gadeira'
was the Greek name for Gades, that is, Cadiz, which is not
far west of the Pillars of Hercules. This Gadeira was the
earliest Carthaginian settlement in Spain.

The constitution of the antediluvian Atlantis does not
tally at all with that of fourth-century Carthage, any more
than that of the antediluvian Athens tallies with that of
fourth-century Athens. Nor, of course, does the location
of Atlantis, far out in the Atlantic. Carthage was well
known to be inside the Mediterranean and less than a

hundred miles from the nearest corner of Sicily. Yet the Greek soldier in Plutarch's *Timoleon* xx taunts the Greek mercenary in the Carthaginian army '...or do you suppose that they [the Carthaginians] have collected an army and are come hither from the pillars of Heracles and the Atlantic sea in order to risk their lives on behalf of the dynasty of Hicetas?' Certainly Carthage employed hosts of mercenaries from Spain and Morocco, but Plutarch makes the soldier speak as if the Carthaginians themselves came from beyond Gibraltar. So perhaps the *Critias* and the soldier's taunt both reflect a tenacious legend.

It will be argued later in this chapter that the original version of the *Republic* II–V, that is, the *Proto-Republic*, had been composed as an advisory address to be delivered before Dionysius I in Syracuse in 367–366. We can now infer that its promised sequel, the *Critias*, was to have been the second of a trilogy of advisory addresses to Dionysius.

While Socrates' *Ideal State* was intended to tell the Elder Dionysius how to reform his body politic by converting his landed 'barons' into propertyless guardians without private family ties, Critias' discourse was to enjoin him by mythical example to lead and thereby to unite Hellas in a Holy War against Carthage. This is precisely the advice that Isocrates meant to give in his address to Dionysius at the very same moment. Isocrates' *Letter to Dionysius I* adumbrates the counsel which his address is to give in full.

The reason why Plato did not finish the *Critias* or even, so far as we know, begin the *Hermocrates* is that he reached Syracuse in late April or early May 367, by which time

Dionysius I had very recently died. Plato had completed the first discourse of his trilogy before leaving Athens; he meant to complete his *Critias* and to write his *Hermocrates* while in Sicily. But he arrived to find that his Churchill-to-be had just been buried and that the Court Festival at which he was to have delivered his trilogy of advisory discourses could not be held.

Supposing, what is argued in the next section of this chapter, that Plato composed his *Timaeus* while in Syracuse in 367–366 and that before leaving for home he delivered it orally to the Court-circle of Dionysius II, why did he incorporate in it so incongruously not merely the promise, but the very preface of an advisory address which he was now never going to use?

Partly, perhaps, because his Syracusan audience would take more interest in a story about the defeat of an antediluvian Carthage than in questions of cosmogony, astronomy, physiology and pathology. The story would serve as topical sugar for a very untopical pill. But also probably because like other authors Plato disliked the thought of a planned and partly written composition going into total oblivion. At least the gist of its message about Carthage, together with that of the message about the Ideal State, could be conveyed in précis to their intended Sicilian recipients. The doricized digest of the *Timaeus*, known as the *Timaeus Locrus*, and Cicero's translation omit the two messages, so presumably the *Timaeus* that was studied in the Academy had been pruned of these irrelevant Sicilian appendages. The young Aristotle studied his cosmogony, astronomy and physiology without being distracted by the first chapter of a yarn about Atlantis. He never mentions Atlantis though he refers to the *Timaeus* much more often than to any other Platonic composition.

It follows from all this that Plato was composing his *Ideal State* and his *Critias* between receiving his invitation from the Elder Dionysius in 369–368 and sailing from Athens in April 367. It is a fair guess that he was writing the *Critias* in the winter–spring of 368–367. He composed the *Timaeus* while in Syracuse in 367–366 and delivered extracts from it there, with a Sicilian curtain-raiser, before sailing home in the summer of 366.

As the *Critias* was unfinished, the book of the *Critias* remained on Plato's shelf during his lifetime. Aristotle never refers to it.

7. THE 'TIMAEUS'

The *Timaeus* has commonly been thought to be one of the latest of Plato's compositions. Some Christian thinkers may have hoped and therefore believed that this was so, since it would have been theologically proper for Plato's final doctrine to be a Book of Genesis. Scholars have argued for the lateness of the *Timaeus* from its stylistic affinities with the *Laws*, which, they have assumed, was still being composed when Plato died. The *Laws* was indeed still under revision when Plato died, but what he was revising was a work which he had already composed. He had composed the first part of it some fifteen years before he died. Its stylistic affinities with the *Timaeus* and *Critias* indicate, if they indicate any chronological fact at all, no more than that these three works were being composed during the same period, not that this period was a late one.

The odd way in which the *Timaeus* is prefaced by a précis of the *Ideal State* or *Proto-Republic* and by the introduction to, and the opening of the *Critias* is, by itself, almost proof that the *Timaeus* was delivered by Plato in Syracuse in 367–366. The gists of the *Ideal State* and *Critias* were prefixed to it, because Plato had been prevented by the Elder Dionysius' death from delivering these two compositions which he had brought with him from Athens. He introduced the burthens of their messages to Sicily as an incongruous curtain-raiser to his allocution *On the Origin of the World and of Man*, which he had been composing during his sojourn in Syracuse, and which, before his departure, he delivered before Dionysius II.

During this sojourn Plato had studied the physical and physiological doctrines of Archytas and Philistion; and these constitute a big part of the scientific content of the *Timaeus*. He brought back to the Academy this scientific harvest, with one extra item, namely Archytas' new doctrine of the spherical shape of the earth and its internal structure. This item Plato divulged to Athens and the world not in the *Timaeus* but as a five-page interpolation into the text of his *Phaedo*, from 108 c to 113 c. We have independent grounds for dating the composition of the original *Phaedo* in 368–367, and the publication of the book of the *Phaedo* in 366–365, immediately after his return from Sicily. The natural place for this new geophysical doctrine would have been the *Timaeus*, but the *Timaeus* was not going to be published to the world outside the

Academy. So the important news about the spherical shape of the earth was interpolated, entirely irrelevantly, into the book of the *Phaedo*. The fact that it was so interpolated quite strongly corroborates the independently based view that, unlike the *Phaedo* and all the earlier dialogues, the *Timaeus* was not published to the world. It suggests, too, that Plato composed the *Timaeus* in the interval between composing the *Phaedo* and releasing its text to the copyists.

The *Timaeus* is drawn on fairly heavily by the *Philebus*, and less heavily by the *Theaetetus*, which was composed after the *Philebus*. Books VI and especially VII of the *Republic*, though composed in substance well before the *Timaeus*, seem to have been supplemented with draughts on the *Timaeus*, when they were being adapted for incorporation in our *Republic*. The discussion of pleasure at the end of Book IX of the *Republic* reads like a post-*Timaeus* addition to a piece originally composed long before the *Timaeus*. Our *Republic* was probably assembled in its final shape late in the 360's. In conjunction these independent bits of evidence seem to establish beyond reasonable doubt that Plato composed the *Timaeus* during his sojourn in Syracuse in 367–366, and duly delivered it with its curtain-raiser to the ears of the Young Dionysius and others not long before he sailed home in the late summer of 366.

The forged *Seventh Letter* says things which partly confirm, but *prima facie* also partly conflict with this conclusion. This *Letter*, 341 and 344 D–345 C, makes Plato speak of a solitary allocution or talk that he had delivered to the Young Dionysius. This talk is twice described as being about Nature, 341 E and 344 D. As the *Timaeus* is the only thing written by Plato on this scientific theme, the *Letter* must be referring to the *Timaeus*. It is his thoughts on this subject, not, *pace* many commentators, his philosophical thoughts on any subject, of which Plato is made to say, at 341 E, that he will never publish them in writing or in speech to the world at large, but only to those who know how to research, that is, to the members of his Academy. Galen says the same thing explicitly about the *Timaeus*, and gives reasons like those of the *Seventh Letter* 341 E why Plato refused to give it to the world (see reference given on p. 25). Maybe Plato kept the *Timaeus* esoteric partly because the scientific ideas in it were not his own, but were the gifts of his Sicilian and Italian friends and teachers. In the geophysical interpolation in the *Phaedo* Socrates makes it very clear that the credit for the new discovery belongs to someone else than himself.

So far the *Seventh Letter* corroborates the conclusions based on our other evidence. However, on the most natural reading of this *Letter*, it was not during his second, but during his third and last visit to Sicily in 361–360 that Plato gave his solitary discourse on Nature to Dionysius. This reading conflicts not only with points already argued, but also with the point that Plato delivered his *Proto-Laws* in Syracuse in 361–360; this would prevent his discourse on Nature, if it had been given then, from being the 'solitary' talk that the *Letter* describes it as being. Indeed, while we have strong reasons for thinking that the concocter of the *Seventh* and *Eighth Letters* had himself heard the *Proto-Laws* being delivered in Syracuse by Plato, he betrays no knowledge of the contents of the discourse about Nature. He gives us instead an amateurish and mystery-mongering exposition of Plato's Theory of Forms, which has no pertinence to the subject-matters of the *Seventh Letter*. Presumably it was dragged in, quite anachronistically, as a signature-tune to satisfy the recipients that the *Letter* really was written by Plato. Doubtless it worked. It still works.

The author of the *Letter* seems to harp on the solitariness of Plato's talk about Nature for one reason and on its unpublishability for another reason. Why Plato gave only one talk was because the young tyrant shirked study. That the talk was not to be published is the ground of a scolding that the notional Plato administers to the young tyrant for subsequently composing, with assistance, and naughtily publishing his own version or plagiary of Plato's esoteric discourse. As Syracuse would have known the facts, the *Letter* must be telling the truth, with its own uncharitable colouring, about this production by Dionysius of a version or plagiary of the *Timaeus*. Probably Syracuse had very reasonably construed the tyrant's literary labour as creditable to him and complimentary to Plato, so the *Letter*'s notional Plato has to pronounce the opposite verdict. Now the time when the young tyrant had shirked his studies was during Plato's second visit in 367–366 (330 B and 338 D–E). His studiousness in composing his version or plagiary was after this visit (341 B). What he was plagiarizing was what he had formerly heard Plato deliver. So, though confusedly expressed, the *Seventh Letter*'s account does require that the *Timaeus* had been given in 367–366. Part of the confusion seems to be due to the fact that the passage beginning at 341 A 9 is not continuous with the pre-tentious passage from 340 B to 341 A 8, in which Plato is made to reveal his 'clear and infallible test' of authentic philosophic fire, namely that slackness proves lack of zeal.

The real reason why Plato had delivered only one talk in 367–366 is that the Palace Festival had been cancelled to which he was to contribute his *Ideal State*, *Critias* and *Hermocrates*. Plato had with him no other composition to deliver until he had completed his *Timaeus*. The young tyrant's shirking of tutorials was the less reprehensible that he was at the time commanding Syracuse in a war (317 A and 338 A). Such facts did not weigh with the author of the *Letter*. The *Seventh Letter* contains other chronological muddles. Plato's reactions to Dion's assassination in 354 are given many pages before the account of Plato's third voyage to Sicily in 361 (334 and 338–9).

There does actually exist a version or précis of Plato's *Timaeus*, and one which tries to be in the Doric dialect, namely the so-called *Timaeus Locrus*. The idea of identifying this quasi-Doric version of the *Timaeus* with the version, presumably in Doric, produced, with assistance, by the young Dionysius is under the ban of the eminent scholars who date the *Timaeus Locrus* four or five centuries after Plato's death. Sceptical inspection of their arguments for this late dating might salve some of its initial plausibility for the identification. Two Doric versions of the *Timaeus* seem excessive.

8. THE 'REPUBLIC'

Plato brought with him to Syracuse in 367 his *Ideal State* and his unfinished *Critias*. His *Ideal State* was the political gist of, roughly, Books II to V of our *Republic*. It was in address style. We seem to get three résumés of this relatively short composition, one at the beginning of Book VIII of our *Republic*, one at the beginning of the *Timaeus*, and one, with criticisms, in Aristotle's *Politics* II.

Aristotle tells us in his *Politics* II 1264b39 that Socrates (*sic*) filled up the *Republic* with 'extraneous discourses', and we can see for ourselves from the three résumés of the original *Ideal State* that this contained nothing substantial, if anything at all, about justice; nothing about theological fables or the dispensability of Homer, the tragedians and the comedy writers; nothing about the higher education of the future guardians; nothing about dialectic, the coping-stone of the sciences; and nothing about the Decline of the State from aristocracy to tyranny.

Only the first book of our *Republic* takes the shape of an elenctic disputation, and just this book had been independently deemed by scholars to have been composed well before the rest of the *Republic*. It belongs to the period of the *Gorgias*. It is only about half the regulation length for a middle-sized dialogue, so presumably Plato had shelved it unfinished.

When did Plato conflate into our *Republic* this torso of the *Thrasymachus*, the attacks on the theological fables and on poetry in general, the original *Ideal State*, the diagnosis of the degeneration of Greek states from aristocracy to tyranny, and the other extraneous discourses?

We have a well-marked *terminus a quo*. Plato could not have begun to assemble our *Republic* out of these elements until he had returned from Sicily in 366. The *Ideal State*, which had been composed for presentation in Syracuse, was brought back unused because of the Elder Dionysius' death in early 367. We have no well-marked *terminus ad quem*. If, which is easily contested, the references in the *Phaedrus* to the books which the true philosopher is licensed to write are references to the *Republic*, then our *Republic* had been assembled, or partly assembled, before Plato wrote the *Phaedrus*. That the *Phaedrus* was delivered at the Olympic Games of 360 is argued later in this chapter; it must anyhow have been composed before but not long before Aristotle inaugurated the teaching of rhetoric in the Academy early or very early in the 350's. So our *Republic* may have been on Plato's hands during part of the last five or six years of the 360's. Several passages in his *Areopagiticus* indicate that the *Republic* was known to Isocrates by about the middle of the 350's. The author of the *Seventh Letter*, written in 353–352, knows something but not much about the *Republic*.

An extra complication needs to be added. If there is truth in the suggestion made at the end of Chapter II about the restricted publication intended for Plato's *Republic* and *Laws* and for Isocrates' *Antidosis*, then there would be no issue of copies of the texts of these discourses. The author would lend out his personal copies of their texts, but he would withhold them from the copyists. There would

then be nothing to prevent Plato from making additions
to or subtractions from his text between one club-reading
and the next. What was delivered to one circle during one
winter might differ from what was delivered to that or
another circle during the next winter.

There are fairly strong reasons for surmising that this
was actually the case with the *Republic*. Our Book VIII
544 B professes to run on straight from the end of the
digression demanded at the beginning of Book V by Polemarchus and Adeimantus. This digression ends in Book V
at 466 D or later. The recapitulation with which Book VIII
opens says not a word about the contents of the last few
pages of our Book V or of any of Books VI or VII. Nor,
despite *Republic* VI 497 B and D, and 501 E, are the begin-
nings of the political decay described in Book VIII said to
be even delayed by the higher education from which the
young Guardians and the State were so greatly to benefit.
Apparently Plato not only initially composed Books VIII
and IX but even incorporated revisions of them in the
Republic without a thought of the contents of our Books
VI and VII. He was still thinking only of the Guardians'
insulation from private property and private family life.

In *The Origin and Growth of Plato's Logic*, p. 324, Luto-
slavski adduces stylometric evidence for Books VI and VII
having been composed later than much of the rest of the
Republic; and these stylistic clues are corroborated by the
facts (*a*) that in these Books, and especially the latter (e.g.
524 A, 529 C, 530 A, 530 D), there are some apparent echoes
from the *Timaeus*; (*b*) that in Book VII 531 D and 532 D we
find the notion of 'Preamble of the Laws', which functions

strongly at the end of Book IV of our *Laws*; and (c) that in Book VII 530D which summarizes the *Timaeus* 47 there is explicit mention of Pythagorean harmonics, with a citation of Archytas' own words 'these are sister-sciences' which we find in one of our few fragments from Archytas, on p. 432 of Diels–Kranz, *Fragmente der Vorsokratiker*, vol. I. It looks as if Plato, some time after 366 and perhaps after, say, 363–362, added the amount of two books and a bit to what had previously been a *Republic* of the amount of not quite eight books.

There is a further pointer in the same direction. At some time, we are not told when, Plato delivered a public lecture or lecture-series on 'The Good', which does not survive. From what we can glean of its contents, it must have been composed after the *Timaeus*, which employs nothing of the *Lecture*'s Number-ontology; and it is likely to have been composed before the *Cratylus*, the *Theaetetus* and *Sophist*, since their concentration on logical and semantic issues seems not to be reflected by anything in the *Lecture*. It had some affinities with the *Philebus*, a dialogue the composition of which, as will be argued in this chapter, must be later than the *Timaeus*, earlier than the *Theaetetus*, and quite likely not far from the *Parmenides*, Part I. So possibly the *Lecture on the Good* belongs to the later 360's. Now in the *Republic*, Books VI–VII, we find the Idea of the Good being adumbrated; and it is represented as being superior both to Thought (φρόνησις and νοῦς) and to Pleasure (505 B). This seems to tie in closely with the *Philebus* 66, where again Thought (φρόνησις and νοῦς), though given higher marks than Pleasure, is still inferior to the Good. As our *Philebus* seems to be a slice out of a longer whole, it could be that the *Republic*'s treatment of the Idea of the Good salvages something out of what had been originally composed as the sequel to our *Philebus* or as its precursor. Our *Republic*, from 504 D, would then contain a stretch resurrected out of the conjectural trilogy of which our *Philebus* is the one independently surviving member. This stretch of *Republic* VI on the Idea of the Good and the Divided Line does seem to be unduly weighty for its role in the current argument, which opens at 487 B. For Socrates is here trying only to explain the notorious worldly worthlessness of actual philosophers. Part of his explanation is that they are dazzled by the superior realities with which Thought acquaints them. The analogy of the Sun is used to illustrate this dazzlement. Ostensibly this is all that the analogical exposition of the Idea of the Good is brought in for. But it had surely been composed for a much more positive end. It does not natively belong in the apologetic and diagnostic discussion-context where we find it. It was inserted into that context to 'preserve it from oblivion'.

Perhaps, even, both the *Philebus* and this stretch on the Good in the *Republic* are revised segments out of the original *Lecture on the Good*. This *Lecture* or lecture-sequence was ill-received by its audience, and maybe for this reason it was not perpetuated in book-form as it stood. The abstrusest parts of this lecture-sequence, on which we have Aristotle's comments, would have baffled any lay audience, and these parts were not preserved from oblivion by Plato. But, on this tentative hypothesis, he did preserve from oblivion some parts of the *Lecture on the Good*, namely in the *Republic* VI and the *Philebus*.

Whether this be so or not, we have reasons for thinking that parts of our *Republic*, Books VI and VII, were revised and incorporated into our *Republic* after Plato had written the *Timaeus* and even after he had begun to compose his *Proto-Laws*. These straws, together with the otherwise apparent philosophical doldrums of the quinquennium after Plato's return to Athens from Sicily in 366, suggest, but do not prove, that the *Republic*, Books I-V and most of VIII-X, was being prepared for delivery to its select audiences fairly soon after 366; and that our ten-book *Republic* was completed later still. The discussion of pleasure at the end of Book IX, from 583 B, seems not only to presuppose the discussion in the *Timaeus*, but also to have advanced a long way beyond it towards the doctrines of the *Philebus*. On the other hand Book VII 528 B–C would seem to have been substantially composed before 369. For Plato here explains the presence in the Academy's curriculum of solid geometry. This was the creation of Theaetetus. The passage indicates that Theaetetus lacked encouragement. But it contains not a hint of the calamitous death of Theaetetus in 369.

So though the great bulk of our *Republic* had been originally composed, mostly in a different literary form, in the late 370's or the very early 360's, well before the *Phaedo* and the *Timaeus*, the young Aristotle knew the *Phaedo* and the *Timaeus* from back to front long before he had access to the text of our *Republic*. To our students the *Republic* is, very unfairly, Plato's philosophy. To Aristotle, even in his thirties, its contents were not more than a rumour. He knew Plato's dialectical dialogues up to the *Gorgias*; he knew very well the *Phaedo* and the *Timaeus*; he had heard and taken notes of the *Lecture on the Good*. But of our *Republic* as a whole he had no direct knowledge before he was middle-aged. In the quite late *Nicomachean Ethics* there is only a handful of stray allusions to points peculiar to the *Republic*; there is no sustained discussion of any of these few points. In the *Topics* and the *De Anima* almost all of their very few allusions to the *Republic* are allusions to the tripartite soul. The doctrine of the tripartite soul would have been known to Aristotle from the *Timaeus*, but the word θυμοειδές, which Aristotle uses, was introduced by Plato not in the *Timaeus* but in the *Republic*. In the so-called *Platonic Definitions* half a dozen definitions are given of justice; the *Republic*'s definition is not among them.

If, in the way suggested, there were two editions of the *Republic*, the first of, roughly, an eight-book, the second of our ten-book *Republic*, then the form of publication given anyhow to the first edition presumably involved the non-issue of written copies, else we should have heard of this shorter *Republic* and probably have been in possession of its text. This gives a bit of corroboration to the hypothesis that the publication of this mammoth dialogue was of an exclusively oral kind. Aristotle's apparently belated acquaintanceship with it slightly corroborates the hypothesis that its audiences were private ones.

9. THE 'PHILEBUS'

The *Philebus* echoes or draws on the *Timaeus* in many places, for example 28 D, 29 B–E, 31 D–32 B, 33 D, 42 C–D, 51 B. Conversely, the notions of the limit and the limitable which are central to the *Philebus* play no part in the *Timaeus*. The analysis of pleasure in the *Philebus* incorporates that given in the *Timaeus*, but advances a long way beyond it. The *Philebus* is later than the *Timaeus*.

In the other direction there is good reason to date the composition of the *Philebus* before the completion of the *Theaetetus*. The *Philebus* is a Socratic dialogue, and the *Theaetetus* is the last dialogue in which Socrates can lead the discussion. In the *Philebus* 38 B–C and 39 A δόξα, opinion, is defined as a conjunction of perception with μνήμη, memory. But in the *Theaetetus* 195 C–196 C it is proved conclusively that the presence of perception is not a necessary condition of opinion, since a person might think that seven plus five equals eleven. Not all cases of something seeming or appearing to be so are cases of sensible appearing. Since a philosopher cannot progress from the conclusive refutation of a thesis to the adoption of that thesis, the *Theaetetus* must be later than the *Philebus*. So the *Philebus* was composed after 366 and before, say, 358–356. Plato was in Sicily in 361–360, and probably composed the *Phaedrus* during his sojourn there. He is likely to have composed or completed his *Cratylus* between the *Phaedrus* and the *Theaetetus*. So there is some time-pressure to date the composition of the *Philebus* before Plato's journey to Sicily in 361. The quinquennium after Plato's return from

Sicily in 366 seems on the other hand to be rather empty, a fact which makes it tempting to find a home there for the *Philebus*.

It is clear from the *Philebus* 15 that the Theory of Forms is now under fire. There seem to be some well-marked connexions between the difficulties here said to be found in the Theory of Forms and the objections brought by old Parmenides against Socrates' juvenile theory in the first part of the *Parmenides*. As this first part of the *Parmenides* seems to have been composed not long before April 361, the *Philebus* may on this score too belong to the later 360's. It should be noticed that as in his *Timaeus* 51 so in his *Philebus* Plato pays compliments to the Theory of Forms but gives it no work to do. He now employs the totally independent theory of the limit/limitable, which almost certainly derives from Archytas. This theory is sufficiently independent of the Theory of Forms for Aristotle wholeheartedly to adopt and develop it without any mitigation of his hostility to the Theory of Forms. We may guess that Plato in 367–366 had found the thinkers of Italy and Sicily not only unamenable to his Theory of Forms but unhampered by the lack of it.

At the time of composing his *Philebus* Plato very likely did not fully realize that his new Italian principle of the limit/limitable led away from a two-worlds view towards a two-factors view; or that the admission that mathematics can be both pure and applicable to things and processes abolishes one previous need for a realm of self-subsistent *entia rationis*. Perhaps it was unbeknownst to himself that Platonism had, in Plato's own heart, cooled down from a passion to a deference. Protarchus' declaration 'I do not know, Socrates, what harm it can do a man to take in all the other kinds of knowledge if he has the first' (62 D) suggests the corollary, unstated by Plato, 'I do not know, Socrates, what good it can do a man to have the first kind of knowledge without taking in the other kinds of knowledge.' The roof has been lifted off the Cave. The demurer representatives even of Pleasure herself are now admitted into the Best Life. In 367–366 Plato had learned from Archytas, Archedemus and Philistion that scientific knowledge of Nature was not only possible but actual. A Transcendent World was no longer needed in order to provide science with a field.

Our *Philebus* lacks both a beginning and a finish. We are not introduced to the participants in the discussion; Philebus has already resigned to Protarchus the defence of pleasure; Socrates and Protarchus have to bring to its conclusion (12 B) a discussion that is not contained in our *Philebus*; Socrates has already given to the gathering an undertaking of which the first that we hear is a reminder at 19 C–20 A. At the other end we hear of a continuation of the discussion 'tomorrow' (50 D–E, 66 D, 67 B); the nature of the Good is only prefatorily adumbrated at 64–7, in order to give their subordinate gradings to Thought and Pleasure. Apparently our *Philebus* is the second part of a trilogy, of which the other parts do not survive, unless part of one of them can be identified with the *Republic*'s treatment of the Idea of the Good; and unless other bits of it are to be found in the reports of Aristotle and others of Plato's *Lecture* or *Lectures on the Good*. We know that

Porphyry found close connexions between the *Philebus* and the *Lecture on the Good* (Aristotle's *Fragments, On the Good* 2, Simplicius *ad fin.*).

Since our *Philebus* is ragged-ended, Plato would not have let it go out into the world in book-form. Like the *Critias* and the *Laws* it remained on his shelf. Doubtless Aristotle had heard the public delivery of the trilogy of which it was a part, but he had not got the book of the *Philebus* to read until a long time afterwards.

This hypothesis tallies well with the following fact. In our *Nicomachean Ethics* we get two sustained discussions of the nature and worth of pleasure, namely at the end of Book VII and at the beginning of Book X. No back-references are made in Book X to the stretch in Book VII. Book VII is one of the books that are common to the *Eudemian Ethics* and the *Nicomachean Ethics*. The *Eudemian Ethics* is earlier than the *Nicomachean Ethics*. In the discussion of pleasure in the *Nicomachean Ethics* X there are plenty of allusions to doctrines in the *Philebus* and of objections to them; and Plato is once mentioned by name, though the dialogue is not. But in the discussion of pleasure in Book VII there are only a few possible allusions to things in the *Philebus*, and even these are not more than possible. They could all be drafts on the *Timaeus*, on the *Republic* IX or on Speusippus, or else on current dialectical debates about pleasure. The idea, cardinal to the *Philebus*, of pleasure as a specimen of the limitable, does not appear in Book VII, as it does in Book X. Nor does Plato's important argument in the *Philebus* that what is improved by the addition of something else is not itself the Summum Bonum. Aristotle adopts this argument in his *Nicomachean Ethics* x. The theory of pleasure as a process or transition, which in the *Philebus* 53 c and 54 d Socrates credits to someone else, is certainly the doctrine of Speusippus. The criticism of this theory in Book vii of the *Ethics*, as well as that in the *Topics* 121 a 30, could therefore be direct criticism of Speusippus, and not criticism of this theory as vicariously expounded in the *Philebus*.

If, when he wrote the *Eudemian Ethics*, Aristotle had known the *Philebus* well, he could not have failed to mention or to quarrel with some of its theses and arguments about pleasure. It looks as if Aristotle's colleagues in the Academy did not yet know the *Philebus* either. For, as in his *Peri Ideon*, so both in Book vii and Book x of the *Ethics* Aristotle gives us what are obviously précis of theses, arguments and objections to arguments originating in some formal Academic disputations. One hedonistic thesis is explicitly credited to Eudoxus. But not one of the debate elements assembled in Book vii hinges on anything that is peculiar to the *Philebus*. The text of the *Philebus* was not in the Academy's hands until after Aristotle had written the *Eudemian Ethics*.

Why did Plato not publish the text of the trilogy of which, apparently, the *Philebus* was the second part? Perhaps like the *Sophist* and *Politicus* the trilogy baffled or annoyed its audience. Plato's *Lecture* or *Lectures on the Good* did baffle and annoy his lay audience. Plato is now thinking above the heads of unacademic Athenians, but he has not discovered how to deliver his thoughts otherwise than in the now Procrustean form of the mime.

Conclusion

The *Philebus* was quite likely, but far from certainly, composed and orally delivered late rather than early in the period 366–361. It was not, however, then or soon issued in book-form.

The 'Pythagorean' stage in Plato's philosophical life, which Aristotle describes or misdescribes in Book I of his *Metaphysics*, from 987b15, developed out of Plato's second visit to Sicily. But Plato issued to the world no writings belonging to this stage. Whether because the Athenian public could not take in the abstruse 'Pythagorean' ideas or because Plato would not publish as his own the ideas of his Italian teachers, we are, save for the *Philebus*, without Platonic compositions to display to us this penultimate lap of Plato's intellectual course. Aristotle was better off only in having heard Plato's *Lecture on the Good*, and in knowing at first hand many of the doctrines of Archytas and Philistion. It would be only natural if this first-hand knowledge over-influenced his expositions of the 'Pythagorean' thoughts of the Plato of, say, 363–362. For these were 'unwritten', that is, no copies had been released, even to the Academy.

10. THE 'LAWS'

Plato died before completing our *Laws*. This fact has often been taken as involving that Plato was still engaged in composing the *Laws* at the time when death or weakness came upon him. Stylometrists have, accordingly, taken the *Laws* to exemplify Plato's terminal style. In fact the position was quite different. Plato had composed the *Laws* in address style eight or nine years before he died. He had nothing, or nothing much to add to it. The task which he did leave uncompleted was the task of rewriting the *Laws*, that is, of converting it from address style to conversation style. This task he began after the Younger Dionysius had been ousted by Dion in 356. Many long stretches of our *Laws* remain totally unconversationalized, other long stretches only patchily or perfunctorily so. There is very little life in the parts which have been rendered into conversation, as, for the same reason, there is not much conversational life in the last nine books of the *Republic*. Allocutions cannot be just tinkered into debates.

It has already been argued in Chapter III that Books III–VII of our *Laws* were composed in address style for delivery in Syracuse in 361–360, and were actually so delivered.

The startling postulation at 710–11 of the young and virtuous tyrant in co-operation with the sage legislator tells us by itself that the *Laws* had originally been meant as a practicable *Code Napoléon* for Syracuse. There are internal and external corroborations for this conclusion. The fictional Cretan colony for which a constitution is designed is, like Syracuse, a Dorian one. The Dionist author of the forged [Platonic] *Letters* III, VII and especially VIII makes Plato prescribe for Sicily's salvation a lot of the contents of our *Laws* III–VII many years before Plato's death and therefore many years before the publication of our *Laws*. The author of the *Third Letter*, which was written before Dion's assassination in 354, knows something about the Pre-

ambles to the Laws. The author of the *Seventh Letter* 337 D
is *au fait* with the differences between the Best State and the
Second-Best State, described in the *Laws* V 739 and VII 807.
He must have heard Plato deliver this part of the *Laws*
when Plato was in Sicily in 361–360.

Aristotle in his *Politics* II comments at some length on
the *Laws*. With other reasons for suspecting that the young
Aristotle was with Plato, Speusippus, Xenocrates and
Eudoxus in Sicily in 361–360 his knowledge only of *Laws*
III–VII suggests the possibility that he too heard this part of
our *Laws* being delivered in Syracuse. Interestingly,
Aristotle makes not the Athenian Stranger but Socrates
the mouthpiece of the *Laws*, so presumably Plato changed
the discussion-leader when he began to render the *Laws*
into conversation style for Athenian listeners. Perhaps
Plato converted Socrates into the Athenian Stranger in
order that the Athenian recipients of the *Republic* should
not be dismayed at finding its discussion-leader surrendering, in the relatively unutopian *Laws*, some of his more
vigorous doctrines, for example about private property
and about tyrants.

Plato had composed the original version in monologue
of *Laws* III–VII by 361–360 and had not yet composed
Books VIII–XII. This second half must have been composed,
anyhow in bulk, by 357–356, when Dion defeated the
young tyrant who was to give Plato's *Code Napoléon* its
realization in a reconstituted Syracuse. Dion nullified
Plato's legislative programme. It was only then that Plato
set to work to salvage something from the ruins by converting his legislative programme for Sicily into educative

literature for some private bodies of senior Athenians. Presumably it was at this stage that he added as a prefatory digression a piece that he had written independently on 'Drunkenness'; as well as another piece, now the body of Book x, on 'Unbelief'. The preservation from oblivion of the latter piece compensates for the preservation from oblivion of the former.

Aristotle may have heard the recitation of the original *Laws*, that is, *Laws* III–VII, in address style in 361–360. He could not have been in possession of a text of our *Laws* until he was nearing forty years of age, and it may have been later than that. He wrote his *Politics* in ignorance of its second half.

II. THE 'PHAEDRUS'

In the *Phaedrus* 243 A, 244 A, 257 A Socrates three times likens himself to Stesichorus, who was struck blind for maligning Helen of Troy and was given back his sight when he recanted. Socrates recants his first speech about Love, which he composed to show that he could not only criticize, but also do better than Lysias. His second speech is his Palinode. But the *Phaedrus* as a whole is a recantation or palinode by Plato himself. For Plato goes back on what he had said in the *Gorgias*, namely that rhetoric is just a knack and not an 'art', and has, by implication, no teachable principles. In the *Phaedrus* he allows that rhetoric is teachable, though the proper teaching of it would take a vastly different shape from that of the rhetoric teaching of the sophists and presumably of Isocrates. The proper teaching of rhetoric would embody instruction in Division, Definition and, let us call it, Psychology. The technical tips collected in the many *Arts of Rhetoric* that the sophists had composed would still have their place, but only a small place in the reformed rhetoric-curriculum which Socrates delineates. In 260E Socrates refers to the view expressed in the *Gorgias* that rhetoric is a knack and not an art. Against this view he now allows that it is a teachable art, if the pupil pays proper heed to philosophy.

Aristotle's *Art of Rhetoric* has been called 'an expanded *Phaedrus*'. It should have been called 'an applied *Phaedrus*'. The curricular prescriptions given by Socrates tally in part very closely with the actual contents of Aristotle's *Art*. Aristotle does produce comprehensive lists of temperaments, virtues, vices and passions; he does distinguish and define these; and he does show what specific kinds of rhetorical argument would be apt to persuade listeners of specific temperaments or in specific tempers. He does also conflate and improve the technical tricks of the trade which the sophists had prescribed in their *Arts of Rhetoric*.

Aristotle's *Art of Rhetoric*, as we have it, cannot be earlier than the middle 330's, but it contains a lot of residues from his early teaching days. We know that he began to teach rhetoric under the auspices of the Academy when he was quite a young man and when Plato was still alive.

There are frequent interlockings between Aristotle's *Art of Rhetoric* and his *Topics*. In both his *Art of Rhetoric* and his *Topics* Aristotle is much interested in some fairly general, though still quite informal differences between types of argumentation. In this respect his *Art of Rhetoric* goes beyond what Socrates prescribes in the *Phaedrus*. In another respect Aristotle's *Art of Rhetoric* falls short of what

Socrates requires. It contains no instruction in the procedures of Division and Definition. The *Art of Rhetoric* is,
indeed, stuffed with definitions and it contains a good
many divisions. But the student is treated as one who is
already quite at home in the drills of dividing and
defining.

We have ample evidence that Aristotle, Xenocrates,
Speusippus and Theophrastus did systematically teach
these drills, since the lists of their works contain scores of
books of divisions and definitions. In the last ten pages of
Diogenes Laertius' *Life of Plato* we have an album of
divisions which Aristotle is incorrectly supposed to have
extracted out of Plato. The generic terms that are there
divided into their species are mostly untechnical terms that
would be familiar to any seventeen-year-old. Some of the
divisions themselves read like juvenile products.

The so-called *Platonic Definitions* seems similarly to be a
class-album of definitions. Here nearly all the *definienda*
are unscientific and unphilosophical terms; but the
definitions offered quite frequently incorporate technical
or semi-technical Aristotelian terms; and the genus-
differentia structure of definition is quite often observed,
though very often not. Only two or three of the definitions are of Platonic origin; a few more are almost certainly of Aristotelian origin. Many of the remainder read
like juvenile essays in definition. We can safely date the
assembly of this album before the composition of the
Topics, especially Book v, where many of the definitions
are properly criticized. Seemingly the systematic teaching of division and definition had become a standard part

of the curriculum for beginners in the Academy, whether they were to go on to dialectic or rhetoric or both. The, to us, infinitely tedious and philosophically unrewarding divisions in the *Sophist* and *Politicus* could be explained and justified as Plato's personal contribution to this preliminary part of the curriculum. 'Dialectic', he may be saying, 'comes later, for those who have been through these propaedeutic drills of dividing and defining.'

Why did Plato write the *Phaedrus*? To announce to the Greek world in general and to would-be students of rhetoric in particular that the Academy was now, despite his *Gorgias*, to go into competition with Isocrates' school as a school of rhetoric. The new curriculum for the rhetoric students would be long and arduous (272 B–C, 273 E, 274 A), but their wits would be trained in a philosophically proper manner. They would learn to speak and write well, since they would learn to think well. As Socrates' own eloquence in the *Phaedrus* is both profounder in content and better organized in form than the speech of Lysias, so the Academy's scheme of instruction in rhetoric will make its students both wiser and more winning than those of Isocrates. In his *Phaedrus* Plato is showing to would-be rhetoric students that the philosopher can defeat the rhetorician in rhetoric. Being addressed specially to such Phaedruses, the dialogue is devoid of philosophical argumentation, though it contains some philosophical rhetoric.

There was another institution with which the Academy would compete. There were available numerous manuals of rhetoric, namely the *Arts* composed by Polus, Evenus,

Thrasymachus, Theodectes and many others; and it is clear that many young men hoped to make orators of themselves by memorization of these manuals. Some of these manuals were versified to assist memorization. Socrates' strictures at 275–6 on books and book-learning were strictures specifically on these manuals of rhetoric and, by implication, on technical cram-books in general. Rhetoric should be taught *viva voce* by teachers who would answer questions and would themselves try out their students by questioning of the dialectical kind (276E). Latter-day tutors have also been known to discourage reliance on books entitled *Teach Yourself So and So*; and to distinguish between learning to think and learning by heart.

Given that the Academy was, despite the *Gorgias*, now to cater for students of rhetoric, it is small wonder that Plato should have broken his general rule and wound up his *Phaedrus* with a tribute by name to a living person, Isocrates. An *amende* was called for. Not only had Isocrates, anonymously, been treated very scathingly in the terminal *Euthydemus*, but now his school of rhetoric was to be in competition with the school of its major critic.

If the *Phaedrus* is the announcement of the Academy's entry into the teaching of rhetoric, then the date of the composition of the *Phaedrus* should be close to the date of the beginning of this teaching. We know roughly when this was. It was when Aristotle was at the start of his teaching career. But when was this? We can be sure that the Academy would not have made this bellicose innovation when Plato, Speusippus, Xenocrates and Eudoxus were preparing for their forthcoming departure to Sicily in the spring of 361 or were already overseas. Aristotle was then only about twenty-three, and anyhow, as is argued at the end of Chapter III, he may have gone with the others to Syracuse.

On the other hand it cannot have been long after Plato and the others returned to Athens from Sicily *via* Olympia in the summer of 360. (*a*) Aristotle wrote a *Gryllus*, as Isocrates, Speusippus and many others are said to have done. These were rhetorical tributes to Gryllus, who died in 362–361, and were partly meant to gratify his father, Xenophon, who died in 354. This would tend to show that Aristotle had already begun to teach as well as to practise oratory only if the story is true that Aristotle's *Gryllus* inartistically contained contributions to the theory of rhetoric. (*b*) Isocrates' pupil, Cephisodorus, counter-attacking against Aristotelian criticisms of Isocrates, levelled his shots at Plato, including his Theory of Forms, since he knew nothing of Aristotle's own philosophical thought. This shows that Aristotle was teaching rhetoric before he had become known for any philosophical doctrines, and certainly before he had published any of his own quite early criticisms of the Theory of Forms. (*c*) From his *Rhetoric* and his *Topics* it is clear that Aristotle taught both sides of the Art of Discourse to the same students. Isocrates' *Antidosis* shows that dialectic was a part of the curriculum of the Academy some time before 353. Plato's *Parmenides*, Part II, seems to be a curricular model of systematic dialectic. Its rigours, like those of the *Sophist*, indicate that some Academic students are already quite sophisticated dialecticians. So the teaching of dialectic must have been in progress in the Academy for some time before Plato composed the *Parmenides*. Unless we credit Plato with very great intellectual vigour in his late seventies, we must date the start of Aristotle's *Topics* classes quite or very early in the 350's. So Plato's *Phaedrus* was probably composed and published near the beginning of the 350's. It was certainly written before the completion of Plato's *Theaetetus*, since the *Phaedrus* is a Socratic dialogue and the *Theaetetus* is the last dialogue in which Socrates can be discussion-leader.

If, as seems likely, the *Cratylus* was written or anyhow completed after the *Phaedrus* and before the completion of the *Theaetetus*, the risk of over-congesting Plato's seventies will incline us to put the *Phaedrus* at the earliest possible date in the 350's. Or even to surmise that Plato wrote it while in Sicily in 361–360 for delivery immediately after his return to Athens in 360.

Perhaps, even, Plato delivered it at Olympia. (*a*) We know from the *Seventh Letter* 350 B that he did attend the Olympic Games of 360 while *en route* for home. Diogenes Laertius says that the eyes of all Greece were on Plato at these Games. (*b*) Olympia is mentioned twice in the *Phaedrus*, at 236 B and 256 B; and in its opening page a gratuitous reference is made to the Temple of Zeus in Athens, the Olympieum, which could have reminded his listeners of the most celebrated edifice in Olympia, which had the same name. (*c*) Zeus, the tutelary deity of Olympia and the Olympic Games, is given markedly solemn treatment four or five times in the *Phaedrus*; as Hera is once, whose temple in Olympia was second only to that of Zeus. Athene gets no mention in the *Phaedrus* and Dionysus gets only one passing mention. (*d*) The invocation to Zeus Philios in the *Phaedrus* 234 E could have reminded listeners of the famous Temple of Zeus Philios at Megalopolis in Arcadia, if this was already built or being built. (*e*) The *Phaedrus*, unprecedentedly save for the *Phaedo*, closes with a devout prayer from Socrates. Somewhat surprisingly he prays to Pan. Now not only was Pan the special god of the Arcadians, but according to Pausanias' *Elis* I xx 9 there was an altar to Pan inside the town hall of Olympia itself. Maybe this town hall was the place where literary compositions were delivered at festivals, as they were in the council house at Elis (*Elis* II xxiii 7). (*f*) In the *Phaedrus* 236 B there is a mention of the Cypselid offering at Olympia. This was a cedarwood chest, the decorations on which are described at great length by Pausanias in *Elis* I xvii 5–xix 10. Its fourth panel depicts Boreas flying off with Oreithyia. In xix 8–9 Pausanias refers also to representations of Centaurs and winged horses; and at xviii 5 of the Gorgons. In the *Phaedrus* 229 B–D, without any obvious dramatic point, Socrates talks anti-sceptically about the stories of Boreas and Oreithyia, of Centaurs, Gorgons and winged horses. (*g*) Two bronze horses, given by Phormis, a beautiful horse and an ugly horse, are described by Pausanias in *Elis* I xxvii 2–3 and these already remind us of Plato's beautiful horse and ugly horse in the *Phaedrus* 253 D–254 E. But the erotic frenzy reputedly induced in real horses by the ugly bronze horse at Olympia very powerfully reminds us of the erotic frenzy that is displayed by the ugly horse itself in the *Phaedrus*. (*h*) In the *Phaedrus* 254E, a very horsey dialogue, we hear of the starting-rope, ὕσπληξ, used in horse-races. Pausanias uses the same rare word in his description of the famous starting device used at Olympia for horse-races (II xx 11).

Socrates' explicit mentions of Olympia, his emphatic pieties towards Zeus, Hera and Pan, and these parallels between what sightseers at Olympia would gaze at and what Socrates mentions, quite strongly suggest that Plato was deliberately putting into his *Phaedrus* bits of local colour and expressions of local religious sentiment for the gratification of an Olympic audience. Even the mention in the *Phaedrus* 267B of the sophist Hippias as 'our friend from Elis' could be a courtesy to the Elian hosts of the Games audience; and it might be no accident that the dramatic scene of the *Phaedrus* is set with some emphasis in high summer, the season of the Olympic Games.

Many of these coincidences, if taken by themselves, would be quite or fairly unstriking coincidences. The conjunction of them all is more than fairly striking. As independent arguments show that the *Phaedrus* was composed when Aristotle was more, but not very much more than twenty-three years of age, this conjunction of possible, likely and certain allusions inside the *Phaedrus* to Olympia and the Olympic Games makes it probable that this dialogue was composed for delivery and was actually delivered at the Olympic Games in the July of 360, when Aristotle was twenty-four or twenty-five. Doubtless the dialogue was a prize-winner. The book of the dialogue was presumably issued directly after Plato's return to Athens.

The hypothesis argued at the end of Chapter III that Aristotle was with Plato, Speusippus, Xenocrates and Eudoxus in Sicily in 361–360, would fit in rather neatly with the idea that it was during the course of this visit that Plato adopted the plan that Aristotle should now start the teaching of rhetoric in the Academy. Perhaps it was during a joint sojourn in Syracuse that Plato got to know his Aristotle well enough to entrust him with the new teaching commission and to discuss with him the composition of its curriculum. _____

There are close connexions between the *Phaedrus* and some orations by Isocrates, particularly his *Helen*. For one thing, in *Helen* 64 we not only get the story of Stesichorus being blinded for his disparagement of Helen of Troy and having his sight restored after his recantation, but Isocrates' words ... τῶν ὀφθαλμῶν ἐστερημένος... γνοὺς τὴν αἰτίαν ...τὴν καλουμένην παλινῳδίαν ἐποίησε are surely echoed in the *Phaedrus* 243 A τῶν γὰρ ὀμμάτων στερηθεὶς...ἔγνω τὴν αἰτίαν...καὶ ποιήσας δὴ πᾶσαν τὴν καλουμένην παλινῳδίαν...Moreover Isocrates, after gently scolding Gorgias for defending instead of eulogizing Helen, says 'But that I may not seem to be taking the easiest course criticizing others without exhibiting any specimen of my own, I will try to speak of this same woman disregarding all that others have said about her' (15). In the *Phaedrus* 235 Socrates too not only finds fault with Lysias' speech, but accepts the challenge to produce a better speech of his own.

Both the *Helen* 54–60 and the *Phaedrus* 250 D–256 contain an excursus on the power of Beauty, with that in the *Phaedrus* vastly excelling in eloquence that in the *Helen*.

In the *Phaedrus* 269 E Socrates' queer phrase ἀδολεσχίας καὶ μετεωρολογίας must be a deliberate parody of Isocrates' ἀδολεσχία καὶ μικρολογία; and Plato concocts other parodies in the *Republic* 488 E and 489 C. Isocrates had first produced his phrase in his *Against the Sophists* 8 in disparagement of eristic. He repeats it in his *Antidosis* 262. That Plato has the former passage in mind is proved by the fact that in the preceding paragraph of the *Phaedrus* 269 D Socrates echoes the sentiments and some of the diction of Isocrates' *Against the Sophists* 14–15. Plato is retorting to Isocrates' rudeness about dialectic by saying that orators themselves are no good without philosophy. That the *Phaedrus* 267 A–B echoes Isocrates' *Panegyricus* 8 was noticed by Cicero in his *De Oratore* XIII 37 and by W. H. Thompson in his edition of the *Phaedrus* of 1868.

In the *Classical Quarterly* of 1937 R. L. Howland argues in much greater detail for the same conclusion that Plato's *Phaedrus* was in some way aimed at Isocrates and particularly at his *Helen*. But why? If we examine the *Helen* we find it prefaced by a seemingly irrelevant attack on some unnamed teachers who teach young men eristic. In the opening paragraph there is an unmistakable allusion to Plato's *Protagoras*, and in 9 these teachers are reproached for laying claim to 'political science', which reproach might well be aimed at Plato's *Gorgias* 521 D and/or *Euthydemus* 291–2. Then, after an ordinary-seeming encomium on Theseus and Helen of Troy, we are surprised to read in

66–7 'Apart from the arts and philosophic studies and all the other benefits which one might attribute to her [Helen] and the Trojan War...it is owing to Helen that we are not the slaves of the barbarians.'

In his *Busiris*, which in some points resembles the *Helen*, Isocrates says on the first page, '...I have thought I should advise you by letter, though concealing my views, to the best of my ability, from everyone else.' Here Isocrates seems to be announcing that his *Busiris* has a double meaning, though it is hard to unravel its hidden meaning. We should consider the possibility that the *Helen* too has a double meaning.

Now in Plato's *Gorgias* Gorgias does put up a defence of rhetoric. So maybe Isocrates is making Helen of Troy stand for rhetoric or eloquence, so that his oration is at once an eulogy of Helen of Troy for whom Gorgias had in real life provided only an apology, and at the same time an eulogy of rhetoric for which the Gorgias of Plato's *Gorgias* had provided only an apology. A long section of the real Gorgias' *Encomium to Helen* is in fact an encomium to Speech or Persuasion. Isocrates' queer assertion that 'Apart from the arts and philosophic studies and all the other benefits which one might attribute to her and the Trojan War...it is owing to Helen that we are not slaves of the barbarians' could then be construed as just a version of what he says in the *Antidosis* 294 '...those qualities by which the nature of man rises above the other animals, and the race of the Hellenes above the barbarians, namely the fact that you have been educated as have been no other people in wisdom and in speech' (cf. *Nicocles* 5–6). In

270

short, Isocrates wrote his *Helen* as a veiled riposte to Plato's *Gorgias*, and Plato's *Phaedrus* is in part a riposte to this riposte. Isocrates' 'Stesichorus' stands for Plato, and so does Plato's. On this interpretation the opening of the *Helen* would not be irrelevant to its veiled point. Its irrelevance to its overt point is noticed by Aristotle in his *Rhetoric* III 14.

If Isocrates' encomium to Helen of Troy was meant allegorically and if Plato was aware of this, it would explain what the joke is in the *Phaedrus* 261 and 269 A, where a number of sophists are given the names of Homeric heroes. As Isocrates uses the equations 'Helen = rhetoric' and 'Stesichorus = Plato', so Plato in parody uses the equations 'Stesichorus = Plato', 'Nestor = Gorgias', 'Odysseus = Thrasymachus or Theodorus', 'Adrastus = (?)Antiphon'.

What would follow from this hypothesis? First, it would follow, what we can establish independently, that the *Phaedrus* is later than the *Helen*, and later, therefore, than 371–370. Next, it would follow that, whatever may have been their private relationships, Isocrates and Plato were publicly sparring. As in his *Euthydemus* Plato says some harsh things about Isocrates, so in his *Helen* Isocrates says some harsh things about Plato; and as in his *Helen* Isocrates gives short shrift to the teaching aims and teaching methods of Plato, so in his *Euthydemus*, *Gorgias* and *Phaedrus* Plato gives short shrift to the teaching aims and methods of Isocrates. There was open feud between the two schools, a feud which Aristotle and Cephisodorus continued. Next, as Plato takes himself to be the main target of Isocrates'

Helen, it would follow that when Isocrates wrote his *Helen* it was Plato who was the main teacher of eristic at whom Isocrates was girding, and therefore that eristic was the sole subject then being taught by Plato that Isocrates thought worth mentioning. He says not a word here about arithmetic, geometry or astronomy, though he mentions these in his *Antidosis* 261–9, *Panathenaicus* 26–8 and *Busiris* 23. This, with other indications, shows that before the foundation of the Academy proper, the curriculum of which is described and explained in *Republic* VII, Plato had been running a one-teacher school for young men, in which a main subject taught was elenctic disputation, or what Plato and Aristotle call 'dialectic'. As the *Helen* is later than the *Protagoras*, *Euthydemus* and *Gorgias*, it would follow that our Academy was started only after these dialogues were published, and after the *Helen* had retorted to them. For reasons debated in Chapter V, Plato now switched from teaching his pupils dialectic to teaching no dialectic at all to the students in the Academy, including Aristotle, until after they had been through the propae-deutic studies described in *Republic* VII, indeed until they were out of their twenties. If Jebb's dating of the *Helen* to the end of the 370's were proved, we should know that the Academy proper began only three or four years before Aristotle joined it in 367.

12. THE 'CRATYLUS'

The *Cratylus* discusses at length the meanings of words and mentions cursorily the composition of sentences out of words. At 429 C it raises the problem of falsehood which is central to the *Theaetetus* and *Sophist*, namely how a sentence can say something and yet say what is not so. At 385 C Socrates had naughtily extracted from his interlocutor an admission that the parts of true and false *logoi* must themselves be true or false. At 386 Socrates makes against Protagoras' doctrine of the relativity of truth objections which he amplifies in the *Theaetetus*, from 161 B and 166–71. The *Cratylus* thus has close links with the *Theaetetus* and *Sophist*, and, being philosophically more primitive than either, it must be earlier than the *Theaetetus*. This priority is proved also by the fact that Socrates is discussion-leader in the *Cratylus*. Between 439 C and 440 C Socrates develops a point affirmed in the *Philebus* 59 A–C and argued also in the *Theaetetus* 182–183 C, namely that even if all things are mutable, still the concept expressed by a word cannot itself be one concept today and another concept tomorrow. We could not describe even the inconstancies of things if the concepts employed in these descriptions were themselves inconstant.

At the beginning of his *De Interpretatione* Aristotle discriminates nouns from verbs and says that in the expression of a truth or falsehood at the least a noun and a verb must be combined (see also *Categories* 1 a 16, 2 a 4). Plato who says this too in his *Theaetetus* 201 E–202 C and 206 D and his *Sophist* 262 D–264 B had done so very briefly in the *Cratylus* at 425 A and 431 B. But his interest in the differences between nouns and verbs manifests itself in the *Cratylus* in a quite different way as well. The bulk of the *Cratylus* is an unserious exercise in extracting the etymological roots of a variety of Greek words. Now though Socrates does not explicitly declare it as his policy, most of the root-words that he proffers are themselves not nouns but verbs. His last sentence in 411 C may be a hint to this effect.

We need not suppose that Plato is here trying to contribute a serious genetic hypothesis to the infant science of philology. But the fact that he is now paying sustained attention to verbs quite strongly suggests that this dialogue, with the *Theaetetus* and *Sophist*, reflects some new grammatical and semantic interests that are now current inside the Academy, interests which Aristotle's *De Interpretatione* and *Categories* also reflect. Parsing has begun, and so has the Theory of Parsing. In the light of all these affinities, it seems reasonable to date the *Cratylus* very early in the 350's, say 359–358.

On the other hand, cogent stylometric considerations have led scholars to collocate the *Cratylus* not with the *Theaetetus* and *Sophist* but very much earlier, with the latest of Plato's eristic dialogues, like the *Meno*. It is tempting to try to resolve the apparent conflict in this way. As Plato had been teaching dialectic to young men up to the time of the *Meno*, so, half a generation later, the young men in the Academy are newly being taught dialectic by Aristotle. Plato writes for the new generation of students of dialectic in the idioms and in the frame of mind in which he had composed for their predecessors some fifteen years before. After a long absence, jollity reappears. Once again Plato can think alongside of dialectical apprentices, though this time their coach is not himself, but Aristotle. Perhaps here too the stretches of elenctic questioning from 385 to 391 A, and from 428 E, are partly drawn from the records of Moots in which Aristotle, his pupils, and maybe his colleagues as well, are now exercising their elenctic muscles.

As there is a dangling 'tomorrow' in the *Cratylus* 396E it may be that Plato had originally planned the dialogue as the first member of a trilogy. If so, the plan broke down. The philosophical content of the *Theaetetus* could have qualified it to be the sequel, but there is no continuity of story or identity of *dramatis personae* between this dialogue and the *Cratylus*. The *Theaetetus* had clearly not been originally intended to be Act I to the *Sophist*. For the *Sophist* itself was to have been Act I in a trilogy of the *Sophist*, the *Politicus* and the *Philosopher*. Only at a fairly late stage was the *Theaetetus*, which is not about a calling, conscripted into a trilogy with the *Sophist* and *Politicus*.

There is no reason to suppose that there was any delay in the appearance of the book of the *Cratylus*. Aristotle does not discuss its contents, but he re-employs some of its etymologies.

13. THE 'THEAETETUS'

It has already been claimed in Chapter II, Section 2(*h*), that the unparalleled dramatic structure of the *Theaetetus* in echoed *oratio recta*, combined with the replacement of Socrates by the Eleatic Stranger in the *Sophist* and *Politicus*, and the near disappearance in these two dialogues of interlocutors' vocatives, proves that Plato had been taken ill very shortly before the oral delivery of the trilogy. As Seneca tells us that Plato did have a severe illness as a result of his Sicilian journeys but a good long time before his death, it is reasonable to conclude that these dialogues were composed and at the last moment hurriedly reshaped, not only some time in the 350's, but early enough in the 350's for the illness to be attributed to the last of Plato's voyages in 360.

It has been argued in this present chapter that the *Theaetetus* is later than the *Timaeus* and than the *Philebus*. Scholars agree in putting the *Theaetetus* later than the *Phaedrus*, which may have been delivered at Olympia in 360. The *Philebus*, the *Phaedrus* and the *Cratylus* have Socrates for discussion-leader; so all three must on this score too precede the *Theaetetus* and the Eleatic Stranger's two dialogues. The philosophical content of the *Cratylus* shows that it is prior, but not much prior to the *Theaetetus*; and the long missing joviality of its style and its brief revivals of the Socratic Method suggest that once again Plato has juvenile students of eristic to listen to and to write for. As Aristotle's *Topics* classes may have begun very near the beginning of the 350's, the *Cratylus* may have been written in 359 or 358. If so, the *Theaetetus*, of which the later parts seem to be moderately sophisticated, might belong to the period 358–357, if not later still.

In the *Theaetetus* 185–6 Socrates draws attention to elements present in our knowledge even of sensible objects, which cannot themselves be the gift of sight, hearing or taste. These are such notions as *existence*, *non-existence*, *difference*, *identity*, *singleness*, *pluralness*, *similarity*, *dissimilarity*, *beauty*, *ugliness*, *goodness* and *badness*. These notions are ubiquitous notions, neutral as between one sense and another sense. They are labelled 'common', 'κοινά'. As early as in his *Rhetoric* and *Topics* Aristotle also classes as 'common' most of these and a few other trans-departmental or topic-neutral notions; and Plato, without again using this epithet, makes these notions the proper subject-matter of dialectic in his *Parmenides* 136. The five Greatest Kinds in the *Sophist* are selected out of this general class of 'common' notions. This discrimination of the topic-neutral concepts from all other concepts seems to have become common ground in the Academy not very late in the 350's. It is quite independent of Plato's Theory of Forms, since Aristotle, who vigorously attacks this Theory, accepts and operates with the doctrine of the topic-neutral concepts. In Book v and in Book x of his *Metaphysics* he subjects the whole range of these 'common' concepts to dissection. In a different way and with a different purpose the whole of Part II of Plato's *Parmenides* is concentrated upon the 'common' concepts.

It is argued in the preceding section on the *Cratylus* and in the succeeding section on the *Sophist* that in the *Theaetetus* and the *Sophist*, and in a small degree in the *Cratylus*, Plato is now operating with some semi-technical terms and some semi-technical grammatical and semantic ideas which are wielded also by Aristotle in works some of which are certainly early works. There are signs that both Plato and Aristotle are here drawing on, and also contributing to an Academic pool of methodological ideas and idioms; a pool to which, among others, Speusippus is also contributing, for example the notions of *genus*, *species* and *differentia*. In this area the septuagenarian Plato is using some of the same dictions, and talking about the same subjects as the young author of the *Categories*, *Topics* and *De Interpretatione*.

The *Theaetetus* is about fifteen Stephanus pages too long, that is, in excess of what seems to be the regulation length of a middle-sized dialogue. Two of these excess pages may be the opening pages leading to the slave's recitation, unless this last-minute supplement had been compensated for by an excision elsewhere. There is also the acknowledged digression from 172C to 177C. Not only is this stretch totally irrelevant to the topic of the dialogue, but it seems to reflect the bitter, self-justifying mood in which Plato had been at the end of the 370's. Theodorus, like many commentators, appreciates this digression as an edifying relief from argument.

If this part of Socrates' conversation with Theodorus is a, perhaps resurrected, addition to the original text of the dialogue, then maybe the whole of Socrates' present conversation with Theodorus is an addition. It is of about the postulated length. It does incorporate some discussion of points highly pertinent to the theme of the dialogue, but it also incorporates a good deal of information about Schools of Thought, namely, Protagoreanism, Heracleiteanism and Monism, information which might have struck a lay audience as over-didactic and not conspicuously relevant to the dialogue's problem.

In his *Antidosis* 268–9 and 285 Isocrates seems to reproach the Academy for teaching the History of Ideas. It is a well-known practice of Aristotle to preface his own discussions of philosophical issues with accounts of earlier views. In his *Cratylus*, *Theaetetus* and *Sophist*, but not his

Politicus, Plato seems to have adopted the same educative policy of putting the issues under discussion into an historical perspective. The political history in the *Laws* III may reflect the same policy. It would be anachronistic to require of Plato or of Aristotle that their essays in the history of ideas be severely scholarly.

The new practice was adopted, presumably, for pedagogic reasons. But what is good pedagogy is bad theatre. So it may be that Plato made these additions to the book of the *Theaetetus* for the sake specifically of students in the Academy. He is now thinking of curricular uses for the books of his dialogues. In the addition to the *Politicus*, 286 B–287 A, which can hardly have been intended for lay listeners, the Stranger says that the prime object of such discourses is to convert their serious hearers into better dialecticians; and this reminds us of Parmenides' advice to Socrates just before he begins his demonstration of the Zenonian Method.

If Plato did add about fifteen supplementary pages to the original dialogue, whether the pages suggested or others, at least he seems not to have kept the dialogue on his shelf very long. The dialogue was out of his hands before he started the hiatus-pruning to which his texts of the *Philebus*, *Sophist* and *Politicus* were subjected, if the hypothesis is correct that is argued in the concluding section of this chapter. Quite likely the text of our *Theaetetus* was in Aristotle's hands when he was a little under thirty years of age. Without mentioning the dialogue by name he draws on it a good deal, though always from the earlier parts of it, in his *Topics*, *De Anima* and *Metaphysics*, especially IV.

It is just worth while considering the orthodox dating of the *Theaetetus*. The battle from which Theaetetus died was in 369, and scholars have argued that Plato wrote the dialogue, as a sort of obituary notice, within a couple of years of Theaetetus' death. No good reason is adduced for this conclusion. The only other dialogue in which a participant's death is mentioned is the *Phaedo*, yet scholars have not argued that the *Phaedo* must therefore have been composed in 398 or 397. But anyhow the opening pages of the *Theaetetus* in which Theaetetus is reported as dying are a late addition to the body of the dialogue, an addition made in a hurry for the very special purpose of getting the discussion into echoed *oratio recta* and thus of making it deliverable, as it stood, from a throat other than Plato's. The dialogue had not been composed with an obituary intention.

14. THE 'SOPHIST'

The philosophical theme of the *Sophist* develops out of a central theme of the *Theaetetus* and an incidental theme of the *Cratylus*. In abstruseness the *Sophist* greatly excels both of those dialogues. Only highly sophisticated listeners could have followed the arguments or even understood the problems of the central core of the *Sophist*. The recipients whom Plato now has in mind are either his own colleagues or else they are his colleagues together with those students whose dialectical gymnastic has already gone a long way. The Stranger's interlocutor is the youthful Theaetetus, so probably the dialogue was meant to teach select young men. As the gymnastic operations deployed by Parmenides in Part II of the *Parmenides* are explicitly recommended for study and emulation by the juvenile Socrates, and as this part of the *Parmenides* seems both to be philosophically ahead of the *Sophist* and to take over from it a few dialectical points, it seems reasonable to suppose that Plato optimistically believes that some of the Academy's students of dialectic are now abreast of the *Sophist's* and the *Parmenides'* problems and arguments. The Eleatic Stranger's young answerer grasps fairly readily the Stranger's subtle and important proof, 237 B–239 B, that what does not exist cannot be spoken of either in the singular or in the plural, and yet that to say this is itself to speak in the singular or the plural of what does not exist. The Academy must now for some time have been training its students in dialectic. But the progressive systematization and formalization of its debates have not only produced a team of dialectically sophisticated twenty-year-olders; they have also shaped the current thinking of Speusippus, Xenocrates, Eudoxus, Aristotle, and of Plato himself. The terminal Plato is partly the product of his own Academy.

In the *Sophist* especially, in the *Theaetetus*, and in a very small degree in the *Cratylus*, we find Plato employing what seem to be nascent Academic technical terms. 'Affirmation' and 'Negation', φάσις and ἀπόφασις, are used in the *Sophist* 257 B and 263 E as they are in Aristotle's *Topics*. The abstract noun 'Quality', ποιότης, is used with a grimace in the *Theaetetus* 182 A. 'Differentia', διαφορά and διαφορότης, seems to be employed, though rather loosely, in the *Theaetetus*, from 208 C, and perhaps also in the *Politicus* 285 B.

More important is the following. In his *De Interpretatione* 16a, 16b20, *De Anima* 430a26, 432a10 and
Categories 1a16, 2a4 Aristotle considers side by side the
grammatical structure of sentences conveying truths and
falsehoods, and the logical or semantic structure of the
truths and falsehoods themselves. As such a sentence consists at the least of a noun coupled with a verb, so the truth
or falsehood conveyed by it consists of the *significatum* of
the noun coupled with that of the verb. These *significata*
are themselves neither true nor false. They are the atomic
components of which truths and falsehoods are mole-
cules. Correspondingly the intellectual apprehension of
these atomic components is not yet believing. In the
apprehension of them there is no being wrong. It is, to
speak with Locke, the bare having a simple idea, Aristotle's *noema*. In his expansion of these points Aristotle
speaks of the *synthesis* or the *combination*, συμπλοκή, both of
words in a sentence, and of *noemata* in a truth or falsehood
(see also *Metaphysics* VI last section, and IX last section).
Plato in his *Cratylus* 425 A, 431 B, *Theaetetus* 202 B and
Sophist 259 E, 262–263 D mentions or discusses the same
matters and uses most of the same dictions, though he uses
the technical word '*noema*' only in the *Parmenides* 132 B–C.
In *Sophist* 259 E Plato speaks of τὴν . . . τῶν εἰδῶν συμπλο-
κήν, combination of Forms, very much as Aristotle speaks
of the συμπλοκὴ νοημάτων, combination of ideas, in his *De
Anima* 432a12 and 430a28. In Part I of the *Parmenides* the
young Socrates, on the defensive, suggests that his Forms
may just be *noemata*.

This atom-molecule model of the sayable, the thinkable and the knowable has always proved very captivating. Locke is as contented with it as Aristotle here seems to be. But Plato is suspicious of it; and he puts his finger on what is wrong with it. For in the *Theaetetus* and the *Sophist* he draws analogies between the simples of which truths and falsehoods are supposedly complexes and the letters, that is the vowels and consonants into which monosyllables can be analysed. He is interested in syllables *qua* phonetic units, and therefore in their letters *qua* voiceable vowels and consonants, and not *qua* written characters. Now a voiced syllable is not a synthesis or combination of independently voiceable consonants and vowels, since consonants are not independently voiceable. They are *consonants*. The syllable 'Top' is not three separate noises; it is a single noise, but one which can in three distinguishable ways resemble or differ from other monosyllables. It is not a compound of components; it is an unit with independently variable features. This phoneme-syllable model and not the atom-molecule model is the right model according to which truths and falsehoods should be analysed, and Plato realized this. So Plato was a long way ahead of Aristotle, who does not here use the letter-syllable analogy in this connexion, though he uses it in other connexions. Aristotle's employment of the notions of *synthesis* and *combination*, συμπλοκή, was then not derived from Plato's employment of them in the *Theaetetus* and *Sophist*. It looks as if the idioms used by Plato and Aristotle in giving their importantly different accounts of the internal complexities of truths and falsehoods reflect, but reflect in independent ways, some grammatical and semantic discussions that were in progress in the Academy some way on in the 350's.

We have a strong reason for thinking that anyhow the *Politicus* and very likely the *Sophist* too were not issued in book-form immediately after the recitation of the trilogy to which they belong. For in the *Politicus* 286 B–287 A there is a clear allusion to a bad reception that had been accorded to both dialogues. The lay listeners had audibly and with some justice grumbled at the length and irrelevance of the *Sophist*'s discussion of Non-Being, and the *Politicus*' treatment of the Backward Rotating Cosmos and the analogy from Weaving. So our *Politicus* which embodies this apology *cum* reprimand must be a second edition, and one not intended for the ears to which the first edition had been presented. Perhaps both of these ill-received dialogues were on Plato's shelf for some time after their delivery. As there obtains an important stylistic difference between the *Theaetetus* on the one hand and the *Sophist* and *Politicus* on the other hand, this possibility of the two latter dialogues having been kept on Plato's shelf for some time may turn out to be of some significance. It will be considered at the end of this chapter.

There is one possible clue which suggests that the book of the *Sophist* had reached Sicily by late 353 or 352. Plato's forcible phrase at 266 C 'a sort of man-made dream produced for those who are awake' seems to be imitated in the last sentence of the *Eighth Letter*.

15. THE 'POLITICUS'

This weary dialogue is the third member of the actual trilogy of the *Theaetetus*, *Sophist* and *Politicus*. It clearly had been intended to be the second member of a trilogy of the *Sophist*, *Politicus* and *Philosopher*.

The *Politicus* was completed after the completion of its two dramatic predecessors, since it refers to them in its opening pages and elsewhere. Like the *Sophist* it largely consists of operations of division. Unlike the *Sophist* it does not also tackle interesting philosophical issues, with one diminutive exception. Between 283 C and 285 B there is a useful little excursus on the difference between *bigger-than* and *too-big*, or between *smaller-than* and *too-small*, which enables the Mean to be distinguished from the mere Measured Amount. This distinction had not been achieved in the *Philebus*. If the view mooted in Chapter IV is correct, namely that the demonstrations of division in the *Sophist* and *Politicus* were intended for the tutorial benefit of beginners in the Academy, then we have to say that while the *Politicus* seems to be designed for beginners only, the *Sophist* is a clumsily assembled sandwich of which the bread could be of educative value only to beginners and the meat could be of value only to highly sophisticated young dialecticians. In the *Politicus* the Stranger speaks to the younger Socrates like a schoolmaster; he had not spoken to Theaetetus in that tone of voice. There is no History of Ideas in the *Politicus*, nor any trace of the Theory of Parsing.

Apart from the political opinions at which Plato pretends to arrive by his Method of Division, the dialogue's chief interest is that the Stranger's instructions in division are now fortified by two principles which had not been announced or observed in the *Sophist*. At 262 the Stranger points out that not all dichotomous divisions succeed in dividing the superior concept into its inferior species. Mankind can indeed be split into Greeks and Barbarians, but these are no more proper species of Man than the numbers below and the numbers above 10,000 constitute proper species of number. At 287C he goes further and points out that not all divisions can be dichotomous. Superior concepts may have three or more inferior species. However, the Stranger's divisions themselves constantly flout both of these excellent methodological principles. The notions of *genus* and *species* are still very indefinite in Plato's mind. There remains much still to be learned, which Aristotle did learn, from Speusippus who took taxonomy seriously. He needed it for jobs of real work.

As has already been argued, the passage in the *Politicus* 286 B–287A must be Plato's somewhat huffy response to an adverse reception by their audience to the *Sophist* and *Politicus*. Our *Politicus* must be a sort of second edition, and therefore have been issued in book-form only some while, short or long, after its oral delivery.

16. THE 'PARMENIDES'

The *Parmenides* is in *oratio obliqua* up to 137C, when it switches over, with just one 'he said', into *oratio recta*. In the first part the audience would be, dramatically, listening to a narrative in monologue from Cephalus. In the second part it would be listening to a duologue between Parmenides and his answerer. The historic dates of the scenes in the two parts are separated by forty or fifty years. The dialogue as a whole would be impossible to represent on the stage. It could not even be delivered as a Third Programme talk, without the intervention of an announcer at 137C to the effect that Cephalus' listeners must now imagine themselves whisked back through a half-century out of the company of Cephalus into the company of the characters whom hitherto Cephalus has been describing to them.

Plato could not have designed either part to be the complement of the other. The first part had been left an unfinished fragment; the second part had been composed as an independent work; and only as a late afterthought did Plato preserve from oblivion the two pieces by tacking them together, without reweaving the dramatic fabric of either. It is a tempting guess that this salvage operation was undertaken when the end of Plato's working life was drawing near. It is better than a guess that the dramatically impossible product was intended not for delivery to a lay audience, but only for the tutorial benefit of juvenile philosophers inside the Academy. For part of this is pretty explicitly said at 135 D and 136 C–E; and we can see for ourselves that the only people who could learn anything from the second part of the dialogue would be senior or junior members of the Academy who were already dialectically sophisticated. It should be noticed that despite the link provided by Socrates at 129, probably manufactured for the purpose, there is no real connexion of topic between

Part I and Part II. Part II is not a discussion of the Theory of Forms. The issues discussed in Part II are good or at least ingenious teasers for any philosopher, whether he accepts or, like Aristotle, rejects the Theory of Forms.

Our dating problem is in consequence a multiple one. When did Plato compose Part I? When did he compose Part II? When did he tack the two parts together?

There are two almost equally plausible hypotheses about the composition-date of Part I.

Hypothesis A

Part I was composed in 362–361, since it is in *oratio obliqua* with a narrator other than Socrates. Like the *Symposium* and *Phaedo* it was designed to be recited to an Athenian audience while Plato would be abroad. So Plato began to compose the piece shortly before his third and last Sicilian voyage. After writing about a dozen pages he shelved the project, perhaps because, very understandably, he could not see how to go on.

Parmenides' objections to the young Socrates' Theory of Forms are all objections to specified relations which Socrates had to postulate as holding between Forms and their instances or between Forms and human intellects. Now in the *Philebus* 15 we hear of some difficulties that had cropped up in the Theory of Forms, and there seem to be similarities between these difficulties and objections which Parmenides develops. This would suggest, but not prove, a chronological adjacency between the two dialogues, and our reasons for dating either dialogue in the later 360's would slightly encourage us to date the other there as well. The *Theaetetus* 183 E and the *Sophist* 217 C both seem to allude to one of the two discussions reported in our *Parmenides*. If so, they show that the *Parmenides* or the earlier part of it preceded the *Theaetetus* and the *Sophist*. We have seen that the *Philebus* must be earlier than the *Theaetetus*. Even if the completion of the trilogy of the *Theaetetus*, *Sophist* and *Politicus* could be brought down as late as the middle 350's when Plato was seventy-three, the composition of the *Theaetetus* must have preceded that completion by a fair time. As the *Cratylus* is likely to have been written before the *Theaetetus* and after the *Phaedrus*, there is not much room in the early 350's for the composition of Part I of the *Parmenides*, short though it is. This Part I contains no trace of the Theory of Parsing which is strong in the *Cratylus*, *Theaetetus* and *Sophist*. It contains no excursus in the History of Ideas.

Hypothesis B

Plato's inferred incapacitation somewhere in the 350's from delivering dialogues in person led him to employ the device of the non-Socratic narrator, not this time because he, Plato, would be overseas, but because, though present in Athens, he would have to have his dialogues delivered from another throat. What had made him invent in a hurry Euclides' slave-*diseur* and the Eleatic Stranger, might have made him at his leisure design a dialogue in *oratio obliqua*, with Cephalus for its narrator. So perhaps the *Parmenides*, Part I, is later than the *Sophist* and *Politicus*, and therefore many years later than the *Philebus*. The apparent allusions in the *Theaetetus* and *Sophist* to Parmenides' discussion in the presence of the young Socrates would then have to be construed as promises and not as reminders.

The philosophical argumentation of Part 1 of the *Parmenides* is unprecedentedly businesslike; its topic is very closely akin to that of Aristotle's *Peri Ideon*; it contains not a flicker of small talk, digression or jollity; and its single theme could not have been a live issue for listeners with only a nodding acquaintanceship with the Theory of Forms. When Plato composed the piece he had in mind not laymen but Academics. It was with such sophisticated recipients in mind that he also wrote the central stretch of the *Sophist*. Doubtless Plato had originally intended to present his *Parmenides* in the regular way to the general public, as he certainly did present to it his *Philebus*, his *Theaetetus*, *Sophist* and *Politicus*, and his *Lecture on the Good*. But his concern for the tastes of the laity was now being displaced by concern for the judgements of the members of the Academy. He was ceasing to work for success as a composer of disputation mimes and correspondingly the Athenian citizens were ceasing to care for his compositions. Plato's dialogues, though still exoteric in form, are now esoteric in matter.

The highly professional spirit of Part 1 of the *Parmenides* seems closer to that of the terminal *Theaetetus* and the central *Sophist* than to the laboriously conversational and homiletic spirit of the *Philebus*. However, on balance, dating the composition of Part 1 of the *Parmenides* very late in the 360's, when Plato was about sixty-five, seems very slightly preferable to dating it near the middle 350's, when he was about seventy-three and the recent victim of a serious illness. Parmenides himself is sixty-five at the time of his discussion with the young Socrates, though he seems to have become very frail by the time he cross-questions the young Aristotle (cf. *Parmenides* 127B with 136D–137B). Perhaps Plato is identifying himself with his new hero, as he had previously identified himself with Socrates.

On either hypothesis this first part of our *Parmenides* did not soon make any difference to anyone else's thinking, since it remained an unfinished fragment on Plato's shelf until he tacked our Part II on to it.

———————

Part II of the *Parmenides* is explicitly produced as a training exercise for future philosophers, and it exemplifies in rigorous form the gymnastic dialectic of which Aristotle's *Topics* is the *Art*. It is meant for the pedagogic benefit of students in the Academy who are already learning dialectic. Its abstractness and difficulty indicate that its intended recipients are already well advanced in the exercise. At 136E it is explicitly declared not to be for Hoi Polloi.

It was Aristotle who began the teaching of dialectic in the Academy, either as soon as he began teaching rhetoric or not very much later, in the earliest or else quite early 350's. We know from Isocrates' *Antidosis* 261–6 that it was an established element in the Academy's curriculum before 353. Even if, what we do not know, Aristotle began teaching dialectic at the very beginning of the 350's, students equipped to learn anything from the central core of the *Sophist* or from the second half of the *Parmenides* could hardly have existed until at earliest 358–357.

If the idea put forward in Chapter VI is right, namely that Plato in his early eristic dialogues drew his argument-combinations from the recorded minutes of recent Moots, then the same may be the case here as well. Here too Plato may not have invented all of the dialectical operations that he assembles. He may have been, in some measure, just their Hansard editor. He may have collected, improved and arranged stretches of the *pro* and *contra* argumentation that had crystallized out of progressions of Academic disputations about unity and existence. The curious mixture that we find in the dialogue of good with bad deductions could be explained in this way. Aristotle's *Peri Ideon* also reads like the systematized digest of Academic Moots.

Parmenides operates almost entirely with what Aristotle calls 'common' notions or concepts, notions, that is, that are ubiquitous and neutral between all the departments of thought and knowledge. Plato notices this class of ubiquitous notions in his *Theaetetus* 185–6 where he too calls them 'common'. The Greatest Kinds in the *Sophist* are a special selection out of these ubiquitous notions, and four of them are listed among the notions on which the future philosopher should learn to operate according to Zeno's procedure (*Parmenides* 136A–C, and cf. 129). This already indicates that the second part of the *Parmenides* belongs, with the *Theaetetus* and *Sophist*, to a period when the Academy has learned to give special treatment to this class of 'common' notions. The Academy now recognizes it to be the central task of dialectic to explore the implications of theses and counter-theses about the topic-neutral concepts. This point is stated in Aristotle's *De*

Sophisticis Elenchis 170a–172a and elsewhere (e.g. *Rhetoric* I ii 21–2, *Metaphysics* IV 1004a–1005a).

There is an extra matter which tends to show that the second part of the *Parmenides* was composed later than the *Sophist*. In the discussion of the Greatest Kinds in the *Sophist* the notions of identity and otherness, being and non-being, rest and motion are discussed substantivally, that is, these abstract nouns consistently appear as the subjects of assertions and denials. We hear, for example, of existence mixing with rest and with motion, and of motion participating in identity. This indigestible idiom is abandoned in the *Parmenides*, Part II. Intolerably abstruse though its whole sequence of operations is, yet abstract nouns, and particularly abstract nouns for the 'common' notions, are now very largely dispensed with. Instead we get complete sentences or clauses of the form '...is identical with...', '...alters...', '...continues to be...', and so on. Consequently the *Sophist*'s baffling ideas of *blending*, *merging* and *mixing* are now replaced by 'if..., then...', and 'since..., therefore...'. As these idioms are clear where the *Sophist*'s idioms are opaque, and as philosophy progresses from the opaque to the clear, the *Parmenides*, Part II, is later than the *Sophist*.

In sum, the second part of the *Parmenides* seems almost certain to have been composed some years after the beginning of the 350's, perhaps near the middle 350's.

When did Plato combine the two discussions into one dialogue? Certainly after the completion of Part II, so certainly, at earliest, fairly well on in the 350's. It is tempting to construe the references to Parmenides' frailty at 136D–E and 137A–B as reflecting Plato's own illness which had forced him to replace Socrates by the Eleatic Stranger in the *Sophist* and *Politicus*. In 361–360 Plato had been vigorous enough to make the two long journeys between Athens and Syracuse and quite likely to deliver his *Phaedrus* to an Olympic audience while *en route* for home. Parmenides himself had, in Part I of the *Parmenides*, been vigorous enough to travel from Elea to Athens in order to attend the Panathenea, and he had requested no rests during his discussion with Socrates.

It seems reasonable to suppose that Plato's motive in combining the two parts into one dialogue was partly a pedagogue's, but also partly an author's motive. He wanted to preserve them from oblivion. But he could not now undertake the labour of substantially rewriting either part. He was near the end of his writing days. There is little save general human probabilities to show whether this end of his writing days belongs to his middle seventies or to the last two or three years of his life, save that in his *De Senectute* V 13 Cicero says that Plato died writing, and Dionysius of Halicarnassus says that he was still polishing his dialogues when he was eighty years old.

Despite his age Parmenides agrees, at 137A, to take his answerer through the chain of *pro* and *contra* arguments, though he will require pauses for rest. This suggests that Plato himself meant to deliver in person our Part II to the Academy's dialectic class—presumably not all in one session, but, say, at the rate of one 'movement' per day. If so, then Plato would be unlikely to let copies go into even

Academic circulation until he became unable to conduct such classes. As this would be the first time that he had conducted a dialectic class since the end of the 370's, it looks as if the old ban has now been lifted. Like Ibycus, Parmenides has been for a long time out of the gruelling exercise.

The text of our *Parmenides* was probably not available to the Academy until Aristotle was well past the beginning of his thirties, or even perhaps after his middle thirties. There are no indubitable or even probable draughts on the dialogue in his *Topics*, although what Parmenides demonstrates is what the *Topics* is the *Art* of, and although cruces about unity and existence are mentioned two or three times in the *Topics*, as they are repeatedly mentioned in the *Metaphysics*, for example 996 a. In his *Physics* I, Chapters II and III, some of these cruces are discussed in a manner and in idioms which must reflect some set disputations about unity and existence. In Part II of the *Parmenides* Plato provides a highly organized and only nominally dramatized digest of just such *pro* and *contra* disputations.

17. A STYLOMETRIC DIFFICULTY

Working on the assumption that death cut short Plato's composition of the *Laws*, scholars have used the *Laws* as the terminus back from which to order the other dialogues according to their degrees of stylistic affinity with the *Laws*. This original assumption is wrong. Plato's death cut short not the composition of the *Laws* but the rewriting of it, and, in particular, the conversion of it from monologue into dialogue. He had finished writing the *Laws* before, parts of it long before he began to reconstruct the whole work for Athenian audiences. There are important affinities of style between the *Critias*, the *Timaeus* and the *Laws*, but these affinities by themselves indicate at most that these works are chronological neighbours, not that any of them or therefore all of them belong to Plato's last composing days. Our independent evidence for the *Critias* and the *Timaeus* having been composed in 368–367 and 367–366 could be evidence that the *Laws* also was being written when Plato was in his sixties; and we actually have strong independent reasons for thinking that his *Proto-Laws* was composed in address-form during the year or two before his last voyage to Sicily in April 361.

It may be doubted whether these stylistic affinities are reliable evidence even of chronological proximity. It might be that these works resemble one another in points of style and diction because they are addresses and not dramas. The author of sustained allocutions in monologue might well take lessons from Isocrates which would be quite inappropriate to argumentative mimes. Conversational cut-and-thrust would be spoiled and not improved by artistries borrowed from the platform, the dais or the pulpit. Conversational exchanges sound unnatural unless they sound vernacular and impromptu. Flows of sustained oratory require just the opposite qualities.

There is, however, one special stylistic feature which the *Critias*, *Timaeus* and *Laws* share not only with one another, but also with the three conversational dialogues, the *Philebus*, *Sophist* and *Politicus*. Isocrates had introduced into rhetoric the elegance of hiatus-avoidance, that is, the avoidance of having a vowel-ending word succeeded by a vowel-beginning word. In the majority of his dialogues Plato is entirely indifferent to hiatus. But in the *Philebus*, *Sophist* and *Politicus*, as in the *Critias*, *Timaeus* and *Laws*, he is systematically economical in hiatus. He does not avoid it altogether, but he uses it with a frequency of about a quarter or a third of its frequency in, say, the *Phaedo* or the *Theaetetus*. Why does Plato economize in hiatus in just those three dialogues?

The tempting hypothesis has often been accepted that Plato only belatedly got into this habit of hiatus-avoidance, with the implication that these three dialogues, together with the three addresses, belong to his latest writing days. It is a difficulty for the hypothesis that, according to it, this literary habit must have grown on Plato almost overnight, namely between composing the *Theaetetus* and composing its trilogy-sequel, the *Sophist*. There is no hiatus-economy in the *Theaetetus*. But anyhow Isocrates' own early practice shows that hiatus-avoidance was a conscious device and not an ingrowing habit. In his forensic speeches he switches from almost total hiatus-avoidance in one speech to almost total indifference to hiatus in another speech temporally quite close to the first. In his *The Team of Horses* hiatus may occur only two or three times on a page, while it may occur a score of times on a page of the *Against Euthynus*.

Whether he adjusted this rhetorical elegance to the social standing of his client, or whether he was differentially fussy about it in subsequent revisions of his speeches for readers, makes no difference. He employed or neglected the device for *ad hoc* reasons. So the possibility exists that Plato too employed the device, when he did employ it, not out of an indurating habit, but for *ad hoc* reasons which need not have been chronologically significant. Perhaps he deliberately employed it when composing addresses, and deliberately did not employ it when composing dialogues even at a considerably later date.

This would still leave unanswered the question What reasons could Plato have had for presenting to the same audience a hiatus-rife *Theaetetus* on Monday and a hiatus-pruned *Sophist* and *Politicus* on Tuesday and Wednesday?

In his *On Literary Composition* xxv Dionysius of Halicarnassus says 'Plato did not cease, when eighty years of age, to comb and curl his dialogues and reshape them in every way' (trans. W. Rhys Roberts). Dionysius wrote over 300 years after Plato's death. If his story is to be credited at all, Plato was, at the very end of his life, not composing new works but tinkering with existent works. What Dionysius says could not have been true of the majority of Plato's dialogues, for their texts were released to the copyists soon after their oral delivery. The published books of such dialogues could not then be recalled for subsequent revision. But what Dionysius says could be true of those compositions which for one reason or another had not been released to the copyists. The *Critias* was not so released, for it was unfinished; nor was the *Timaeus*, for it was reserved for study in the Academy. The *Laws* was still on Plato's shelf when he died. The *Philebus* is ragged-ended at its beginning and finish, and we have seen that Aristotle and the Academy were unfamiliar with it when Aristotle wrote his *Eudemian Ethics*. The *Politicus* cannot have been released immediately after its oral delivery, since it contains a reference to its own unfriendly reception. As the *Sophist* was also ill-received, Plato might have kept this failure back, with the *Politicus*, from an uncordial public.

So these particular compositions could have been 'combed and curled'; they were still on Plato's shelf. The *Laws* certainly was under revision, since it was partly but only partly converted from monologue into dialogue. The lifelessness and incompleteness of the conversion strongly suggest that its author's hand is now a tired one. Perhaps, then, the hiatus-economy of the *Philebus*, *Sophist* and *Politicus* is the result of a pruning applied to them after their original composition; perhaps the audience that had heard a hiatus-rife *Theaetetus* had also heard a hiatus-rife *Sophist* and *Politicus*.

But for what literary reason could Plato have given the suggested Isocratean polishing to these three shelved dialogues? Well, conceivably there was no literary reason. The writer's hand does not drop the pen the moment invention dies in him. Write he must, since this is his one hold on life. But all that he can do is to rewrite. He polishes and repolishes his unpublished works, even sentence by sentence, not because they need it, but because it is his only hobby. The aged sportsman in his beloved gunroom assiduously oils and polishes the guns that he will never use again. On this pathetic hypothesis, which is hardly more than a *faute de mieux*, the Academy would at soonest have read these dialogues when Plato was past discussing their philosophical contents.

If Plato also polished even his *Critias* and *Timaeus*, this interesting consequence would follow. Since our *Timaeus* would then differ somewhat, at least in expression, from the *Timaeus* from which the young Aristotle had been taught during the 360's, some of Aristotle's assertions about the *Timaeus*, which notoriously do not tally with our text, might after all be true. That Plato did touch up his *Critias* is shown by the fact that he did write a new and sadly feeble opening to it, to replace its original beginning that had been borrowed in 366 to be the opening of the *Timaeus*. What stopped him from tidying up the end of the *Critias*, that is, from finishing it may well have been the uncreativeness of old age. On this unprovable hypothesis the texts of some of these six compositions would not have been seen by Aristotle before he was well on in his thirties; those of the *Laws* and the *Critias*, and perhaps also the *Philebus* and the *Republic*, only when he was near or in his forties, that is when Plato's executors published them. As Aristotle was far away from Athens during the years following Plato's death in 347, he may not have come into possession of these posthumously published books until some time after they had become procurable in Athens.

ACKNOWLEDGEMENTS

1. Chapter IV of this book is a modified version of an article entitled 'Dialectic in the Academy', included in *New Essays on Plato and Aristotle*, edited by J. R. Bambrough, and published by Routledge and Kegan Paul, 1965. The editor and publishers are thanked for kindly giving permission for the re-employment of this article.

2. The many English translations of citations from Greek works are drawn, for the most part, (*a*) from the Loeb Classical Library's Editions of Hippocrates, Isocrates, Plato, Aristotle, Xenophon, Plutarch and Diogenes Laertius; (*b*) from Jowett's Translations of the Dialogues of Plato; and (*c*) from the Oxford Translations of the Works of Aristotle, edited by Sir David Ross.

3. Special use has been made of the following works:

Sir Clifford Albutt, *Greek Medicine in Rome*. Macmillan, 1921.

R. Bosworth Smith, *Carthage and the Carthaginians*. Longmans, Green and Co., 1879.

Harold Cherniss, *The Riddle of the Early Academy*. New York, Russell and Russell, 1962.

I. Düring, *Aristotle in the Ancient Biographical Tradition*. Göteborg, 1957.

I. Düring and G. E. L. Owen, *Aristotle and Plato in the Mid-Fourth Century* (esp. article by Glenn R. Morrow, 'Aristotle's comments on Plato's *Laws*'). Göteborg, 1960.

G. C. Field, *Plato and his Contemporaries*. Methuen, 1930.

E. Frank, *Plato und die Sogenannten Pythagoreer*. Tübingen, Max Niemeyer, 1962 (2nd ed.).

D. Harden, *The Phoenicians*. London, Thomas and Hudson, 1962.

ACKNOWLEDGEMENTS

W. Jaeger, *Diokles von Karystos*. Berlin, Walter de Gruyter and Co., 1938.

W. Lutoslawski, *Origin and Growth of Plato's Logic*. London, Longmans, Green and Co., 1905.

W. D. Ross, *Plato's Theory of Ideas*. Oxford, Clarendon Press, 1951.

E. G. Turner, *Athenian Books in the Fifth and Fourth Centuries B.C.* An Inaugural Lecture given at University College. London, H. K. Lewis and Co. Ltd., 1951.

INDEX

A. GENERAL

B. PERSONS (REAL AND MYTHICAL)

C. PLACES (REAL AND MYTHICAL)

D. INDIVIDUAL TEXTS OF ARISTOTLE, DIOGENES LAERTIUS, ISOCRATES, PLATO, PLUTARCH AND XENOPHON

310